T0245728

INCLUSION
Revolution

INCLUSION Revolution

THE ESSENTIAL GUIDE TO
Dismantling Racial Inequity in the Workplace

DAISY AUGER-DOMÍNGUEZ

WILEY

Published by John Wiley & Sons, Inc., Hoboken, New Jersey.
Published simultaneously in Canada.

For general information on our other products and services or for technical support, please contact our Customer Care Department within the United States at (800) 762-2974, outside the United States at (317) 572-3993 or fax (317) 572-4002.

Wiley also publishes its books in a variety of electronic formats. Some content that appears in print may not be available in electronic formats. For more information about Wiley products, visit our web site at www.wiley.com.

Library of Congress Cataloging-in-Publication Data:

Names: Auger-Domínguez, Daisy, author.
Title: Inclusion revolution : the essential guide to dismantling racial
  inequity in the workplace / Daisy Auger-Domínguez.
Description: Hoboken, New Jersey : John Wiley & Sons, Inc., [2024] |
  Includes bibliographical references and index.
Identifiers: LCCN 2023055159 (print) | LCCN 2023055160 (ebook) | ISBN
  9781394259151 (cloth) | ISBN 9781394259175 (adobe pdf) | ISBN
  9781394259168 (epub)
Subjects: LCSH: Racism in the workplace. | Diversity in the workplace. |
  Discrimination in employment. | Equality.
Classification: LCC HF5549.5.R23 A94 2024 (print) | LCC HF5549.5.R23
  (ebook) | DDC 658.30089—dc23/eng/20231214
LC record available at https://lccn.loc.gov/2023055159
LC ebook record available at https://lccn.loc.gov/2023055160

Cover Design: Paul McCarthy
Cover Image: © Getty Images | MirageC

SKY10066038_012924

In memory of my late grandfather, Ramón Arcadio Fernández Domínguez—Te digo adiós para toda la vida, aunque toda la vida siga pensando en ti.
—Poema de la Despedida

To Christopher and Emma, siempre.

Contents

Acknowledgments

This book is a love letter to my family. It honors the legacy of my late grand-uncle Rafael Tomás Fernández Domínguez, who played a key role in leading the Dominican Republic Civil War of 1965 and was recognized as a hero by the government in 1999 for his dedication and respect to democratic ideals.

When I sat down to write these acknowledgements, one word kept running through my mind—Ubuntu. Ubuntu is an African concept in which your sense of self is shaped by your relationships with other people. In South Africa, they call Ubuntu: I am because of you. Thank you, Michael Gross, for introducing me to this concept and always reminding our Coro Fellows class of 1998—Lisa Cowan, Zander Grashow, Amy Sweet, Ken Young, Jason Gill, Valerie Santos, Kiran Makam, Yoojin Lee, Saran White, and Alix Saint Amand—about our shared humanity.

I am because of so many amazing humans in my life. It would take writing another book to name all those who have shared their love, wisdom, compassion, and kindness. These are a few who have been especially pivotal on my journey.

Writing a book can be arduous and isolating, but I had Kathleen Harris in my corner every step of the way. Kathleen, you helped me get out of my head, push past my corporate speak, and give life to my stories. I am forever grateful for your heart, talent, wit, and friendship.

I owe a debt of gratitude for my formative learning in social justice, race, intersectionality, and equity to Teresa Amott, John Ernest ("Ernie") Keen, Linden Lewis, and Walter Stafford.

To Rossana Rosado, Luis Miranda, the late Lisa Quiroz, Fred Terrell, Ella Bell, Roz Hudnell, Freada Kapor, Anita Hill, and Lorraine Cortés-Vásquez, whose sage wisdom and generosity have paved the way for me and countless others.

To the many DEI leaders and practitioners who inspire and teach me every day to be better, do better.

To my sheroes, Yrthya Dinzey-Flores, Tiffany Dufu, Cindy Pace, Diana Cruz Solash, and Helene Yan, whose vision, grit, and friendship always push me to dream bigger.

I was lucky to meet my terrific agent, Johanna Castillo, before the world was forced into quarantine. Your belief in me, my story, and Latinx voices meant everything. That coffee meeting changed my life!

Emi Ikkanda for championing my work and the story I wanted to tell.

To everyone who agreed to be interviewed for this book: Bob Alotta, Emily Best, Aubrey Blanche, Tiffany Dufu, Keesha Jean-Baptiste, Freada Kapor, Lisa Kenny, Lucinda Martínez, Brian O'Kelley, Cindy Pace, Katica Roy, Vanessa Roanhorse, Bird Runningwater, Reshma Saujani, Deepti Sharma, Meghan Stabler, Sherice Torres, Alicin Williamson, Cid Wilson, Jamia Wilson, Kenji Yoshino, and many others whose experiences I drew on.

To the bosses who showed me it was possible to lead with heart and courage: Nicole Johnson, Chee Mee Hu, and Steve Milovich.

To Phil Clark for always being willing to give me golden editorial feedback—bluntly and kindly all at once.

To Bart Oosterveld and Adam Whiteman, my first white male allies.

To my Planned Parenthood Federation of America, Brooklyn Children's Museum, and Robert S. Clark Foundation board partners who are doing the work, every day.

To my VMG work family, for engaging with me in this work and believing that change is possible

To Rha Goddess, who emboldened my sense of what's possible.

To my sister friends, Dominique Jones, Erica González, Elizabeth de Leon, and Katy Romero, for always having my back. Mi *hermano del alma*, Angel Tirado-Morales, *e mi fratello*, Antonino D'Ambrosio.

To my childhood friends who first showed me what it means to straddle multiple cultures and identities—Rie Arvesen, Anneke Schalpelhoumann, and Chi Wai (David) So.

To my Bucknell peeps, Chhavi Seth, Rich Shiu, and Natalia Espinal, my first social justice learning partners

To Brandy Baucom, who helped this "island foreigner" navigate the "tough" waters of New Milford HS.

My Auger family, Ric and Joan Auger, Matt and Ursula Auger, Karyn and Josh Banke, and my niece and nephews, Ellie and Aidan Auger, and Jordan and Luke Banke.

I was raised in a nontraditional family setup, and it made all the difference in my life. My dearest grandparents/mami y papi, Ramon Arcadio Fernández Domínguez and Elena Miniño, my father Ramón (Cachito) Domínguez—what a journey we've been on, the best wicked stepmother, Haydee Domínguez, my fierce *tia/madres*, Maritza Siegel and María Elena Domínguez, the most awesome "little" brothers Sonny Ray and Legend Domínguez, my beloved *primos-hermanos* Petal Carr, Laksmi, and Visnu González, Natalia Báez, Brisa Siegel, and Melissa Machado, my aunt Josefina Miniño, and my late uncle Papa Molina, whose inimitable talents and courage paved the way for many artistic rebels, *mis primos* José Antonio y Evangelina Molina, my uncles Michael Siegel and Víctor Báez, and the new generation who fill us with hope, Valentina and Lia.

My husband Christopher Auger-Domínguez, the single best person I know. Thank you for holding me, spoiling me, pushing me, teaching me, nurturing me, and anchoring me. *Te amo.*

And to Emma Auger-Domínguez, with whom I have been madly, deeply, and intensely in love since the day you were born. I gave you life, and you gave me mine. To witness you becoming who you are—your humor, curiosity, wisdom, and kindness—is pure joy. I love you more.

Introduction

Sitting at a sleek white conference table at Google's equally gleaming Silicon Valley headquarters, surrounded by some of the most credentialed HR executives in the world, a humming laptop in front of me and a free chai latte from one of the ubiquitous Google cafés in my hand . . . I'd felt as if I'd finally arrived. I was hired specifically into a newly created global diversity recruitment role—a role that was elevated to an executive level to recruit me specifically—with an ambitious charge to "hire the most diverse talent." As a Dominican Puerto Rican woman in a leadership position at arguably the world's most powerful company, here was my moment to achieve the type of change I'd dreamed of since growing up in Santo Domingo, the capital of the Dominican Republic.

My team's mission was to build a workforce that better represented our world and users by increasing the hiring rates of female, Black, and Latinx Googlers. We enthusiastically set out to redesign how to find, cultivate and convert a robust and steady stream of female, Black, and Latinx candidates. We based our recommendations on detailed analysis of the experience of Black and Latinx software engineers. These included solutions for reducing bias in job descriptions and the interview process and expanding our talent markets beyond traditional target schools and companies largely lacking in racial and ethnic representation.

Minutes before I unveiled my biggest, boldest diversity hiring initiative yet, I paused to think about the experiences, experiments, wins, and losses that led me to this moment. This has been my life's work for nearly two decades. I was ready for this. But what happened next shattered my natural optimism. Our plan was quickly thwarted when the big bets we presented—such as expanding our offices in communities rich in Black and Latinx talent—were perceived as impractical and unimaginative. This was 2016, and upper management wasn't ready to take bold action.

I was presenting to a room of mostly white men and women. The team leader, who was of Indian descent, and my own manager, a white man, dominated the conversation, and clearly signaled to the rest of the team whose opinion mattered. After what seemed like hours of an intellectual debate over the root cause of our inability to hire more Black and Hispanic software engineers at scale, dismissing the changes I was proposing as not scalable or tractable enough, I nearly lost my mind when I was asked, "What's the root cause?" for what seemed like the millionth time and finally blurted out, "RACISM . . . The root cause is racism. Our recruitment process was designed with a racist lens, and we need to reexamine and rebuild every stage of the hiring journey with an anti-racist lens in order to achieve different outcomes."

The room went qui-eeeet. The discomfort was palpable. It was the truth that no one wanted to hear. But it was the truth. Up until that moment, I didn't dare to speak my whole truth because I was afraid of being misjudged or penalized, like many underrepresented and marginalized employees feel every day, regardless of their place in the pecking order. I shared the truth that causes even good people to become defensive and dismissive. And they did.

Many well-intended and brilliant Googlers before me had designed a highly efficient recruitment process to hire the brightest minds. Many also had advocated for changes to enhance the company's overall people systems and culture. While the company doubled in size and saw increases in hiring and representation for women globally, and Black and Latinx employees in the US, turnover rates for underrepresented employees of color remained just as high, if not higher. Clearly, the culture at Google needed to change if the company wanted to retain gender- and racially diverse talent. But the tolerance for behavioral and operational change is low, even in organizations that brazenly set out to "change the world."

During a brainstorming session that we coined "reimagining the hiring process," a group of experienced engineers, staffing team members, analysts, and other colleagues came together to share and reconsider their long-held innovative ideas. Despite many of these ideas being discussed or experimented with for years, few executives were open to truly listening or acknowledging the underlying reasons why our current practices had barely moved the needle in achieving compositional diversity. And suppose you're one of a handful of employees with limited seniority daring to propose changes that could potentially incur significant financial costs and discomfort for white executives. Under such circumstances, gaining leadership's attention, let alone their commitment to action, is intellectually and emotionally arduous.

This resistance is even more challenging when confronted with the adversities of an economic downturn, political turmoil, and social instability. As we've seen repeatedly, the easiest path is ignorance or resistance during such moments of uncertainty and upheaval. However, I urge you to rise above the challenges and push for change.

One place we can all start is taking a close look at our workplaces.

Everyone has a relationship to work. It is how we get paid and are able to put food in our children's bellies. Work is where we spend the majority of our days outside of the time spent with our families and loved ones. Over the years, I've worked for managers and leaders who emboldened my sense of what's possible. They went beyond saying, "I want you to be successful" to "I am going to ensure that you are successful." They said: "I see you. I value you. You matter. You make a difference." You can never hear "I believe in you" too often. But I've also had managers and peers who have set up roadblocks for my success and questioned my value on a daily basis. Even as I fought to bring more seats to the table, I have had to fight to earn and keep my own while watching white colleagues face far fewer hurdles.

Inequity in the workplace is a problem you can solve. I want you to be the people manager who shines a light on others, not the one who dims it. The leader who uses their power to combat stigma, promote accountability, and acknowledge the shared humanity within their teams; the leader who embraces allyship, minimizes implicit bias, dismantles systemic exclusion, and fosters healthy and meaningful connections among your employees; the leader who creates platforms for nuanced discussions about identity, power, and restorative justice; the leader who models and shows the power of recognizing our commonality.

Despite the progress made since the summer of 2020, when corporate America and the philanthropic sector pledged substantial financial resources to combat racial injustice and address historical harm inflicted on Black people, the United States is now witnessing a resurgence of efforts aimed at undermining the rights, opportunities, and freedoms of historically underrepresented communities. While there are many progressive measures such as appointing chief diversity officers; implementing anti-racism and belonging training; hosting listening series and educational forums; providing talking points, guides, and other resources; diversifying talent pools; and establishing supplier diversity programs, many of these advancements have regressed. Book-banning attempts to erase our history, disproportionate voting restrictions targeting BIPOC (Black, Indigenous, and People of Color) individuals, legislation diminishing hard fought-for LGBTQIA+ rights and women's bodily autonomy—especially women of color—and outlawing of affirmative action in public colleges and universities by the Supreme Court, coupled with the reversal of diversity, equity, and inclusion (DEI) initiatives across various organizations, pose significant challenges. These circumstances are a powerful reminder that the ongoing work for equality across every sector requires unwavering vigilance. In the face of these obstacles, how can we seize these cyclical moments as opportunities rather than succumbing to threats?

Revolutionizing workplaces goes beyond superficial one-and-done approaches that provide temporary comfort to those content with maintaining the status quo. The evolving world of work requires managers and leaders to adapt and transform their approaches. This includes reimagining how work is done, reevaluating the environments in which work occurs, and reconsidering the individuals prioritized, accommodated, and harmed in these spaces. This transformative journey must align with the dynamic changes in work relationships, practices, and expectations.

Employees now hold employers accountable to higher fairness, vision, courage, safety, purpose, and autonomy standards. The nature of their work, creation, and contribution has shifted, requiring new, radical, inclusive approaches to leadership and management. This calls for a fundamental change in mindset, approach, and practice.

Good intentions can fall short. Merely ticking off the checkboxes and appearing to prioritize diversity, equity, and inclusion doesn't exempt companies from making decisions that inflict massive harm on marginalized communities. Moreover, as companies face resistance and criticism of their

DEI efforts from right-wing groups and a decline in executive support for DEI initiatives, leaders and managers must grapple with the shifting agency within their workforces. Workers everywhere, especially those from Black and Brown communities, are voicing their collective sentiment: "We've had enough. We demand real and substantive change. And we're keeping score."

Quick-fix attempts are often short-lived, wasted efforts like one-off diversity training and conversation series. Those executing these well-intentioned solutions must discuss the underlying reasons—the *why*—and be prepared to take action based on the sometimes uncomfortable truths to achieve substantial and meaningful progress.

The urgency is clear but the road map is not.

The "diversity" problem many are trying to solve is addressing racial and gender imbalances, harm in the workplace, and, most fundamentally, power imbalances. It affects what products, services, and content companies create, who they are designed to serve, and who benefits. It elicits the question: What can be done to dismantle centuries of discrimination and anti-Blackness globally? And how can more fair workplaces be achieved? The starting point is a recognition of their own deep, long-standing, and systemic racial inequities. This should prompt reflections about how they need to change to achieve a fairer and healthier future for all, with many taking action to become the companies where we all want to work. This should be the time for institutions to tip toward fairness and belonging finally and put an end to systemic racism and other "isms." However, it is important to acknowledge that resistance and backlash are real challenges in this pursuit.

Diverse hiring sprees and solely focusing on listening and learning alone won't change organizational behavior, systems, and cultures perpetuating inequity and exclusion. Why? Because we cannot hire our way out of exclusive hiring practices, just as we cannot rely solely on listening to transform deep-seated organizational issues. Instead of filling the void with short-lived promises, organizations must confront the root causes of racial inequity and address the opacity of institutional practices. And let's not forget people are no longer satisfied with empty promises and don't want to associate themselves with brands that underdeliver on their promises. They seek tangible evidence of progress—receipts, concrete results, not mere "diversity theater."

Merely striving for diverse representation in the workplace is not enough to ensure that all employees feel a sense of inclusion, equal value, and both physical and psychological safety. Instead of making fleeting promises, we must approach this endeavor with empathy and determination, delving into the root causes of racial inequity throughout the entire employee lifecycle—from recruitment and onboarding to development, retention and, offboarding. We must establish inclusive values and clear behavioral expectations, challenging the status quo—"the way things have always been done"—and embracing transparency in tracking our progress toward our goals. In other words, we need a fundamental shift in organizational thinking, culture, norms, processes, and practices.

An entrenched culture like the one I experienced at Google, and that exists at many other organizations, can be masked by a company's strong financial performance or brand. A company can appear from the outside to be forward-thinking and progressive, while its internal culture quietly erodes the morale, well-being, and professional advancement of BIPOC employees, as well as the effectiveness of its DEI programs.

Organizations frequently find themselves trapped in one or more of these pitfalls:

- Uninformed leadership teams taking charge of DEI decisions, disregarding the expertise of DEI professionals, and witnessing the continuous turnover of highly competent BIPOC talent.
- Misdiagnosing "diversity and culture problems" as separate problems, failing to recognize them as ultimately stemming from leadership and management deficiencies.
- A misguided emphasis on "quick wins" without the necessary financial resources (read: budget) and support from leadership (such as speaker series, or "Rooney rules," which are practices borrowed from American football (NFL) that require teams to interview minority candidates for head coaching and senior football positions, with the goal of promoting diversity and equal opportunity in hiring) resulting in efforts, and valuable time and energy, directed toward solving the wrong challenges.
- Manager incompetence or resistance when it comes to engaging in difficult conversations related to racial or gender disparities.

The obstacles to fostering diverse, equitable, and inclusive workplaces are often glaringly evident—characterized by insidious exclusionary cultures infused with bias, power struggles, prejudice, bullying, discrimination, and harassment. Additionally, there is an increasing shortage of experienced modern leaders and managers and misaligned human resource programs. Instead of addressing the root causes of these issues, organizations continue to blame the lack of representative diversity on a supposed "supply issue." They ignore the influence of subjective hiring practices ("Hey, this kid played lacrosse at Dartmouth, and he interned at Goldman, he knows how to compete . . . "), as well as flawed performance and pay processes, not to mention toxic behavioral norms. Most disheartening, they are reluctant to hold leaders and managers accountable for their lack of competence, toxic behaviors, and inadequate actions.

How do we reduce the structural inequities that limit people's access and potential, and what would it take to change? These have been central questions throughout my career. Inspired by historian Ibram X. Kendi's work and pioneering scholars Walter Stafford, Kimberlé Crenshaw, Dr. Ella Bell, and Anita Hill, I believe that eliminating racism requires challenging it before and when it appears. White supremacy not only influences who gets hired, included, and promoted in an organization, but it also influences what we think of as normal and acceptable, whether we are white or not. Instead of working toward populating organizations with more racial representation—a common aim of DEI practices—we should address and dismantle the root causes of how racism systematically advantages white workers and disadvantages BIPOC workers.

We have all witnessed acts of passive racism. When I entered the workplace, I watched talented women and BIPOC employees be sidelined, marginalized, and silenced. These experiences led me to spend the past two decades designing and executing DEI strategies across large, global companies, and in more recent years also at start-ups and nonprofit institutions. I worked at companies known and revered such as Google, Disney, and Viacom, companies at which we got some things right and got some things wrong. This has been my journey, but I can guess that many of you reading this right now have experienced something similar in your own lives and careers.

My commitment to creating workplaces that work for everyone comes from a personal place. I know firsthand how companies and organizations are strengthened when they make their cultures more inclusive and equitable, and I know why that shift is hard.

The greatest gifts my family gave to me, at the expense of their own comfort, were the educational tools to access and navigate a wide range of professional environments, including spaces not designed for people like me. I have been sought after and hired at some of the most admired companies because I've learned how to navigate predominantly white spaces. But that doesn't mean that I have always felt welcomed and valued. The real shame is that it has been up to me—and others like me—to neutralize passive, and sometimes outright, racism and construct our own personal safety nets (employee resource groups, private "catch-ups," etc.). Now it's time for everyone to step in.

What Is Change?

To create fair and inclusive workplaces, we must understand and break free from hidden power structures and toxic workplace cultures and commit to changes in management practices such as hiring, compensation, benefits, and performance management. While we each have a role to play, I want to be clear that the onus is on the privileged white male leader and manager to address the varied sources of inequalities that exist for marginalized people at work. Throughout this book, I'll offer tangible advice to dismantle exclusive practices throughout the employee lifecycle. You have to put in the work if you believe this is important to you, your teams, and your organizations. I will show you how to do this work step-by-step.

Real revolutions are the ones no one sees coming. But in the case of the ongoing struggle for racial justice, the signs have been evident for all to see. The United States carries a complex history scarred by slavery and racial segregation that has long fueled racist ideologies. We have witnessed and personally experienced the repetitive cycles of action and inaction. It is no shock that those most affected by racial hierarchies are raising their voices and demanding fairness. White supremacy has insidiously embedded itself within our institutions and systems, permeating every facet of our lives, from everyday interactions to overarching systems and structures. Media messaging often perpetuates the protection of white Americans while inflicting harm upon BIPOC communities. In other words, we unwittingly absorb racism, internalizing its effects. However, understanding the underlying causes of our biases spurs us to question our ingrained beliefs and drive meaningful change. It is no longer an option for any of us to remain passive.

Throughout my career, I've contributed my voice, experience, and bits of my soul to solve complex issues of workplace culture, identity, access, opportunity, and power from the inside. Many of my fellow DEI leaders and practitioners have also been at this for a long time, frustrated, and burned out. Yet I am more hopeful than ever. Why?

Because of *you.*

I'm writing this book for you, the white or BIPOC manager, the leader who recognizes that DEI is necessary for your teams; the leader who wants to dismantle old systems in your workplace from the inside out and build bridges and connections; you, the manager sandwiched between the C-suite and entry-level workers, who may feel that you don't have the power and influence to effect change. I have been there. And I am here to tell you that you do have the power.

This book is for you, who are often given mandates instead of time, support, and resources; you, who often feel unable to move forward because you lack answers to your questions about purpose, values, and process; you, who want to ensure that everyone who works with you feels better after an interaction with you, not diminished and depleted; you, who want to clear the pathway for success for everyone on your team.

So what's in it for you? Think of this book as a how-to manual for building a more inclusive company or organization. If you've picked up this book because you're either anxious about this work, worried about the backlash, or dismayed with the lack of progress, this book will share stories to ground and inspire you. If you want to support this work indirectly or take it on as part of your responsibility, this book offers tools and resources to help you do that. And if you've picked up this book even though you doubt this work is worthwhile or valuable, well, enjoy!

We all interact in workplaces and have a million opportunities to influence change. Fostering fair, respectful, and inclusive workplaces requires dedicated effort. Despite overwhelming demands and challenging decisions, we hold more agency and influence over reimagining our work environments than we might initially perceive.

Throughout this book, I will expose the hidden trip wires, failures, secrets, and missteps that impede inclusive management practices. Through intentional examination, I will share policies, practices, and ideas that anyone can implement to chip away at bias, challenge prevailing norms and behaviors, and transform outdated processes and systems. I will shed light on the experiences shared by thought leaders and marginalized workers who navigate those trip wires daily, sharing a path toward creating workplaces that embrace and uplift the diverse individuals who form the heartbeat of organizations. Moreover, I will share my personal stories, drawing from my journey where I have found myself on both sides of the equation and how I have grown and learned from my mistakes. You'll need to identify the interventions most relevant to your unique culture and business and approach their execution with unwavering dedication and discipline.

While you may not hold the authority to reprimand leadership misconduct or single-handedly replace your company's leadership, there are significant steps that managers and leaders, both white and BIPOC, can take today to cultivate diverse, equitable, and inclusive workplaces and organizations that thrive both commercially and culturally. This book serves as a guide for action, intended for courageous people to pursue equity within their organizations and confront the pervasive whiteness at work. It is a resource for those grappling with the challenges of moving past the trending hashtags, navigating political landmines, and addressing the pervasive blind spots that hinder lasting change. The insights shared within these pages are designed to help you effectively recruit, hire, engage, retain, and grow diverse talent, ultimately building a truly inclusive workplace where every employee can thrive.

Change means creating a fervent sense of belonging for everyone, no matter your background, ethnicity, gender, sexual identity, religious beliefs, physical ability, or any other identity. Everyone is welcome to this inclusion revolution, and the invitation explicitly states to show up as you.

I've encountered many leaders eager for actionable frameworks and advice to create more inclusive cultures. But again and again, I find one thing plaguing their attempts: fear. They are utterly terrified about messing up and saying the wrong thing to all their stakeholders—employees, board members, funders, clients, customers, or the wider public via social media.

They have fear of losing their jobs, livelihoods, and ability to provide for their families—they're paralyzed into inaction. In today's workplace, there is a heightened fear of being "cancelled." Managers, leaders, and CEOs are acutely aware that their companies, personal reputations, and share prices are one social media cycle away from ruination. Acknowledging and addressing the blockages created by these fears is vital for creating more inclusive environments.

There is a very special energy in organizations where fear doesn't exist; when people feel seen, heard, and valued; when they feel that they can engage, perform, and contribute without judgment and retaliation. It keeps workplaces from feeling dark and heavy. It keeps the mistrust out of the air. It keeps employees from leaving the organization or, worse, sustaining repeated trauma to survive financially. It breeds the highest levels of creativity, innovation, and collaboration. That is the workplace I want for you!

Over the years I have tested and developed different models for dismantling inequities across many organizations and industries. I have seen what works and what doesn't. I've learned that best practices and research are starting points, that there are no silver bullets or shortcuts, but you have to start somewhere. The model I present in this book is intended to help you on your journey toward organizational culture change, and it's rooted in four steps:

Reflect: Get clear on your truth and the truths of your coworkers—the variations in your points of view, feelings and identities, your motivations, and how these affect your teams and organizations. Why are you enthusiastic or hesitant? What is possible?

Vision: Use your knowledge of the organization's climate and systemic and structural barriers to build a way forward. What does DEI look like when it is no longer a challenge or a problem to be solved? This is where you frame the work ahead for yourself and others.

Act: Approach this work from a place of ideas and values and from a place of pure pragmatism—fixing one part of a broken system at a time. Create your own best practice learning lab through rigorous testing and iteration, and define the role you want to play. This is where you invite engagement and collaboration.

Persist: Discomfort and shame are a common response when we realize that we have fallen short of our personal expectations. You should feel uneasy when you learn about the times that you or your organization have let employees down. Lean on courage and fortitude to stay the course, respond proactively, track progress, and celebrate your wins. Make small tweaks over time—you need to see what sticks.

Your approach has to be specific, tangible, and responsive to your unique workplace barriers. I believe this model can be cultivated in every company and organization. Use it as your guide on your own journey.

If this sounds intimidating, don't worry. Small, repeatable, and consistent actions can deliver the most lasting impact. I'll show you how to come at it with a compassionate, realistic, and accessible approach. Your goal is not to change your entire organization overnight; it's to make a plan that reflects your values and aspirations. It's to increase the capacity of others to do good.

Embrace the Revolution

I want to inspire new levels of ownership, to strengthen our collective capacity to drive change, recognize the pitfalls, and keep going. This is about how we as a people can learn to work together. That has always been the revolution. At a fundamental level, it's about how we learn to work together and how we drive change, together. This is not about a culture by default but instead about building a culture with deep intention and action. What does it look like? It is work that feels purposeful, effortless (despite the "work" you do), productive, and yes, joyful.

What works, what has proven to work for generations before us, is millions of people acting in millions of different ways and across millions of moments. To dismantle inequity in the workplace, we must translate good intentions into powerful and sustained actions and generate better decisions, better strategy, better conversations and debate, better risk and performance management, better investments, and better career and business outcomes.

The model for achieving the workplace change I'm presenting is a revolutionary but incremental approach within our reach. It does not require us to tear down the existing structure and create something from scratch. It is meant to increase our capacity for driving change. The building steps of this model are incremental enough that everyone can do it, including *you*, regardless of your position, education, or influence.

Inclusion revolution is not a blueprint for check-the-box diversity training; it's not a prescription to being politically correct in the workplace. This is a book of action for those who are willing to confront the pervasive inequities at work. Let's raise the bar by fighting back against the attacks on building equitable workplaces, the lack of sustained attention and effort coupled with fatigue and inertia that comes from years of trying to get DEI right. Let's turn goodwill and intent into real results. And let's build change that lasts, because through the best teams, and the broadest client/customer/investor/audience reach, companies can build a stronger future.

Welcome to the *inclusion revolution!*

1

Your Inclusion Ambitions

There's a famous story about President John F. Kennedy visiting the NASA space center in 1962. Kennedy noticed a man carrying a broom, and when the president introduced himself, he asked the man what his job was. The employee, a janitor, responded, "Well, Mr. President, I'm helping to put a man on the moon." Achieving that sense of shared purpose is a foundation for true and lasting inclusion and belonging in the workplace.

Right now, diversity, equity, and inclusion (DEI) is our moon landing, and to make this mission successful we need everyone, from interns to executives, to contribute to creating a culture of belonging. Imagine that you have the ability to make work easier for all kinds of people in your organization, to allow them to use their skills and thoughtfulness for innovation and problem solving. Imagine that you can create a sense of psychological safety where everyone feels confident and comfortable to take risks, make mistakes, contribute opinions, and be candid about what they are up against. Managers have this power. You have this power. It starts with making a visible commitment to inclusion and belonging across your teams because work cultures are not all created equal.

Some people experience the workplace as it should be: challenging—it is "work" after all—and rewarding, if you're lucky. For others, that same workplace can consist of daily acts of microaggressions, gender violence, systemic racism, and discrimination, and the nagging feeling that you're going crazy as you try to get through each day. Underrepresented employees across many workplaces feel that their ideas and experiences are routinely dismissed. These feelings of exclusion are among the primary reasons there is a revolving door of talent for employees of color. Over and over, outstanding people are hired for their magic—and then that magic is sucked dry when they are excluded for not fitting in in the majority culture. And when that happens, they underperform, quit, or get pushed out. Those are the circumstances for so many, and that's what I want to change. If you're reading this book, you do, too.

This book is full of actions, practices, and policies that will help you transform your organizations to be more diverse, equitable, and inclusive. But before you roll up your sleeves and start to act, I have found that reflection before action is the most effective path toward creating a culture of belonging. This first chapter is an essential moment of truth that will encourage you to act with intention.

We first need to clear the air and be honest with ourselves, and our colleagues, about why corporate America is so white. White people have enjoyed decades of advantages in professional workplaces, mostly through the systemic segregation of neighborhoods, schools, and social and professional networks, resulting often in white people only moving through all-white spaces, having all-white friend circles, and all-white colleagues. This chapter is about being willing to interrogate why and to understand how ill-prepared everyone is, white and BIPOC managers alike, to discuss the true root causes of this fact in a constructive way.

"What's one thing you like about being white?" That's the question writer, scholar, and TV host Dr. Marc Lamont Hill (2021) asked his guest, a conservative activist, in a discussion on race theory. The guest didn't respond, deflecting the question. Still, if every white person took a moment to stop and consider their answer, you could begin to understand why it's essential to confront racial inequity in workplaces.

I'm hopeful because I believe more and more managers are beginning to understand that they must first create a psychologically safe environment where their team members feel encouraged to be themselves and speak up at work, a sense of connection to their work and their peers, and that they have a fair chance to succeed. When you understand this and why it's necessary to create a culture of belonging, why these actions will work, what challenges they are helping solve, and how they will benefit everyone, you will become a stronger champion, a better ally, and an enviable leader.

Get on the Balcony

Goals are necessary, and milestones are measurable, but the real transformation comes when you align them with the spirit of why it's important to hire, retain, and engage a diverse workforce. This requires you to recognize the biases and practices that have kept you from making progress and then designing changes to mitigate bias and microaggressions. That's when the work of creating a fair, equitable, and inclusive organization gets clear.

Ron Heifetz and Marty Linsky (2017) coined the leadership skill "getting off the dance floor and going to the balcony" in their book *Leadership on the Line*. They describe getting on the balcony as the practice of gaining a clearer perspective on the bigger picture by distancing yourself from the action. That is, asking, "What's really going on here?" The operational pressures of DEI work, such as needing to show nearly immediate results in workforce representation, often mean that those tasked with achieving a company's DEI aspirations must rely on quick-fix approaches that do not address the root cause of racial disparities in their organizations. They are pushed and pulled by events, people, and complex and often conflicting agendas. This often leads to misdiagnosed problems and well-known yet inadequate stand-alone solutions, such as diverse candidate slates, employee resource groups, culturally immersive programs, and unconscious bias training, and ultimately you're back on the dance floor.

When you're feeling lost or stuck, bring it back to the *why*: define it, and then refine and redefine the opportunities. Get clear on how DEI will contribute to your mission and performance, how you can solve smaller gaps before they turn into hard-to-manage ones, and what you will do to make your insights a reality for your business.

Getting on the balcony as both an observer and a participant takes discipline, courage, and a willingness to stay the course. Allow yourself the time to think, reflect, and observe the patterns of behaviors, norms, actions, and inactions to understand what is or might get in the way of dismantling inequity in your workplace. The best leaders, managers, and individual contributors learn how to move gracefully between the balcony and the dance floor. Try this exercise to help you get on the balcony:

Define what you're trying to solve for and why:

- What motivates me to build a diverse workforce and inclusive culture?
- What makes me nervous or confused?
- What gets in our way as an organization, a team?
- What am I missing or have been unwilling to see?
- What can we accomplish that we have not thought of yet?
- What's working, and what can we share with/borrow from others?
- How do we bring others along?

Then get back on the dance floor to make interventions based on what you've gathered. Try building an opportunity statement:

- Creating a more diverse, equitable, and inclusive workplace at _____ is critical because _____.
- As a(n) (individual contributor, team leader, senior executive) at _____, I will _____ and _____ and _____in the next 6 to 12 months.

You can move back and forth, dynamically and collaboratively. When employees clamor for public statements, ask them to challenge their assumptions about how and where work gets done and the behavioral norms and expectations across teams. When executives are eager to jump into action, encourage them to pause, before jumping to action, to listen to what their team members need, to build solutions based on the insights they gather, and to show evidence of care even when they don't know what to say.

Center on what you want to achieve. Performative action won't do. You must answer that core question: Why do I want to do this? Followed by, Where do I want to enter this work? If your answer is: "I want to avoid being cancelled" or "I'm told it's important," you will not make the right choices or investments. Achieving a more diverse, equitable, and inclusive workplace is not a box to check off. A common answer is that it's the right thing to do, but achieving an inclusive workplace is not just about ethics and morality.

"The work has to start with an internal focus before it turns to an external focus," Freada Klein Kapor said to me in a conversation on October 15, 2020. Freada is founding partner at Kapor Capital, a venture capitalist, social policy researcher, and philanthropist, who has advocated for diversity and inclusion in tech since the 1980s. She adds, "While there might be a well-meaning leader in every organization, I think right now that the motivation is not to be the last one standing who doesn't have a Black partner or a Black manager" (Kapor 2020).

Think about your vision; write down your mission; get grounded in your motivation so that you can better define your role in the inclusion revolution. Let's start by acknowledging that we all have a lot on our plates, and that training, research, and resources should help lighten our loads as we explore new ways to be at work. So think about leaning into this work as a lifelong learning process to become a better leader and colleague. Don't conflate perfection with your commitment to build a more inclusive and equitable organization. It's a classic growth mindset, and having one is vital on this journey. "I'm not an inclusive leader . . . yet," is what an elementary school teacher would emphasize; that's what I want you to remember, too.

If you're not yet sure of your why, know this: When we improve belonging and inclusion at work, success follows. Belonging improves retention: 42% of employees who feel that they are able to bring their whole selves to work are less likely to plan on leaving for another job within a year. That's because, as data from Culture Amp confirms, people who feel they belong perform better, become more willing to challenge themselves, and are more confident and resilient. The positive stats keep on coming: workplaces with inclusive cultures are six times more likely to innovate and weather market change, and workplace engagement (an additional indicator of belonging) is closely correlated with increased productivity, profit, and innovation, as well as decreased employee turnover (Culture Amp n.d.). *Harvard Business Review* attempted to quantify this impact, stating that increased job performance, reduced turnover, and fewer sick days for a 10,000-person company would result in annual savings of more than $52 million (Carr et al. 2019).

That's $52 million in savings just to help someone feel comfortable and safe in their place of work. The message is loud and clear: diversity and inclusion will bring profits and innovation. But it's still not breaking through.

Doing good and doing well are not mutually exclusive. You should frame the value proposition of nurturing a diverse, inclusive, and equitable workplace as both the right and smart thing to do. You should aim to be the company that everyone else wants to emulate, the one receiving awards for the best workplace because your employees can share ideas openly, explore disagreements, and talk through tensions as a team, not because you had the greatest number of press stories. People feeling included, connected, and embracing belonging is not just a nice thing to do. It's necessary to heal the harm across workplaces, and it's a critical role of leaders who wish to build innovative and agile teams. It's essential to understand your motivations, aspirations, and privilege as a manager or coworker to eliminate disparities and inequities. This drives empathy, understanding, and, in the end, improved innovation, experimentation, and productivity. You reflect. You think and then act. Being at the forefront of this revolution will make you a better, more in-demand leader.

Your Mindset Matters

This work is hard, complex, and triggering. It fundamentally requires you to acknowledge your personal blind spots and your organization's cultural and systemic sore spots. You're going to have to confront deep-seated beliefs and unconscious habits, including guilt and shame, common obstacles to change. You're going to have to explore your identity and privilege in relation to others and ask for feedback you may not want to hear. You're going to have to build new muscles, including the capacity to interpret new information; to sit in ambiguity, conflict, and discomfort; and to determine what's possible when you witness workplace inequities. You're going to have to act on the new knowledge you gain and embrace and admit your fears about what change means for you. You're going to have to come face-to-face with the moments when you have been complicit by looking away or letting something slide. I know that may feel like a lot, but when you open your mind and heart to the possibility of making a difference in someone's life, the future looks bright.

"In any given moment, we have two options: step forward into growth or step backward into safety," said psychologist Abraham Maslow, the architect of Maslow's hierarchy of needs. Safety looks like short-term policies and public campaigns; growth is working toward finding the best solution, not the fastest one. Instead of clinging to what we can or can't control, or a fear that we will be dismissed for trying to be helpful, we can meet this overwhelmingly complex DEI work with curiosity, openness, and a willingness to adapt and build resilience and agility. I invite you to think more expansively and imaginatively about your role as a leader and individual contributor, whether conscious or unconscious, in creating feelings of exclusion or inclusion.

We all have the capacity to lead and collaborate fairly and with compassion. Whether you're a DEI professional or a leader, ally, or accomplice trying to cultivate a diverse, equitable, and inclusive workplace culture, here's how you can get in the right mindset:

- **Embrace courage.** Know you're going to make mistakes along the way. Don't let the fear of putting your foot in your mouth keep you silent. Don't let it set you back—learn from your gaffes or things you might have not done right in the past, and make a promise to yourself to do better next time.

- **Tame your defensiveness.** Defensiveness is a natural by-product of feeling uncomfortable and questioning your privilege or your habits. Sit with those emotions, ask yourself what you are trying to protect and why, and watch for any tendencies to make excuses, deny facts, or blame others.

- **Be transparent.** If you don't know an answer, or are genuine about your desire to do better, say so. Transparency and vulnerability build trust, which is an essential tool in this work. Be frank about what you do not know, what you wonder about, what scares you, and what blind spots you are working on.

- **Own your power.** Know that you can make a difference and that it will take time to radically transform your organization—it's worth it. While it's crucial that your CEO and senior executives drive change from the top, a survey from BCG analytics found that 80% of a company's workforce is mid-level managers who influence most day-to-day decisions and culture building. Whether a manager or an individual contributor, you can be a leader for change.

- **Think like a beginner.** A beginner's mindset stems from a concept in Zen Buddhism called Shoshin: "Having an attitude of openness, eagerness, and lack of preconceptions when studying a subject, even when studying at an advanced level, just as a beginner in that subject would." It's crucial to have an open mind and a growth mindset that enables you to be willing to experiment, seek feedback, and admit your fears and mistakes.

An important first step is to put your mind in an inquisitive, reflective state. Be ready to ask why; go deeper, question norms, assumptions, policies, and procedures. Question everything—even what I write here! Observe yourself and look for blind spots. Challenge my assumptions and yours at every step. Brain scientists have shown us that a remarkable number of things you do every day operate outside of your awareness—how you engage with the people around you; the way you conduct yourself in a meeting; the candidates you select for jobs; and even where, what, and with whom you eat. You do them automatically. You do them by habit. This is implicit bias, and you do it because your brain creates biased shortcuts to help you make decisions quickly.

Hold Up a Mirror on Bias

We can build real solutions only after we are honest about inequities and assumptions in our workplaces. Holding up a mirror (on you) and a magnifying glass (on unexamined behaviors, processes, and systems) can reveal discriminatory practices and blind spots. It will help you recognize how access and opportunity are granted or denied and the structures in place that enable some to be always tapped for opportunities, while others remain stubbornly invisible and at the margins. You will see whose conduct is challenged or welcomed regularly and how anti-Blackness (accepting the stereotype that Black Women are intimidating or angry), Latinx erasure (reinforcing immigrant and language stereotypes), or Asian expectations (buying into the stereotype of Asian employees' lack of assertiveness) holds back BIPOC leaders.

Workplace inclusion, let alone a complete inclusion revolution, is a challenging endeavor because in-groups tend to reject or resist out-group efforts. Research on brain science has further confirmed the existence of an "us versus them" bias. Take this quote from Mary Casey and Shannon Robinson in their book *The Neuroscience of Inclusion*: "When we meet someone and the brain doesn't like their differences—the way they think, the color of their skin, what they believe, how they dress, or any other characteristics the brain perceives as outside its comfort zone—this is no small event. When the brain registers differences as discomfort, it sends an 'away' impulse and even regards these differences as potential threats" (Casey and Robinson 2017).

UC Berkeley professor John A. Powell's work on belonging asks, "How do we build bridges?" In short, How do we move to a "we," not "us vs. them," mindset? He says that belonging requires us to hear others' stories with compassion, and he believes that we can achieve belonging through "bridging"—the practice of turning outwardly to connect with others. This contrasts with what we currently see in the workplace: we turn inward, relating only to what we know and who we know, diminishing our capacity to listen and collaborate (Powell 2017).

This lifetime of social programming and biased mental shortcuts can prevent people from reaching their full potential and cause harmful setbacks. You can avoid the invisible barriers caused by implicit bias by pausing, reflecting, and taking different actions. It requires a deep examination of history, motives, and intentions. Preconceived notions, biased interpretations, and social conditioning can foster unjust practices.

The first step is rewrite the old rules. Stop saying (and thinking), "That's how it's always been done" or "That's the 'right way' to do something." Question a practice or policy's origin. Does it still make sense to do things that way?

For example, when writing a job description or asking for referrals for a new role, ask yourself, "Why am I doing it this way? What am I missing? Whose voice or experience am I discounting? Who could I be creating access for?" We don't have to continue with oppressive practices that allow inequities to persist. We can transform our organizations for good and in the process show up differently in our workplaces, families, and in our communities.

This requires a willingness to interrogate the ways your behavior or organizational habits may reinforce advantages for white coworkers and marginalization of BIPOC coworkers. It means recognizing that anti-Blackness harms and holds back Black coworkers. And that, as I've learned from Mimi Fox Melton and Karla Monterroso in "Equitable Workplaces

Require Getting Over Fear of Conflict," it is up to you—the white or BIPOC manager—"to develop the skills and learn tools to help you discern between when you experience an emotional reaction because (a) someone has violated a legitimate boundary of yours, versus (b) you expect coworkers to comply, appease, and defer, and you're not getting it" (Fox Melton and Monterroso 2021).

It's rare for a manager, even BIPOC managers, to have received racially sensitive management training to understand how to do this; instead, we come up in a working world built for white workforces, and very few organizations have culturally challenged their racial norms. Unsurprisingly, women and BIPOC feel that to achieve professional success, they must act like white men.

Every employee deserves a workplace culture and manager that brings out their best professional performance. And no employee can bring their best selves and talents to the table if they feel they have to armor up and overcome their manager's low expectations from the start. But just because you're a person of color doesn't mean you've known what it's like to create an inclusive and welcoming workplace. You've likely learned to put up with a lot to survive all-white spaces, and there is a danger that you could be normalizing bad behaviors ("He didn't mean it that way").

My thesis, one that is widely shared in the DEI community of practitioners, is that racial inequity across all industries is a systematic problem; that a misuse of power is at the root of inequity; that to achieve inclusion in the workplace, we need to dismantle the stereotypes, practices, and systems that exclude; and that we live in a white supremacy culture that privileges white norms, values, and behaviors. When I say we need to adopt an equity mindset, that means committing to advancing fair outcomes for your coworkers. For all your coworkers.

Create a Road Map for Change

Companies are made up of people, and people are the agents of change. Period. For far too long, managers have believed that creating a fair, inclusive, and equitable working environment is somehow not central to their core job as a leader—that's what chief diversity officers are for, right? As if their only job is achieving a particular operational goal.

Employees have become more vocal and persistent in challenging leadership on controversial issues—including immigration, harassment, reproductive health, and pay equity—yet we are all stuck in the gray space between awareness and effective action. There are reasons: a fear of saying the wrong thing, confusion over what to prioritize first or where and how much to invest, and frustration about the lack of impact of previous efforts. We need to get out of this space.

We all interact in workplaces and have a million opportunities to influence change. You can create change in your organizations through small and constant actions that change hearts, minds, and systems over time. Activist and author Angela Davis says we need to "make the radical imaginable" and empower ordinary people to put pressure on the existing state of affairs to create conditions for change (Capece 2018). She calls these practices "reform tactics," though you may think of them as operational practices, such as designing new hiring policies, launching new management training programs, and setting targets for achieving representational diversity. I think of it as attaining the conditions for change, one effort, conversation, or key performance indicator (KPI) at a time.

Waiting for change to happen means releasing your responsibility to lead transformational, revolutionary change and be part of a thriving workplace. You must act—there is no other choice if you believe that building inclusive, equitable, and diverse workplaces is the priority of the decade. Reading antiracist books doesn't magically turn you into an antiracist leader, just as reading about inclusive practices doesn't make you an inclusive leader. But you can gain meaningful lessons and connect new ideas from reading books on DEI that can serve as catalyzers for personal change.

A thoughtful, committed call to action is what's needed. Acting quickly and reacting defensively can feel right. But more often, a thoughtful response and an action plan to make things right is far more necessary when, for example, you receive a report of harassment or toxic behavior. Your key ingredients for success are introspection, thoughtful responses, and commitment to meaningfully and materially change what needs to change. What works best is not always what comes first—it's what has the most lasting impact.

"This work needs to be done in the true spirit of reparations if we're going to do anything differently," says Kapor (2020). An exploration of reparations acknowledges that institutional and structural inequities exist and that they limit people's professional opportunities. "It is as though we have run up a credit-card bill, and having pledged to charge no more, remain befuddled that the balance does not disappear," said Ta-Nehisi Coates (2014) in his article "The Case for Reparations." "The effects of that balance, interest accruing daily, are all around us."

What do reparations practically look like in the workplace? In relation to work, it is not about placing guilt on white people or as an excuse for BIPOC employees not performing their job duties but acknowledging that 400 years of slavery and subsequent racial segregation in our schools, neighborhoods, and workplaces has stunted economic and social outcomes for Black communities. So what's a business leader to do?

Shift your mindset to achieve fair outcomes for all of your people. What do they need to feel a sense of belonging and connection to you and your organization? Start with these questions:

1. **What do your customers want?** The global audiences you build for, sell to, and speak to are diverse, and they want to feel represented. You can't do that if your company doesn't reflect their voices, culture, perspectives, and needs. If a high percentage of your customers are Black, doesn't it make sense to have Black employees contributing to marketing plans? They may be the best suited to understand the demographic and what they value from a personal and professional lens. Profitable companies understand that they must create room for diverse voices to be welcomed and challenged, for creative tensions to exist, and for excellence, innovation, and inspiration to thrive.

   In 2014, Apple made a strategic acquisition to engage the Black consumer market, 71% of whom own smartphones. They purchased Dr. Dre's Beats for $3 billion to add a product line favored by a Black audience and featured celebrities such as Kendrick Lamar in advertising. Apple recognized the purchasing power of their consumers.

   Every company has a customer, and the most successful companies know to put that customer—no matter who they are, what they believe, where they are from, what they identify with—first. Diversity of thought, experience, and background is good for business, but it's also better for your customers, who are your business.

2. **Who are you leaving out?** The "smallest" changes can have the most significant impact on the most people. For a LGBTQIA+ event at Twilio, a cloud software company, an organizer taped a sheet of paper on a bathroom door that declared it "all gender" for the day. They never took it down. A candidate who interviewed there reportedly joined the company because of that sign; it was a literal signal of inclusion, and the candidate felt comfortable coming out as transgender. In response to that feedback, Twilio added gender-neutral bathrooms across the office.

   Some diversity advocates use historic moments throughout the year to make inclusion sustainable in the form of Black/Hispanic/Asian heritage months, Pride month, women's history month, and so on. This must be done tastefully and sensitively—having Taco Tuesday during Hispanic Heritage Month is one big eye roll. Do something more meaningful. Several organizations such as Barclays UK have held global Wikipedia edit-a-thons where teams get together to literally change the narrative of history. Less than 20% of Wikipedia biographies are about women, and an estimated 90% of Wikipedia editors are men, so they set out to fix this and write and upload articles about women. Art + Feminism, a national campaign to improve coverage of cis and transgender women and the arts, teamed up with UC Berkley's Race + Justice edit-thon to fire up their laptops and add or edit articles.

3. **What do your managers need to know?** Everyone in corporate America has gone through some type of diversity training. The truth is it's not working. Little research-based evidence demonstrates the effectiveness of generic training and cookie-cutter DEI practices. Instead, you need to tailor solutions to the individual needs of the people in your workplace. And you need to provide reinforcing mechanisms—such as continuous nudges and suggested resources for managers—to help teams integrate the learnings in their day-to-day operations and accountability expectations.

DEI initiatives that include bespoke educational opportunities can be a practical first step. At VICE Media Group, at the height of the racial reckoning that rocked organizations in the summer of 2020, I received multiple employee demands for anti-racism training. Why weren't we doing it, when everyone else was?

My response: We must get to the basics of how people manage, lead, operate, and hire inclusively. As an organization, we need a shared understanding of what we're trying to solve for and by whom. We have to be careful of what we expect to get out of training and research and the impact it will have. Training can introduce complex, nuanced emotions, new vocabulary, and an expectation for immediate expertise, as if a one-day exploration of racism at work is all it takes to turn managers into inclusive leaders.

Instead, leadership and management development should prioritize giving managers the tools to spot where changes can happen: Where are the most significant gaps in your company culture? What direct or indirect experiences at work cause racial disparities? What specifically do you want people to do, think, or feel differently after the training? Start by determining your focus, where your most significant opportunities are, and where you want to make an impact.

At VICE, we spent a summer listening to employees from traditionally underrepresented backgrounds and reviewing our employee data. We discovered that the biggest problems were caused by a lack of constructive performance feedback, transparency on how to achieve career progression, and management modeling of respectful and inclusive behaviors. My team worked around the clock to vet vendors and co-design curricula that addressed these management practices. In the fall, we launched training designed specifically for middle managers—inclusive management and belonging in the workplace—to strengthen essential management skills. Our goal was to avoid generic statements about bias and microaggressions and instead share targeted and practical tools so that white and BIPOC managers could better support and grow their staff of color.

By focusing on how to develop effective teams, we set a tone for a transformed culture that held managers accountable for leading diverse teams inclusively. For phase two, we strengthened management muscles through training focused on creating psychological safety and a sense of belonging through effective race, identity, and culture conversations.

Everyone's favorite part of the programs was interacting with their colleagues across the company. I also received the following feedback from white managers: "A very helpful tool to have on hand as we learn to develop new and better habits of inclusion." "The most impactful training I've attended in a long time." "I have already implemented some of the tips in my weekly recaps and am receiving better feedback from my team."

BIPOC managers also responded positively, mostly commenting on how glad they were to see these learnings delivered broadly across the organization. I know the feeling. I have attended my fair share of diversity workshops as a participant. While my colleagues of color and I often joked, "Hey, you're also here to learn about how to work with yourself?" we also learned about our own blind spots. When delivered with care and aligned with ongoing organizational commitments to DEI, this training can help build better managers of all backgrounds.

One of the critical blind spots many white people have is that all people of color come in at the same baseline into meetings and group discussions. Use these trainings as an opportunity to point out that women and BIPOC are conditioned over a lifetime to take up as little space as possible—so while white colleagues assume that colleagues are not interrupting or talking at length because they have nothing to say, the reality is that many women and BIPOC staff are reluctant to speak, even when they have great ideas. A useful leadership hack is setting up a norm where women and BIPOC are asked to speak first and are brought in by explicit invitation from someone in a leadership position, rather than expecting them to interrupt and dominate the conversation. Note: this doesn't work for everyone; ask your BIPOC colleagues if they're willing to engage or not.

Many BIPOC have had to conform to white norms to rise, so BIPOC managers may also need to find ways to create paths for people to succeed as themselves. For example, ideally BIPOC won't have to code-switch (the act of adjusting one's style of speech, behaviors, appearance, and expressions to mold oneself to society's expectations of a professional) in the future to seem "professional"—it can be damaging if BIPOC junior staff meet senior BIPOC staff who pressure them into respectability politics and encourage code-switching to fit in.

To help teams understand the nuanced and often conflicting emotions and experiences across our workplaces, I like to share these statements I've gathered over the years in one-on-one conversations and presentations. How many resonate with you?

What We Feel

- "I'm afraid of being hurtful to others."
- "I'm exhausted by having to constantly explain my lived experience in a way that others can understand."
- "I'm over white men getting a trophy for showing up while I need to prove myself over and over again."
- "I want to attract, develop, and retain a racially diverse workforce, but I don't know where to start."
- "I'm tired of being asked to do additional unpaid labor to solve diversity problems, when I should already be walking into an inclusive workplace culture where I can do my best work."
- "I'm afraid of saying the wrong thing and making a mistake."
- "I want to be an ally, but I don't always know how to support BIPOC colleagues."
- "I'm constantly worrying about being misgendered or dead-named.

What We Wonder

- "I look for underrepresented talent—why can't I find any?"
- "Why are we talking about people dealing with injustice in the workplace?
- "Are our recruiting efforts lowering the hiring bar?"
- "How do I respond to being called out without doing further damage?"
- "Do leaders really care about DEI?"

The Belonging Effect

Belonging—a word I'm sure you've heard a lot—is key to creating environments where everyone feels they can thrive. Belonging is not just getting in the door and being invited to a meeting; belonging is the feeling that you're respected, valued, and essential. An MIT study, "Acute Social Isolation Evokes Midbrain Craving Responses Similar to Hunger," found that our brains crave belonging and social interactions the same way we do food (Tomova et al. 2020). Our words and actions must signal to others that we really do care enough to notice—to see and welcome them for who they really are. To belong is not just to be a team member but to be able to participate in cocreating the workplace that you belong to. It's also consistently and universally tied to a person's workplace commitment, motivation, and pride, according to Culture Amp (n.d.), a culture-driven people analytics platform. Asking the question, "Will this help someone feel like they belong?" is a good starting place throughout all the work we will do together.

When I joined the workforce in 1998, I quickly learned that to survive, I needed to put on emotional armor every day. For years, I had to leave parts of myself at the door because it wasn't safe for me to bring my whole authentic self in. Like many women of color and other marginalized identities, I know what it feels like not to be included or welcomed into the social circles where networking and advancement thrive. And I was one of the lucky ones because I had managers who empowered me to do my best work, often advocating and opening up doors for new opportunities. But even they were unaware of the racial power hierarchies that kept so many talented people sidelined and marginalized. They were ill equipped to understand the stress of being stereotyped.

Covering, as coined by Kenji Yoshino (2006), is a form of identity camouflage where an individual downplays part of themselves, and code-switching has a profoundly negative effect in the workplace. I've seen too many women and people of color exhaust themselves by being constantly on-guard to cope with discrimination. Forty-two percent of women of color, 40% of men of color, and 40% of women of all backgrounds cited being, "on-guard in anticipation of racial or gender bias," according to a 2016 study from Catalyst. Other people responded that they felt on-guard because they felt as if their physical appearance, disability, age, or religious beliefs diminished their opportunities (Dnika, Thorpe-Moscon, and McCluney 2016).

Workers of color tend to be more socially distant in the workplace because they carry the burdens of past mistreatments or even just a lack of caring. When BIPOC staff are routinely forgotten on invitations to essential meetings, confused for event staff, or not approached to join after-work events, that stings. I've been there. When employees have to expend boundless energy to survive in their environment, what do you think happens to their output? To their relationships with colleagues and supervisors? They cannot give their best 100% because they are working from a mental and physical deficit—they spend the majority of their energy on emotional and corporate politics, all of which can lead to heightened responses at the wrong times.

As I've shared earlier, as humans our need to belong is innate. We all want to feel seen, heard, and valued—that we deserve to be "here," wherever that is. Have you ever felt left out, underestimated, or sidelined at work? Maybe it was when you shared an idea in a meeting only for it to be co-opted by someone else or simply ignored. Perhaps it was when you found out that a new team member with less experience was hired at your level and with a higher salary. I will never forget when I was brought in on a major project in my department, only to realize that I was asked to lead and execute a team project that I had in fact been previously excluded from for months. My teammates were already in the ideation process long before I was asked to bring my ideas. It seemed like including me had been an afterthought. In that moment of realization, my ego deflated, my shoulders slumped, and I felt socially rejected.

That isolation and lack of connection is the dark side of corporate culture, and most of us have been both victims and perpetrators. Hypocrisy runs deep: As someone who has been the leader of global diversity and inclusion initiatives, tasked with solving for and being the face of diversity programs across many organizations, I have faced my own inclusion battles. I have felt invisible and disposable, my voice muted by white men who had no trouble taking up all the space and air in every meeting and hallway conversation. Their sense of entitlement is rarely checked or questioned. But perhaps most painful was the silence and denial surrounding racial privilege and abuses of power that I have experienced from white women who advocated for diversity and inclusion but enforced expectations that I needed to conform to white cultural norms for how I dressed and behaved. Those who actively challenged gendered microaggressions but failed to do the same when I faced racially biased and inappropriate comments.

Barriers to inclusion tend to be invisible to those already succeeding in an organization. If you've navigated your organization successfully, it may be difficult to see how systemic and cultural barriers prevent some people from successfully navigating your workplace. You've become so accustomed to fitting in to the dominant culture that you miss the cues and roadblocks others experience.

You may now be asking yourself, "Okay, I've reflected and have a vision of where I want to go. Where do I begin?" Use this book as a guide to starting to chip away at personal and organizational bias in norms, behaviors, processes, and structures.

Your road map to reflect, vision, act, and persist is unique to you and will serve you on your journey well past reading this book. I will share practices that can help you drive impact in your organizations. It is up to you to be selective by choosing what will move the needle for your organization and be disciplined in the execution. Make sure to pause and reflect as I've mentioned earlier. Inclusion nudges, unbiasing moments that matter, and small behavioral shifts can deliver change. Think of this book as a series of actionable nudges on your journey to culture transformation.

Your Road Map to Revolution

I believe that ongoing micro-moments of learning and action can change behavior. How we listen, teach, assess, train, embody, and test our courage affects our success in developing the cultural mindset shift required to dismantle racial inequity in the workplace. It can be done. It may feel overwhelming to want to do everything, to try everything, and not know where to begin. At the end of every chapter, you'll find nudges toward action to help create your own road map to revolution.

- Reflect and get clear on your ambitions. Ask yourself, "Why do I want to do this work? Why is it important to me? What can make it important? What are the roadblocks here?"
- Craft an opportunity statement. Creating a more diverse, equitable, and inclusive workplace is critical because _____. Refer back to it when you're feeling stuck or tired. This will keep you focused, efficient, and effective.
- Confront your fears. What am I nervous or uncomfortable about? Will you let that stop you? Embrace courage, and know that you will make mistakes along the way. That's okay.

- Focus on your mindset. Go into the journey with an open mind and willingness to learn and grow. Practice saying, "I don't know." Think about what you can do to educate yourself, model inclusive behaviors, or change your mindset.

- Understand how deep bias runs in your workplace and the world. Start by recognizing your own blind spots and assumptions— question why things are done a certain way and how they might be done differently. Rewrite the old rules. Ask: "What behavioral changes and interventions will have a greater chance of achieving my desired results?"

- Stop one-size-fits-all training. Listen to your employees, learn from the data, and ask for what your specific organization and managers need to create a more inclusive workplace. Ask: "How can we provide support, surface issues, or push for changes through our day-to-day interactions with others?"

- Build bridges to and connections with your customers, your team, your managers. What do they need from you to feel valued, empowered, and connected to a shared vision and goals? Think about them as you seek to build inclusive teams where everyone feels a sense of belonging.

- Remember to take a beat. Look before you leap. Give yourself some grace to reflect before you act.

2

Build the Best Teams, Period

Why do we hire people? Because we need help, ideas, skills, and support to build and grow. But what if we take a step back from the nitty-gritty of the hiring process—a grueling operation that's laden with bias, privilege, secret handshakes, and unfair treatment—and focus on the larger purpose of hiring? As you approach this work, your first thought shouldn't be: "I need to get more Black and Brown people on our team." It should be, "I want to create the most successful team ever." And what does success look like? To me, it's a team that is reflective and representative of our country at large where nobody is excluded because of their differences.

You can design and implement the most inclusive hiring practices. Still, if your managers are unwilling to champion DEI across the business, you will struggle to attract and retain diverse talent. Reactive hiring practices aren't sustainable. Telling people they "have to hire a Black person" doesn't work because that language focuses on a binary, quantitative measurement of success, which only produces short-term, non-inclusive results—they follow the script once and believe their work is done. This hire is labeled a diversity hire, is automatically laden with low expectations, and is thus doomed from the start. The working biases and assumptions of the company have not been discussed openly, and so this Black hire has been set up to fail. Since this person will inevitably feel misunderstood and undervalued, they will no doubt fail or quit, reversing the company's original compositional diversity lift.

One female senior executive I know who works at a global beauty company was directed by her CEO to hire the sole Black woman being evaluated for the job because she didn't currently have a Black woman on her team. The candidate had a noncompete that wouldn't allow her to start at the company for six months, so the manager was frustrated that she was strongly instructed to hire someone that wouldn't be able to ease operational stress for half the year. I advised her to stop focusing on the fact that she was asked to hire this specific candidate to fill out her team's compositional diversity and put pressure on her recruiters to find a broader selection of viable candidates to choose from. This woman is not the best hire now because of her noncompete, and the CEO should look beyond optics and recognize that there are many other talented individuals with professionally solid backgrounds across all racial and ethnic groups. When pushed to yield, I say, push back.

You can't just focus on quantitative results and tackle diversity without first addressing the need for an authentic culture of belonging. That means BIPOC staff's unique challenges need to have already been openly discussed, as well as any roadblocks for BIPOC staff advancement. That is before sourcing, selecting, and onboarding underrepresented candidates. If a BIPOC hire is brought in, only to be socially isolated and treated as if they won't rise in the company because they don't "really" belong, they will leave.

I have yet to speak to a Fortune 500 company that has not implemented a diversity hiring strategy as one of their first diversity and inclusion initiatives. It's often the first move companies make to course-correct and attempt to build a pipeline of diverse talent in entry-level, management, technical, and executive roles. Big and small companies have diversity goals in place. They try to revamp the status quo of hiring by expanding the demographics of their talent pools and changing their processes. There is an ever-growing list of companies striving to help them remove bias, track metrics, and accelerate their progress through their technologies. I've seen many of these strategies in action; many of them fail; and I've experimented with many of my own.

Fair and transparent hiring mechanisms are an essential driver of diverse representation, but we're not doing it right. According to the Society for Human Resource Management, 57% of recruiters say their talent acquisition strategies are designed to attract diverse candidates, yet their processes and results say otherwise (Ideal n.d.).

To desegregate workplaces, hiring managers must be willing to question their choices at every stage of the process—from sourcing, screening, interviewing, selection, and onboarding. Then they need to move in a different, actively anti-racist direction. If your current hiring practices have shown years of majority white hires, whiteness has been privileged in your hiring practices. Instead of asking, "Why aren't there more qualified BIPOC candidates?" you should ask yourself, "Why are we allowing this company to be a whites-only space at every level of the organization?

A diverse team doesn't happen overnight. Cultural change takes time, and representation is only one measure of progress. We need to start somewhere. To set yourself up for success, you need metrics (what you'll measure), transparency (to keep you honest), and accountability (Who is responsible? The recruiter? The hiring manager? The team leader? The colleague who made the referral? Quick tip: the answer is all of the above).

It's time for a new hiring playbook. A new corporate playbook, too.

The following few chapters will tackle the hiring process and suggest tried-and-tested and emerging strategies to create more opportunities and align your intent with your practices.

Help Underrepresented Talent Envision Themselves at Your Company

Most companies have a solid hiring process and a stated commitment to diversifying their workforce. More recently, many have claimed to be sharpening their focus on hiring more Black leaders across all levels of their organizations. Knowing the business case for diversity is not enough: you must align your mission with your hiring goals. Even if you're not the CEO, you must clearly state to your team what DEI means to you. You must explain why it matters to build a diverse team of diverse leaders to deliver the best outcomes for your organization. Your team members need to connect to your organization's mission and values. And the talent you seek to hire needs to feel convinced that they will contribute and grow on your team.

Salesforce promotes equality in its diversity mission statement ("We're greater when we're equal"); T-Mobile says, "Uniqueness is powerful" (T-Mobile Career Site n.d.). These are beautiful sentiments, and I applaud them for promoting this message. What comes next is most important: after you craft a statement that packs a punch you must deliver on it. Your hiring mission should amplify your overall values and goals and act as a guide or reminder throughout the process. It should be bold and specific. It should describe what it's like to work at your company from the perspective of various voices and identities.

For example, Disney's company mission is: "To entertain, inform and inspire people around the globe through the power of unparalleled storytelling, reflecting the iconic brands, creative minds and innovative technologies that make ours the world's premier entertainment company" (Walt Disney Corporate Site n.d.). Their hiring marketing tagline, "Where will your story begin?" succinctly reminds candidates about the promise of being part of the treasured stories associated with the brand. But if you haven't seen yourself reflected in those stories before, well, perhaps being more direct, as in "Every story matters. Where will your story begin?" can help candidates see themselves as active agents in telling *new* stories. That's how you get the attention of those who think in terms of their complex identities, values, and passions.

Translate and discuss this with your whole team, not just your hiring team. Word-of-mouth referrals often carry the most weight, which makes everyone a recruiter. Companies that succeed onboard *all* employees in their mission to increase BIPOC, LGBTQIA+, and female or nonbinary job opportunities. Ask yourself, How does your hiring mission contribute to company goals? Why should everyone on the team care? For Disney, this could look like: we need more perspectives to tell better, more authentic and relatable stories. For Salesforce, it could be: when our sales teams reflect and create for the communities, voices, and movements of our time, our clients grow.

Common People United, a digital strategy company focused on facilitating community works and activism, translates its company philosophy, "Work that matters," into an HR mission. On their website, they write:

"We absolutely need big thinkers, big personalities, and big movements to see positive change on a national or global scale. We also need small groups of people doing work that matters on a day-to-day basis, and we try to surround ourselves with people who feel the same way" (Common People United website n.d.). When you connect this to an inclusive hiring mindset that helps prospective candidates see themselves at Common People United as the big thinkers, personalities, and movement makers who will be welcomed and allowed to drive change, you have a winning recruitment strategy.

If your CEO is not doing this, get them to listen to what achieving racial representation means to you and your business and how to get untapped talent in your organization. As the tech start-up AppNexus grew, there was a persistent impression that they didn't have enough women in leadership. "There were always 'reasons' why," says founder and CEO Brian O'Kelley, but he wanted to understand the root cause of this leadership gap. Flimsy excuses of a shortage of talent weren't enough. When he was invited to a meeting held by the AppNexus Women's Network, he jumped at the chance to listen in . . . until they started talking. Brian was confronted by their stories, the reality of their experience at the company, he was peppered with questions about the lack of women on their board, the lack of growth opportunities. "It was really hard to hear," Brian says. "It would have been so easy to walk out of there and do nothing. But I was the CEO and sitting in that room, I had the realization that it was my responsibility to fix" (O'Kelley 2020).

Brian credits a change in his vantage point for the company's transformation. Instead of focusing on the *why not* (why aren't we hiring more female leaders? Why don't we have a woman on the board?), he shifted his focus to the *why* (having a female board member will make us more attractive to VC firms; putting women in senior roles of responsibility will help us recruit more female talent; when we have women on the team, our sales grow). That mindset soon became contagious throughout the company.

Like O'Kelley's team, you can invite your CEO or senior executives to an affinity group meeting, email them, share your thoughts with your boss, ask a question at a town hall—use your boss to hold the higher-ups accountable. It's also imperative to tune in to what is not being said. What are people's fears, blind spots, or obstacles to hiring racially diverse talent?

"For years, McKinsey has been putting out rigorous international data on the financial performance of companies with diverse leadership, diverse boards, and that those companies outpace and outperform everyone," says Freada Kapor Klein (2020), partner of Kapor Capital. "So if business was truly rational, they would have seized on that years ago. But it's not rational, and instead it's packed with fear."

When you build an inclusive hiring strategy and mission, if you dig deep enough, at some point you have to ask yourself, Who's going to give up their seat at the table to make room for someone else? That's the elephant in the room; that's what everyone is afraid to say. If people in positions of power are invested in the change they claim they wish to see, they will remove themselves from the equation and ensure that those who have been ready to take on these roles be considered to replace them and are given the resources and timeline to succeed. We increasingly see white male board members give up their seats following sexual harassment allegations. Does it need to be only then? In other words, do you care enough to get out of the way for someone's advancement? And if you haven't addressed the anxiety that comes with that and the shared responsibility required to make it happen, your DEI strategies are set up to fail.

I've often heard that people don't fear change; they fear loss. When talking about your DEI mission, you need to reduce the fear of loss, fear of being replaced and misunderstood, fear of losing the privilege and power often taken for granted, fear of being uncomfortable. Instead you need to invite others to be part of the change through a shared sense of purpose and benefit. A scarcity mindset believes that if one person wins, another person loses; an abundance mindset focuses on the limitless opportunities available. It can be hard to believe in an abundance mindset when the economy dips and threatens job security or when opportunities are in fact limited due to racial bias. Still, an abundance mindset focuses on the fact that each of us does better when we all do better. That's why this work matters.

Confronting Privilege in the Hiring Process

Privilege is a word that's tossed around a lot, but it's essential to understand that the privilege you may hold because of your race, sexual orientation, gender or gender identity, ability, socioeconomic status, or religion can lead to shortcuts for you while creating obstacles for others. In short, a white person's professional achievements are shaped by systems of privileges that funnel them forward, such as having access to white professional networks that come with job references. "I have come to see white privilege as an invisible package of unearned assets that I can count on cashing in each day, but about which I was 'meant' to remain oblivious," writes Peggy McIntosh, author of *White Privilege: Unpacking the Invisible Knapsack*. "White privilege is like an invisible weightless knapsack of special provisions, maps, passports, codebooks, visas, clothes, tools, and blank checks" (Davis 2021).

It's normal to be resistant or defensive about admitting your privilege. Privilege is the ability to look away; I'm asking you not to look away. Tension erupts because privilege threatens people's two central desires: we want to live in a fair, meritocratic system and to feel like a good person. When the concept of privilege doesn't fit with your self-perceptions, you tend to justify your privilege and deny its existence or dynamics. Michael Sandel (2020), professor of political philosophy at Harvard University, coined the term "Tyranny of Merit," and urges individuals to take a look in the mirror—at their "meritocratic hubris"—and stop believing in their success as their own doing while they look down on others who haven't made it.

"How do we have an honest conversation about dismantling this idea that we have meritocracy and that every white man who is in a position of power earned it, because he didn't?" says Reshma Saujani (2020), founder of Girls Who Code and author of *Brave Not Perfect* and *Pay Up: The Future of Women and Work (and Why It's Different Than You Think)*. "We don't touch that or address that, and until we do, we are going to have the same conversation. As a South Asian woman, I acknowledge my privilege, but people assume facts about me that allow my voice to not be heard. I'm often overlooked, or bumped into. I have had my hand raised real high, but no one really saw it. I'm assumed to be smart, but not violent. No one is crossing the street when I come walking down." Privilege is a transient concept—you can be privileged in one room and not the other.

When people are perceived to "be different" from the majority, privileged culture, their potential and contributions are also perceived differently. Many Black women have felt pressured to conform to European standards of straight hair because Black people's natural hair has long been considered "unprofessional." As reported in *USA Today*, several states and cities have passed or proposed laws banning policies that penalize people of color for wearing natural curls, dreadlocks, twists, braids, and other hairstyles that embrace their cultural identity (Terry and Jones 2019). However, this overwhelming racist bias in notions of professionalism continues to plague our workplaces.

White men and women, for the most part, know their power grants them access and safety that will be largely unquestioned. But it's easier to deflect blame than to face white supremacist views because you have convinced yourself that only others hold those unpleasant views. Dismantling racism, sexism, and all the isms means disrupting the status quo. Anti-racism requires white people to sacrifice a comfort created through someone else's oppression. That includes the ease of moving through majority white spaces. White and BIPOC managers must believe diverse colleagues when they speak uncomfortable truths. And all managers need to leverage our privileges—seniority, whiteness, heterosexuality, or wealth—for change.

I'm not asking those who currently hold most of the power—namely, white, male managers—to be powerless. This is about a redistribution of power. Yes, in some cases, you may need to move on to create space, but what would be truly revolutionary is for everyone to use their power for good. Once you can see how systems and structures create inequity on the individual level—both the advantages and disadvantages—then you can start fixing them.

For example, your privilege can grant you the power to speak up and act on behalf of others, and research shows that when you do, your words and actions can be particularly effective (Dnika, Thorpe-Moscon, and McCluney 2016). The raw truth is that advocating for a new hire or a policy holds more weight from a white senior manager. When BIPOC colleagues do the same, they are held to a higher standard of results. Research from the Academy of Management found that when a white male manager made a hiring decision, it had no impact on his performance rating—even if that candidate did not look like him. But when a BIPOC male manager hired someone who looked like him, he took a hit for it (Ibarra et al. 2010). That's privilege in action.

Use your privilege to:

- Examine your hiring process with a critical lens toward reducing bias. Suggest changes to recruitment and hiring systems—how we identify, research, generate pipelines, and network with potential job candidates and how we recruit, select, hire, and make offers to candidates—that have been rigged to keep so many locked out.
- Diversify your professional network. Most people are hired through referrals, and most white people have all-white social circles and professional networks. Seek out diversity-focused professional organizations that you could use for referrals, and encourage your colleagues to do the same.
- Be vigilant about identifying and removing obstacles so racially diverse talent can move through the hiring process fairly and consistently.

Everything from a job description to your company's profile in career sites to your website's career section should reinforce your company's inclusive culture and ethos. Removing bias from hiring practices and opening up job opportunities to people who might not traditionally have had access to them are critical parts of reducing inequities in organizational operations. Relinquishing unfair advantages in the hiring process is not reverse discrimination. Racial progress and confronting white professional norms do not mean that white people are under attack. It's time to broaden the definition of "us" and refocus our hiring habits toward broadening opportunity, belonging, and equity.

A word about white privilege: White privilege does not mean that if you are white, you have not experienced hardship or exclusion. If you were the first in your family to go to college, you didn't have access to workplace navigational tools either. It simply means that you have not experienced racism, and that racism has not been a barrier to entry and opportunity. White fragility is when white people experience discomfort when faced with their role in perpetuating white supremacy. We all have to get better at sitting with discomfort and not allowing it to block action and change.

Metrics for Hiring Success

An inclusive and equitable hiring process requires that you evaluate the funnel through which candidates move through, understand how privilege affects access, set ambitious goals, hold people accountable for pass-through rates, and monitor progress. Below is a simple recruitment metrics format adapted from Ian Cook (2016) and many of the great recruiters with whom I have worked over the years:

1. *Who is moving (and dropping) through each hiring stage?*

    Metrics: Intersectional diversity demographics by hiring stage (pass-through rates).

    Monitor applicant and candidate progress across all hiring stages (sourcing, screening, interviewing, and offers) to accurately track the health of racially diverse applicants and candidate representation (note: an applicant becomes a candidate when they move to the screening stage). Suppose your initial candidate pipeline has a high level of BIPOC talent and you notice a significant drop after the screening interview. That may mean you need to address potential biases in how recruiters or hiring managers are reviewing job applications when they meet potential candidates.

2. *Who is doing the interviewing and making offers?*

    Metric: Intersectional composition and inclusive hiring skills of interviewers and those making offers.

    A balance of interviewers representing various demographics will bring unique viewpoints to the process and help candidates feel more comfortable in various recruitment settings. Have your interviewers been trained in inclusive hiring? Are they using behavioral and competency-based interviewing techniques? Or are they making decisions based on their biased ideas about how an ideal candidate should look and behave? Are those making offers equipped to consider biases in final decision-making?

3. *Who is accepting (and rejecting) offers?*

    Metric: New hires by demographic versus existing workforce by demographic / New hires by demographic versus available labor pool.

An inclusive hiring process aims to deliver a healthy acceptance rate of racially diverse talent. You should also assess the impact on your workforce demographics. Suppose you're hiring racially diverse talent, but your workforce demographics do not shift meaningfully. In that case, you need to assess turnover rates by demographic, or as I call it, the "diversity revolving door."

Set Bold Goals

Everyone needs accountability. Without KPIs or measurable goals at every stage of the hiring process, talk of increasing compositional diversity is just talk. Hold your company accountable to your revitalized mission with diversity hiring KPIs and objective goals that can be measured and tracked. The bolder, the better. These should be lofty goals and not a minor percentage increase, which produces superficial data that "our diversity numbers are improving." Let's stop using dated standards to define success in diversity hiring outcomes such as overemphasizing the diversity composition of entry level talent and focusing solely on hiring white women without recognizing the intersectional barriers for women of color.

In 2018, AppNexus's O'Kelley kicked off their annual global customer conference, encouraged by the women's network demands that he do better. O'Kelley looked at the 2017 conference lineup and calculated that only three out of 20 speakers were women, establishing a goal to double that number. "I was so proud at the end of that conference," O'Kelley says. "Not only was it a robust, seamless event packed with great content, I was thrilled that we had increased the number of female speakers. I thought I made a big difference." But then O'Kelley got a call from a colleague. "She told me that the Women's Network was livid because even though there were more women on stage, men still spoke for 90% of the time and there was never a woman on stage without a man. I felt like I was punched in the gut. Initially, I got defensive and mad. I thought, 'Are you kidding me?'" (O'Kelley 2020).

O'Kelley admits it took him an hour to cool down and realize the error in his thinking. He called back and said, "Okay, tell me again." He realized that even though the overall representation metrics were a dramatic improvement over the previous year, the measures of success failed to take into account status quo blind spots that assumed men were still the stand-ard go-to. "That's Diversity 1.0," Kelley says. "At that conference, I was the best Diversity 1.0 CEO, but the women of my company rightly decided to change the standard so I failed them as a Diversity 2.0 CEO. Diversity 2.0 is about equity. When I did a conference post-mortem with the team, I praised them for crushing every metric we set out, and then told them it still wasn't good enough. We needed better metrics."

So what's good enough? What should be expected? At a minimum, your racial+ (race, gender, class, ability, age, nationality, ethnicity, etc.) diver-sity goal should be 50% of your total workforce; or try double what it is now. When setting goals, consider possible growth, contraction, promotion processes, and restructuring plans. Will hitting your goals require massive turnover, or is there a budget for a hiring spree? Will every new hire have to meet one of these representation gaps? While corporate recruitment direc-tives can't legally require that every new hire be female, Black, or Latinx, targets such as these can create a shared sense of accountability for recruit-ment practices and internal restructurings.

Project Include has for years advocated for setting specific demographic targets in the technology sector. In 2019, Ellen Pao, cofounder and CEO of Project Include, provided guidance to Silicon Valley start-ups and tech companies for setting four D&I targets (10-10-5-45) in two years: 10% rep-resentation for Black employees, 10% for Latinx employees, 5% for nonbi-nary employees, and 45% for women. They set these targets after reviewing representation gaps across their roster of start-up clients over several years and to avoid watering down the definition of diversity, which has histori-cally resulted in hiring more white women, and maintaining a vastly white workforce. "The most encouraging result we've seen is that hiring teams with gender and race diversity early on creates a flywheel effect that makes attracting, hiring, and retaining candidates from all underrepresented back-grounds dramatically easier," reported Ellen Pao (2019) in a Medium post.

When setting goals, top-down and bottom-up can be equally successful. For example, the BBC's 50:50 Project, a grassroots effort to reach gender parity in journalism, helped reset the organization through a common goal and the voluntary sharing and tracking of data. What started as a simple idea introduced in one program in the BBC newsroom unleashed a movement, a revolution! Here's how it started: At the end of each night's primetime news program, the production team would take two minutes to count and record the gender split of guests, with monthly reporting. In January 2017, during its first month of counting, the show reached 39% of women as contributors. Three months later, it hit 51% for the first time. Following proof of concept, Ros Atkin, founder of the 50:50 Project, and his team shared instructions, guidelines, measurement templates, and checklists with other programs. In March 2020, two-thirds of teams reached at least 50% women in their output, an increase of a third from where they began.

To add this level of powerful strategy to your numbers, consider critical mass theory. While it has been highly debated in academic circles, I favor Rosabeth Moss Kanter's articulation of it as a threshold to guide organizational transformations (Childs and Krook 2008). *Critical mass* is a term borrowed from nuclear physics that refers to the quantity needed to start a chain reaction, in this case, the idea that one-third or more representation of minority groups can influence or "tilt" the group's culture. As a guidepost to close racial and gender gaps alone, this won't solve for unequal treatment, but it can shape your aspirational goals. It is possible to get to critical mass, but it needs to be a widespread, cross-company effort. Otherwise, you end up with a misshapen workplace.

For example, in tech, the BIPOC representations on marketing, legal, and HR teams are generally higher than in engineering. Those individual groups will boost a company's representative diversity. Still, you're not going to eliminate biases and barriers across the organization until you've also achieved critical mass in the engineering functions—the core revenue-generating sources of power.

"There is a tipping point in organizations. When between 20% to 33% of a company is made up of underrepresented groups, there is the sense of critical mass," says Kapor Klein. "That is transformative, especially when it exists from the top to the bottom in the hierarchy, especially in more prestigious parts of the organizations" (Klein 2020).

Tackling the Fear of Reverse Discrimination

I am often asked if it's illegal to set a goal tied to representation gaps. Many companies worry about the tension between legitimate efforts to promote representational diversity and reverse discrimination. The aim is not to make hiring decisions based on any single demographic consideration. However, we have long been giving undue recruiting advantages to white men and women in the workplace. That is what we're essentially being asked to rebalance. So yes, we need to add more demographic diversity to the mix—the slates from which you are to draw from in searches, high potential, and succession pools—to ensure the final selections are representative of the workforce you aspire to build.

Diversifying talent pools, whether for promotions as noted in Korn Ferry's "Five Classic (and Overlooked) D&I Mistakes" (Tapia and Kirtzma 2019) or for recruitment practices, is about leveling the playing field so that there is ample diversity in the selection process. Goals or targets that consider race, gender, and other protected traits are legal, acceptable tools for combatting underrepresentation. These efforts may be lawful if they (1) seek to eliminate imbalances in traditionally segregated jobs, (2) do not unduly harm nonminority workers, and (3) serve as a temporary measure to eliminate imbalance and are not intended to maintain a new balance.

That said, this is complicated. I have never met an in-house legal team who didn't fret at the idea of establishing representation goals for placing people in specific jobs. Even if an employer is using an objective hiring assessment, results could be perceived as discriminatory. If you somehow depart from those practices to increase diverse representation in your workforce, it can create a claim of reverse discrimination.

In short, you can ask for BIPOC candidates, but you cannot demand to hire one. There should be an equal pool of candidates to evaluate. You can tweet that your company is seeking to hire diverse talent for an opening: "We're actively seeking diverse candidates for a new account management position" or "We're committed to inclusive hiring practices—apply to be our new Creative Director." However, it cannot be the sole consideration when you are trying to fill a job opening. Under federal employment discrimination laws, a decision not to hire someone because of race, color, sex (including pregnancy, sexual orientation, or gender identity), age, religion, national origin, disability, and genetic information (including family medical history) is illegal. Again, you can approach a friend outside your company and say you'd love some BIPOC candidate recommendations for an opening. Then add them to the mix for consideration based on qualifications.

An excellent way to avoid discrimination claims is to not discriminate in the first place.

Talk about this with your teams and train them often to combat the fear that you're doing something wrong by being specific in your recruiting goals. Explain the legality of it. Companies such as Google and HPE have long offered diversity recruitment training to ensure all employees are well versed in the do's and don'ts of diversity hiring practices.

Share this talking point, "It's not illegal to focus your talent search when trying to correct a diversity gap." But you should understand the risks; as Julie Levinson Werner (2020) from the law firm Lowenstein Sandler LLP notes, "There is a difference between committing to hire and promote a certain percentage of individuals on the basis of their race or other factors and committing to interview and/or consider these individuals for hire or promotion."

What's illegal is making a decision based on a protected class. The challenge is that when you put those practices in place, hiring managers can sometimes game the process by only selecting Black candidates for a specific role, for example. Beyond being illegal and creating legal risk for the company, it also doesn't set up the candidate for success when hired. This practice can reinforce negative stereotypes. The perception of being the "Black hire" becomes their burden to carry unfairly. Setting diversity-focused hiring goals is always perceived as tricky legally, but I believe in sharing transparent goals based on representation gaps in distinct areas, say content creation, senior leadership, and software development, and then applying specific and measurable interventions to address those gaps as we've discussed in this chapter.

When in doubt, always seek the advice of HR or your employment counsel. Lawyers stick to the letter of the law because that's their responsibility. You should aim to build a relationship with your HR and legal partners and work together to create the best workforce. No one wants to get sued, but you also want to make sure you're pushing when you can to address system failures. The irony is that equal opportunity laws were established to create more opportunity for more people—and to protect everybody the same way! It's all in the expectations you set and the operating mechanisms you put in place to reduce adverse impact.

Spelling out a commitment to fair hiring practices, such as your equal employment opportunity (EEO) statement in job descriptions, is basic and necessary—it's now become standard to use language such as "We encourage people from traditionally underrepresented groups such as Black, indigenous, Latinx, Asian, Middle East, and North African talent to apply." Kapor Capital's job postings are an excellent example. They read: "In keeping with our beliefs and goals, no employee or applicant will face discrimination/harassment based on: race, color, ancestry, national origin, religion, age, gender, marital/ domestic partner status, sexual orientation, gender identity, disability status, or veteran status. Above and beyond discrimination/harassment based on 'protected categories,' Kapor Capital also strives to prevent other, subtler forms of inappropriate behavior (e.g. stereotyping) from ever gaining a foothold in our office. Whether blatant or hidden, barriers to success have no place at Kapor Capital."

Incentivize Goal Achievement

Academic researchers Iris Bohnet and Siri Chilazi (2020) have shown that behavior change requires transformations along two dimensions: the *will* and the *way*. It's not enough to be motivated to be an inclusive leader or to publicly commit to anti-racism if you do not have the knowledge and the skills to act on that ambition. Goals have the potential to transform behaviors because they provide both the will (motivation) and the way (understanding and skills) to change.

When goal setting, how you incentivize and hold people responsible for achieving the desired outcome can be the difference between success and failure. Accountability is key; there is no other route to success. Goals help motivate behavioral change by promoting accountability and transparency; boosting pride, recognition, and competitiveness; and shifting perceptions of desirable outcomes.

Diversity hiring goals should be a part of every employee's job description and annual performance review and should be factored into compensation and promotion decisions. Meeting the company diversity hiring goals should be stressed explicitly for middle managers and executives whose positions enable them to change company hiring practices directly.

In five years, Nike has achieved more than 50% BIPOC representation through inclusive hiring practices such as holding leaders accountable for representational growth in their teams by attaching key metrics to hiring. Now, Nike has its aims on senior leadership positions and has pledged in the next five years to increase the representation of women and BIPOC in those roles, tying executive compensation to the success of hitting them (Thomas 2021).

A top-bottom approach of linking hiring goals with executive compensation, such as Accenture's, Johnson & Johnson's, Nike's, Mercer's, and other companies', can be equally successful in engaging the whole company. In an article for *Fast Company*, Jennifer Jordan and Sonal Lakhani shared examples of charges made by global forums aimed at shifting the representation of women founders, including how "the World Economic Forum called for venture capitalists, limited partners and accelerators to target 30% of funding for teams with at least one woman founder, and called for media organizations to make the "30% airtime" pledge—advocating that 30% of on-air, quoted or panelist experts be women" (Jordan and Lakhani 2021).

Even if you're unable to influence new hires across departments, or even have the approval for your own hires, you can, as a manager, set your own metrics of success for what you can control. What is the composition of your team, and what do you think it should be? When you have an open role on your team, clearly define the opportunity to shift composition—for your business and culture. Be as specific as possible to align your recruitment plans with business needs. Also think about what other aspects of the business you can "hire" for, whether it's a product vendor, a freelancer or contingent worker, or speakers at a conference.

Next, communicate them broadly. Studies have shown that when you share your goals with others, you are twice as likely to achieve them. And when you share them publicly with the world, millions of people watch and keep score.

Joe Biden publicly committed to hiring a female VP (and he did!), and Reddit cofounder Alexis Ohanian recently stepped down from its board and via Twitter urged his colleagues to fill his seat with a Black candidate (CNBC 2020). Some parliaments around the world achieve fairer gender representation (at least 50% female) through various reforms such as fining parties every year if they don't have gender parity, or by using a "zipper" method, where a seat alternates between male and female leaders.

In 2015, April Reign was watching the Academy Award nominations while getting ready for work. "It struck me that there were no people of color nominated, so I picked up my phone and tweeted '#OscarsSoWhite they asked to touch my hair,'" she told *The New York Times* (Ugwu 2020). It was the tweet that started a movement. In turn, the Academy of Motion Picture Arts and Sciences (aka the Oscars Council) acknowledged they had work to do to address their membership which was 94% white and 77% male. The proof was in the envelope: the 2015 nominations and best director snub for Ava Duvernay for *Selma*, reflected a supreme lack of diversity and was reflective of who had voting power.

But a year later, all 20 Oscars acting nominations went to white performers again. This is often the case in corporations when hiring initiatives fluctuate given shifting priorities at the leadership level and lack of focus on retention. At an emergency meeting, the board of governors launched A2020, a plan to double the number of women and ethnically underrepresented members in four years. They had to hit these goals; the Twitterverse was watching.

And they did. In 2020, the Academy invited 819 new members, 36% of which were BIPOC and 45% women. To balance the compositional diversity throughout the organization—not just at the bottom, they also added six new governors, three women, and one BIPOC.

Besides mandating unconscious bias training for all governors and a commitment to building an anti-racist and inclusive organization, it set new and transformative rules for membership: New members will be eligible for a 10-year membership and must remain active in the film industry in some capacity.

This means that aging white men no longer have membership for life, a practice that has for decades reduced opportunities for non-white men and women seeking access to executive and board positions. If we continue to focus our diversity hiring efforts on the entry-level candidates alone, it will be decades before change happens at the senior level. These thoughtfully targeted new measures aimed at tackling the bespoke needs of the Academy show that there isn't a one-size-fits-all solution to diversity hiring—practices have to be tailored to the organization.

According to a McKinsey report on the Black workplace experience in the US private sector, it will take 95 years for Black employees to reach talent parity (or 12% representation, equal to their current population percentage) (McKinsey Institute For Black Economic Mobility 2023). Why do companies continue to prioritize investing their capital in semi-retired white men instead of hiring racially and ethnically diverse emerging talent? One step is to acknowledge the systems that keep institutions such as the Academy overwhelmingly old, white, and male and create a new system, such as term limits. The Oscars also released new inclusion standards for its best picture nominees, whereby a lead actor, subject matter, or percentage of the cast must highlight an underrepresented group. While these standards fall short at transforming an industry whose entire ecosystem is based on sustaining white male power, it's a start to thread diversity in all business layers. We can all learn lessons from these tailor-made goals to reach critical mass for all aspects of your work life.

Your Road Map to Revolution

As Robert Livingston (2020) notes in "How to Promote Racial Equality in the Workplace," people wrongly assume that increasing workforce diversity means sacrificing principles of fairness and merit, because it requires giving "special" accommodations to BIPOC candidates rather than treating everyone the same. I, and other DEI practitioners, have long argued that a racially sensitive management team reduces systemic disparities and treats people fairly by sometimes treating others differently. To recruit a more diverse workforce, everyone involved in the hiring process needs to understand the hiring goals and why they matter and be held accountable for hiring with DEI in mind. Every recruiter knows how painful it is when someone in the chain—the hiring manager, the interviewers, and leadership—breaks the systems of accountability. These practices should be just the starting point for you and your organization.

- **Gain clarity on your hiring mission.** Explain why it matters and that building a diverse workforce is an organizational priority. This mission should be bold and specific. Discuss and share it with your team to ensure everyone is on board.

- **Identify how bias and privilege appear in the hiring process.** If you have it, use your privilege and power for good! Measure the percentage of underrepresented talent at every stage of the hiring funnel—sourcing, screening, interviewing, and selection—to determine what works and what needs adjusting.

- **Design ambitious hiring goals.** To do so, take a look at your current workforce and look for representation gaps. Create bold targets (at least 50% growth) based on minimizing those gaps plus your capability for adding headcount. Discuss critical mass theory to help your team understand the importance of setting such goals.

- **Discuss the legal dos and don'ts of the hiring process.** How can you be an equal-opportunity employer while aiming to correct representation gaps? Offer training for all employees to better understand how to do this.

- **Hold people accountable to your goals.** Tie them to compensation and rewards or other metrics of success. Share them publicly to keep yourself in check.

3

Overhaul Your Recruitment

Soon after I left Google in 2017, engineer James Damore posted a fiery 10-page memo to an internal message board that argued that women aren't a "personality fit" to be an engineer and that the company was not inclusive, especially when it came to the ideas of conservative white men. Basically, he felt threatened by diversity initiatives. This was a white man who was arguing that white men were experiencing reverse discrimination. The full memo was posted to tech blogs and analyzed by mainstream media (Wakabayashi 2017).

This was not the first time that this tech giant was charged with the incongruencies of its diversity approach (perhaps the first time from a conservative white male POV though). But this was the first time it was forced to confront its inability to effectively address biases and barriers for underrepresented talent, while facing internal and external turmoil. If you can organize the world's information, how can you not better reflect it in your workforce? I had raised the issues of an ongoing culture of racism and sexism with Google leaders, and now they were very publicly being confronted with their years of inaction.

There's nothing like a PR crisis to put a fire under a CEO and senior leadership team. In February 2020, over three years after that contentious meeting where I presented our diversity hiring strategy, I was happy to see

41

that one of our biggest asks came to fruition. Sundar Pichai (2022), the CEO of Google, announced a $9.5 billion investment in the expansion of data centers across the United States to cities such as Atlanta, and southern states such as Texas, Alabama, South Carolina, Virginia, and Tennessee to create access and opportunities for a talent pool that has been there all along. In the tech industry there is a persistent assumption that failures in diversity hiring efforts result from limited Black talent. I'm hopeful in light of the trend toward a more remote and geographically dispersed workforce due to COVID 19 that more companies can follow suit and remove similar barriers to entry for hiring. And that Black professionals looking to break into these fields may no longer have to move to inhospitable tech hubs such as San Francisco, known for its lack of diversity and unaffordable housing markets.

Google took its time to get this right, but the time is now. We may all want to believe that our organization's hiring practices are fair and unbiased. But racially diverse candidates often face barriers and biases, including being held to higher standards, in the interview process that negatively impact hiring decisions. We have an opportunity to address with rigor what's needed to be anti-racist (thank you, Ibram X. Kendi) in our hiring process and enact real and sustainable change.

It's time to let go of recruitment processes that yield the same results year after year. Creating a new hiring process from beginning to end, including updating your recruitment applicant tracking systems, is hard work. Don't be afraid to abolish what doesn't work and add what does. In their application flow, Policygenius, an online insurance company, asks candidates to check off their preferred pronouns and record the pronunciation of their name. That small feature immediately conveys the sense of a welcoming, respectful culture.

Be willing to remove bias from recruiting and hiring and refine your process to fit the needs of different groups and individuals; otherwise, you risk remaining in the status quo instead of a revolution for good.

Building better teams is everyone's responsibility. Pay attention to what matters. We have historically focused on hiring pipelines but not on the deeper issues with workplace cultures with regard to access, opportunity, voice, pay inequities, and insensitive approaches to diversity and inclusion that cause people to leave or avoid working in certain industries. Consider these barriers for underrepresented groups, regardless of your role or level in the organization, as you take a closer look at your recruiting policies.

Stop Using Résumés as Gatekeepers

Ah, résumés, that one-page summarization of your greatness to prove your worth. They're also among the largest contributors to implicit bias and pattern matching in the hiring process. Rampant résumé bias at the screening stage—where recruiters and computers weed through résumés to find candidates that best meet hiring manager's job criteria—leads to a wealth of talent slipping through the cracks.

Let's name bias for starters, the highly documented practice of skipping over candidates with ethnic-sounding names that don't fit into the traditional white standard of professionalism. A Tamika may get passed over for a Tanya; a Sayed may get passed over for a Sam. Economists Marianne Bertrand and Sendhil Mullainathan (2004) found that white-sounding names such as Emily Walsh or Greg Baker received, on average, 50% more callbacks for interviews than African American–sounding names, such as Lakisha Washington or Jamal Jones. Or, as a study has found, Jamal needed eight more years of experience than Greg to be considered equally qualified (Williams and Mihaylo 2020). That's why African American and Asian job applicants who mask their race on résumé have better success getting job interviews, according to research by Katherine DeCelles and colleagues (Gerdeman 2017). This stereotype-based bias means that from the very start, the recruiter already sees someone that, whether they want to admit it or not, they may already feel is less competent or likely to fit in with the company culture—to meet their "hiring bar." These biased standards for professionalism are based on white norms, white European standards of what work is, what it should look like, and who belongs within those spaces. So a candidate has to spend more energy trying to sound and look like the candidate the company wants, rather than just be the talented individual they are.

I have managed several recruitment teams, so I understand that you can receive on average hundreds, if not thousands, of résumés for every open position, and that to get through growing piles of résumés, you need some gut check to make sure that applicants meet key qualifications. On average, recruiters take 7.4 seconds to scan a résumé, according to career website The Ladders' 2018 eye-tracking study (Lepore 2020). In less than 10 seconds they determine if an applicant is a "suitable match" based on first-impression information such as current job titles, company names, universities attended, and potential internships. This gut check, this gray area, is where bias rears its head.

Think about the last time you looked at a résumé—What details caught your eye and helped you decide if this candidate was worth talking to? Did you fall into the Ivy League, top-tier university, instant credibility trap? Many managers do and still believe that hiring Ivy League alum means hiring "the best," which in their minds will translate to stellar performance. But, of course, most of the country does not have an Ivy League degree. It's a poor determinant of performance, yet perhaps the most consistent exclusionary recruitment practice in both the screening and selection process. At Google, when they increased the number of universities from which they recruited for internships to non–Ivy League schools in 2014, they significantly increased the pool of talent from historically underrepresented backgrounds and, no surprise, the pool of interns that summer was far more diverse.

Some companies leverage technology to enact fairness at scale. At least 98% of Fortune 500 use applicant tracking systems to collect and sort thousands of résumés and redact key information or use AI technology to scan résumés for skills, eliminating potential bias. But the process in which résumés can earn bonus points for matching keywords in the job description or other preselected terms to eliminate unqualified candidates and filter the "best" résumés to the top is equally problematic.

Wharton assistant professor of business economics and policy Corinne Low, who conducted a résumé audit study, cautions against the reliance on machine scanning: "Firms need to remember that if you have some of these biases, they're going to get hardwired into the algorithm. You have to think very carefully about how to strip that out" (Knowledge at Wharton Staff 2019b).

Here's what will make a difference: stop putting so much weight on résumés. They're not a good indicator of success, as proven by researchers from Florida State University who found that previous work experience is a poor predictor of future job success and that there was zero correlation between experience, performance, or retention at future employers (Heller 2019). Résumés don't reveal soft skills either, which are a valuable asset in leadership potential. So why do we continue to use résumés as an evaluation tool? Because it's how we've always done it and because they provide easy shortcuts for assessment when you're hiring thousands of workers.

Some companies have stopped the practice entirely such as Greyston Bakery and The Body Shop (DeLong and Marcus 2021). Similarly, many colleges and universities have stopped requiring ACT or SAT scores because they recognize that performing well on these tests may be more indicative of one's privilege rather than intellect. Instead, these institutions are upping the stakes for interviews. I understand that companies have limited resources and simply cannot interview every single applicant, so they try to make it easier to filter people out. Here's what to do instead.

Emphasize the Cover Letter or a Creative Pitch

Cover letters have lost their favor in many industries or are seen as a perfunctory step in the process, but this is the real sales pitch—not a collection of facts about where you were lucky enough to go to college. At VICE Media Group, when we launched The 2030 Project, a fellowship seeking curious and passionate individuals whose career plans had been affected by COVID-19, one of the most creative pitches was a TikTok video that intrigued everyone about the applicant's potential. Ask candidates to tell you who they are and why they want this job—what will they bring to the table? What's not being said on their LinkedIn profile? What's their real story? *That* is a better indicator of someone's readiness and eagerness for the job than any listing of accomplishments.

Use a Q&A Platform as Part of Your Application Process

Whether via video or writing, ask a standard set of questions of every application. What are the top three questions you would ask in an interview? Use these as a first-round review. Wepow, for example, is a video interviewing platform company that allows you to meet more candidates without having to read mountains of résumés. Candidates can record responses to interview questions in their own time, eliminating the need to schedule interviews with recruiters. We used it at Viacom for sourcing entry-level candidates and found it to be an excellent screening tool to evaluate soft skills, the ability to problem-solve, work styles, and more for other roles.

Try a Skills Test or Neuroscience-Based Brain Games

Tech companies are infamous for their cognitive interview practices. Still, many others such as Tesla, Accenture, and LinkedIn have worked with a company called Pymetrics, which created a 30-minute game-playing scenario to evaluate a person's cognitive and emotional capabilities. Candidates take on puzzles and quizzes, which measure a person's problem-solving skills, fairness, generosity, and other critical abilities customized by the hiring manager. It's a relatively painless experience for candidates that helps companies select talent based on specific traits required for the job. To detect bias in its questions, Pymetrics continually analyzes answers to ensure the same demographic groups aren't "missing" the same answer.

Give a Work Sample Test

Assignments highlighting the type of work the person will be tasked with can offer key insight into their potential performance. In journalism, there's a practice of giving candidates an edit test where they are asked to complete a variety of tasks, from copyediting a paragraph to brainstorming ideas for a new section. Some of these tests are laborious, and there are stories of companies using the ideas in future projects without crediting the original thinker. But the essence of the assignment—to see the kind of work a candidate can produce, whether it's a creative brief or a market analysis—is a valuable screening tool. It can also weed out candidates who aren't serious about the position and don't want to spend the time.

Stop the Friends and Family Program

Representational diversity hasn't shifted because personal recommendations often outweigh a recruiter's sound hiring plan. Hiring managers turn to their friends or family for referrals (per some studies, 70% to 90% of positions are filled this way), and when that circle looks way too white (75% of white people have zero friends of color), you can draw a direct line as to who is benefitting from word-of-mouth hires. This is called shortcut bias.

"It is well known that non-diverse, particularly white employees, are far more likely to refer other white employees to their companies," says Cid Wilson (2020), president of Hispanic Association on Corporate Responsibility (HACR) and former Wall Street executive. "Companies give greater weight to these employee referrals than external applicants because it's the feeling that the employee is a stakeholder of that company and is not going to recommend an employee that won't succeed."

Success in this case is code for "fit," which is an overused, bias-inducing term in the interview process. We refer who we know. We refer what we're comfortable with—that is, people who look, think, and act like us. So ask yourself, What does achieving fit really mean to you and your teams? How many times have you inadvertently made decisions that were comfortable for you but not in the best interest of the team or business? What reasons have you told yourself to support your decision, and are they true?

"Your recruiters just can't compete with that unless there is systemic change that internal recommendations must emphasize diversity-focused employer referrals," says Wilson. "Every employee can join in and help drive this change, but unfortunately, very few companies are telling all of their employees to send diverse candidates as part of your referrals" (Wilson 2020). Or even requiring it as part of formal referral programs.

One that does is Pinterest. In 2015, Pinterest publicly announced that they wanted to expand the number of engineering roles to hit 25% women and 8% from underrepresented ethnic groups, and non-tech roles to reach 12% from underrepresented groups. To hold themselves accountable, Pinterest partnered with Paradigm, a diversity and inclusion consulting firm, who implemented strategies such as unconscious bias training and requiring diverse interview panels. Paradigm also enrolled current employees in their mission to hit these goals by asking them to be mindful of who they were recommending for new hires. Were they recommending diverse candidates? Could they start doing that and expand the Pinterest network? (Rose Dickey 2015).

Pinterest employees welcomed the challenge, and in just six weeks referrals from underrepresented communities increased 55%. Three years later in 2018, Pinterest nearly hit all their goals (they reached 7% of engineering hires from underrepresented ethnic backgrounds instead of 8% but succeeded on their female engineering and ethnic background non-engineering goals).

Yes, Pinterest had the budget to hire an outside (read: expensive) partner to help them get there, and the learnings from that training were not ground-breaking, but challenging and enrolling its own base—the employees that call Pinterest home—moved the needle.

Another strategy to reduce the unconscious bias system of employee referrals: push back on the volume of internship referrals. When I worked at ABC News, internship recruiters took great pride in building a robust and diverse pool of top college-level talent. It didn't matter. The intern pro-gram manager was handcuffed from selecting among terrific candidates we received from minority organization internship partners because the spots were quickly filled internally with "must hires"—that is, those that came as a favor to a sales client or an exec's niece or nephew. After an analysis of past practices, these "strongly recommended" (read: must hire) candidates surfaced as the majority of historic intern classes. While the active part-nership with minority intern groups was there, we often could not open the door widely and place these candidates in the internships that would open doors for them.

To fix this, we enabled managers to hire diverse interns by capping what I called "the Friends & Family Program" at 10% of the total number of intern hires. I let policy be the buffer. When we established and shared these new norms, we more than doubled the representation of diverse talent from the prior year. Reducing the standard practice of interns-as-a-favor protocol was a real, concrete action the company took to improve hiring outcomes. This is an action every manager can implement now.

Another way to immediately create more equity in your intern class: pay them a minimum wage or small stipend. College credit doesn't do the trick. Offering paid internships will allow you to attract more candidates, especially those who cannot afford to work for free. The United States Labor Department has passed laws to protect interns (and others) from unpaid roles, explicitly stating that the employer cannot derive an immediate advantage from the intern's activities. Therefore, pay up. It's just the right thing to do.

Attract Diverse Talent Like You Mean It

In 2019, the PGA partnered with Jopwell, a career advancement plat-form for Black, Latinx, and Native American students and professionals, to collect feedback on perceptions of the golf industry and career access and opportunities. Jopwell discovered that there wasn't a lack of interest in golf, but rather two-third of respondents shared the perception that golf isn't an inclusive or diverse industry. That coupled with a lack of awareness of open roles (27% of respondents) and access to contacts in the industry (26%) created a significant barrier to entry. However, once respondents were told explicitly that the PGA of America wanted to create a more diverse workforce and broaden its hiring reach, the likelihood of applying went up from 46% to 64%, according to Jopwell and the PGA (Cross and Braswell 2019).

To break down these barriers, the PGA launched a job awareness initiative. They actively promoted the PGA WORKS program, a fellowship for people from diverse backgrounds, on social media; they increased the visual representation of BIPOC golfers and talent on their website; and they launched strategic partnerships with media companies such as Black Enterprise to attract new audiences. The result? The PGA saw a direct increase in applications from underrepresented communities and continues to partner with Jopwell as they work to diversify the golf industry, says Jopwell CEO Porter Braswell. My former Google colleague Suezette Robotham said, "We need to help people see themselves here." Additionally the two organizations partnered together to create a joint photo collection to increase the visual representations of BIPOC in golf. That collection has been viewed over 100 million times, and the photos are reused throughout the PGA's website.

The pre-applicant stage of the talent acquisition process is perhaps one of the most important. Suppose you want to attract more racially diverse candidates. In that case, if you want to reach a broader applicant base, you must build a robust and transparent talent-focused marketing strategy that enables candidates to see themselves in your roles, hallways, and meetings.

Look at your careers page: What are you saying? Can prospective candidates see themselves in your organization? And if they can't right now, don't lie to them about it. When I was global head of Diversity Staffing at Google, I was asked to consult on a career website redesign to ensure our recruiting marketing language and approach would land well with diverse talent communities. I'll never forget a planning meeting where we were asked to consider the Facebook career page for competitive intelligence, which boasted a rainbow of employee photos. I had to scroll to the bottom to see one white guy, Mark Zuckerberg. Now, I know the stats on Facebook. I appreciated the intent to promote inclusivity, but you must tell candidates the truth. Yes, it can be through an aspirational lens but it also has to reflect reality—false advertising simply won't work. Candidates are savvy. They will dissect what you're showing them and question your language and stories, what's included and omitted, so be bold, be inclusive, be honest.

This goes for universities as well. I remember being asked to pose for marketing photos when I was a student at Bucknell University in the 90s. Here we were, a group of Black, South Asian, and Asian friends, and they added a white guy, also a friend, for good measure. We were tickled pink when we saw the shiny brochures prominently featuring us. But we also thought, "Oh boy, we're not fooling anyone. Once they are on campus they'll know just how white everything is."

Why should someone want to work for you? Your employment value proposition (EVP) describes what makes your organization a desirable place to work. Relevance, uniqueness, and authenticity are the key qualities of a strong EVP. Bonus: these qualities generate better candidates. Ensure you promote your company's most desirable EVP qualities (honestly!). "We provide safe working environments for all employees" sounds like a minimum, and it does not captivate. "Increasing diversity, equity, and inclusion in hiring, compensation, promotion, and workplace culture is our top priority"—now that's how you attract the best and brightest.

If you aren't the kind of place where underrepresented talent wants to work, no amount of outreach will help. You have to start at the top: Are your company's diversity, equity, and inclusion objectives and values publicly available? Does the employment brand reflect the lived experience of employees and the communities they work in? Does it signal to diverse communities that they would be welcomed and valued in your organization? Do current staff of color feel valued and groomed for success to the point where they feel confident in recruiting more BIPOC staff into a racially welcoming environment? Are you building genuine partnerships and relationships with the groups and communities where diverse talent thrives? And how clearly can any of your peers and colleagues articulate to a candidate their career path once they join the organization? If you can't answer these questions—or feel that your organization is lacking here—before going out to market for talent, think again, regroup, share your thoughts with your people and culture teams (aka HR), and then get out there.

If you want to understand the perception of your company but don't have the budget for a consultant or staff for a task force, try data-driven survey tools such as The Muse BrandBuilder, which can help you uncover the unique aspects of your employee value proposition by collecting employees' stories about working with your company. Another idea: simply survey current and prior BIPOC applicants. What do they think the company stands for? What influenced their decision to apply? What do they think would be the most significant opportunities and barriers for their success? We won't have the answers until we start asking better questions.

Four Recruiting Don'ts

1. Using the phrase "diversity hire." It's racist. Also, try to avoid saying you want to hire "more diverse talent," and instead be specific about your representational gaps and the strategies to close them. Instead of using the phrase "We need to hire more BIPOC employees," say "We have hired too many white people in X department or function and need to address that imbalance by hiring X Black or Latinx or Asian or LGBTQIA+ (insert the demographic background that can address gaps)" to help paint a clearer value proposition and dismiss the elephant in the room that pops up when you say, "Diversity."

2. Referencing inequitable data. Don't blame the pipeline of qualified applicants. That ignores the historical inequality and institutional roadblocks that have left marginalized individuals out of elite colleges and companies to begin with. Instead, set benchmarks that reflect where you should be and where the country and your industry are headed. By 2040, according to the US Bureau of Labor Statistics, the majority of the US workforce will be ethnically diverse, with women of color accounting for a significant share of that growth, and the post-millennial generation (Gen Z) is on track to be the most diverse and best-educated yet.

3. Failing to look internally. Is anyone ready for a promotion or expanded role responsibilities? Can you use an open role as an opportunity to provide a growth experience for someone whose strong performance or potential has gone unnoticed?

4. Taking a check-the-box approach. That is, if you fail to contextualize and acknowledge the interconnected strategies and barriers to this work and simply go after changing optical representation, you will be at this again and again.

Change the Spec

The job description is often the source of racial bias in hiring. Hiring managers often complain that their recruiters are not bringing them enough "qualified" diverse candidates. This is the point when I will likely ask a clarifying question: What does "qualified" mean to you? The answers I often receive are muddled, defensive, and rarely consistent with the job description. We must redefine "qualified" or even eliminate it from our vernacular. Qualified is subjective when there are no checks and balances on bias. Qualified emphasizes past accomplishments instead of potential for future success. Qualified is a lazy and unclear statement used to defend decisions without reflection.

One way to secure a higher number of applications from traditionally underrepresented talent is to emphasize purpose and culture beyond solely relying on the standard checklist of skills and experience. Focus instead on what the candidate will experience and achieve in the essential components of the role. I've seen recruiters and managers screen for qualifications that are proxies for must-have qualities (read: what's necessary to get the job done) when they're nice-to-haves (read: extra skills not required to carry out the core functions of the position such as having 10+ years of experience in a related industry). Examples of core requirements include: masterful project manager: can manage multiple projects at once and communicate across a wide variety of stakeholders with often uncoordinated expectations; analytical and data-driven: strategic thinker who uses data to tell a story and provide insights. Recruit for *those* key capabilities. Write your job descriptions with *that* language. And screen consistently for those qualifications.

The more we rely on preferences and "this is how we've always done it" shortcuts, the more we compromise on a diversity of experiences, perspectives, and approaches. There's nothing wrong with preferences or conventional approaches except when they become embedded expectations that only you know and can change at your whim. Candidates who are more like you or who are from similar networks are more likely to pick up on those expectations. Conversely, candidates who are less like you are less likely to read the playbook in your head.

First impressions matter. Your job descriptions must feel compelling and, most important, accessible. Otherwise, you're not genuinely enticing BIPOC talent to apply for your roles. For starters, don't limit hires to those with college degrees, X years of experience, and work experiences within your industry. At VICE Media Group, we put a lot of energy into redesigning our recruiting process, which includes updating our external branding and ensuring our job descriptions more accurately describe what success looks like in each role regardless of gender identity, race/ethnicity, or any other identity. We don't always get it right, but we apply discipline to this process by regularly auditing our job specs.

Over the years, I've learned from DEI practitioners and recruiters alike on what works best when recruiting diverse talent. My colleague Aubrey Blanche has noted that hiring inclusively is also about being more thoughtful about your word choices—avoid buzzwords and clichés. In "Eight Ways to Make Your DEI Efforts Less Talk and More Walk," she highlights words such as "rock star" and "ninja" in the tech industry, male-dominated and racially insulting culture signals (Blanche 2019). Likewise, highly corporate language often signals exclusive white professional norms to members of underrepresented communities. You must be mindful of the incredibly subtle language differences in your role descriptions. For example, as Aubrey further notes, when you describe a position as *managing* a team, research shows that you increase the likelihood of a more significant number of male applicants. For *developing* a team, there's a strong likelihood of increasing the number of female applicants. You can guarantee a more balanced and qualified applicant pool by considering a more gender-neutral approach of *leading* a team. In STEM fields, the language around "genius" is gendered;

math skills are learned, not something only men are born into. To attract more women to STEM fields, Harvey Mudd College launched a marketing campaign that focused on applicants' potential for growth rather than expectations on ability (Weisul 2017). The fact is that if someone doesn't have inborn skills, they can learn them. As always, it's about how you invite others to be part of your journey. Do your homework, and skill up on this critical practice.

In "5 Examples of Racial Bias in Hiring," the authors share an internal wiki page built by Amazon engineers with alternative phrases to help remove unconscious bias. They suggest replacing "brown bags" with "learning session" or "lunch and learn." Other racially biased terms such as "catwalk," "blacklist," and "grandfathered in" can be easily replaced with "easy task," "blocklist," and "exempt from regulations." Similarly, Twitter engineers shared a list of coding terms often used in database-related job ads, the same ads that should feel welcoming for racially diverse talent, which they swap out for more inclusive terms. For example: "whitelist" changes to "allowlist," "blacklist" to "denylist," and "master/slave" to "leaders/follower, primary/replica, primary/standby" (Shankland 2020).

Here's a tip they share: Use Job Description Text Analyzer when reviewing your job descriptions for non-inclusive language. It flags racially biased words and recommends bias-free language. Another widely used tool, Textio (n.d.), is according to their site, "The world's most advanced workplace language guidance" that helps organizations see where social bias may exist in their job postings and how to fix it. In an increasingly competitive and distributed talent market, every bit of edge helps.

When done right, in just a short amount of words, job descriptions have the power to attract and catalyze a more diverse pool of candidates. This is where you can tell the story of the job, make your company feel like an exciting place to work, and use language that feels accessible to all. Organizations have gotten much better at writing compelling job descriptions. When I first joined Viacom, some of our job descriptions were so bland and standard that I often thought, Who would want to work here! So we partnered with our communications team to teach us how to apply the same level of energy and enthusiasm they did to our press releases. That helps people see themselves in an environment consistent with the company brand and is far more helpful at attracting a rich candidate pool that is excited about joining you for what you have to offer.

If your industry is vastly white, you can look to related industries for BIPOC talent. For example, book publishing should attract candidates from journalism, magazines, online media, book awards, book store staff, advertising, literary agencies, literary scouts, TV/film, and more. Write job descriptions with that type of openness and eliminate any descriptions that mandate a certain number of years in a specific industry (i.e. instead of saying X years working at an ad agency, write X years having experience building creative campaigns with clients).

Broaden your reach, and you'll broaden your talent pipeline.

Go Where the Talent Is!

In 2020, Wells Fargo CEO Charlie Scharf announced the company's goals to double Black leadership and align compensation with DEI efforts. Cue the applause. But then, during a call with employees, he reportedly said that he understands there is "a limited pool of Black talent to recruit from" (DiversityInc Staff 2020). And there it is: that ubiquitous and offensive statement from the top that excuses leaders from hitting their DEI goals and doing the work necessary to source and evaluate candidates fairly. Institutionalized racism buffers white people in self-segregated social, educational, housing, and employment circles—to the point where they don't notice that they are constantly moving through all-white spaces.

There's not a lack of talent, there's a lack of effort. When I hear, "We can't find any Black engineers," "There are simply no Latinx coders," "The other candidates were stronger," I see excuses for lazy sourcing. What if you were in sales and you told your boss, "I can't find a company who is willing to advertise with us." Would your boss just shrug and say okay? No, they would question your methods, ask you to look harder, find out why companies don't want to work with you, and then encourage you to adjust your pitch and approach. You must do the same for recruiting diverse talent.

To do so, seeking out racially diverse candidates by securing referrals from diversity-focused organizations is a good step for diversifying the candidate pool. I've hired BIPOC executives with various competencies and skills for every role imaginable. Sometimes I lean on my network, sometimes on the network of others, but never have I been unable to find an incredibly talented and overqualified candidate from an underrepresented background. We are everywhere, really.

Talent is equally distributed; opportunity isn't. Companies can and should dedicate resources for diversity hiring. Many have and continue to do so, but the most successful programs don't silo the effort. At Google, for example, we had a team of 60 recruiters dedicated to sourcing predominantly Black and Hispanic software engineering candidates. That number might seem large, but it simply wasn't enough, especially considering that the entire sourcing organization consisted of more than 300 sourcers tasked with building a global talent pipeline across all of Google. There was no way my relatively small team could scale by being solely responsible for finding Black and Hispanic software engineers.

In fact, we would often come into conflict with other teams when it came to who could claim credit for who found the candidate first (oh, the gaming risks of KPIs) because sometimes the non-diversity recruitment-focused sourcing team would want to claim credit for initially securing or helping close the Black or Latinx candidates. Of course they should! Everyone should share in the win. But is it a shared win when only one team is dedicated to that outcome? I made the decision to decentralize my diversity sourcing team and place those with subject matter expertise (hiring Black and Latinx talent) inside each hiring vertical (i.e. software engineers) to build up everyone's skills and ensure everyone would have skin in the game to diversify candidate pools, at scale. I fundamentally believe that everyone needs to be able to recruit with an inclusive mindset and skill set and be held accountable for process and results.

The Ford Foundation has been committed to social justice since its inception, and the culture they have built has led to diverse representation across every level up and down the organization. "One of the things I admired most was the HR department," says Bird Runningwater (2020), a former program associate at the Foundation who is now a senior director at Sundance Institute. "Even back in the 90s when they were hiring for positions, diversity was the first and foremost goal. They used headhunters, they sought out people, they sifted through applications, they interviewed people, and if they didn't find a diverse candidate to fill the position, they started over." They didn't throw in the towel because it was hard.

This is time-consuming work; I get that. Especially when you work at a small nonprofit or are a recruiter in a start-up where hiring needs and recruitment resources change before, during, and after a round of funding. When you don't have the capacity and support to be proactive in your search, that's when you must tap into your network to do some of the work for you.

But what does your network look like? When you share a job posting on your LinkedIn page, who sees it? Hiring managers should not just audit their networks—they have to actively research, share, and recruit from racially diverse communities and organizations. Like eradicating the Friends and Family program, you need to broaden your networks and organizational affiliations and question your assumptions about go-to job sites and platforms. Otherwise, you will always reach the same people. I've had recruiters beg me to speak to their managers so they stop hiring from their alma maters. I once told our head of sales at Viacom, "I know you had a good experience at Brown but about eighty percent of your staff are Brown alumni. You can't complain to me about not having diversity on your staff when you're forcing my team to hire from an almost all-white pool." At first, he resisted. He had an emotional connection to Brown that biased him positively toward their graduates. But when we stopped sourcing from Brown and other similar schools, we found equally talented, if not more talented, racially diverse candidates. Sure, they were not versed on Brown shorthand, but that was not a requirement for the role and certainly not for engaging with the many non-Brown graduate clients they were trying to land.

Look harder and consider who you're asking for help. Start within your company, inclusive of employee resource groups and partner organizations and influencers. Then look outward: get creative (and don't be afraid of some gentle stalking) for diverse communities who may not currently consider your company or industry a potential employer. I've worked with recruiters who have joined niche industry communities of color, such as WomeninTech, Black Professionals in Tech, or ColorComm, a diverse network of women in the communications industry, to gain proximity to this talent and to more effectively post targeted job announcements on their social media and career sites. If you're recruiting for an engineering role, research or ask BIPOC engineers which job sites, organizations, and clubs they follow, and make sure you're building pipelines from those networks.

When Trevor Noah was hiring for The Daily Show, most agents sent only white clients. At first he worried that Black writers didn't want to work with him, but then he met with some of his Black comedian friends who revealed that they never heard about the opening because they didn't have agents (Phippen and National Journal 2015). They didn't even know the opportunity existed! Talent agencies are notoriously white and have operated as the primary gatekeepers across Hollywood for far too long. So Trevor had to actively ask everyone he thought might know a Black comic to refer people his way. It's easy to assume that every comedian has an agent, but it's not true.

Similarly, when Issa Rae asked executives why there were no BIPOC available to work on her show, she was told, "We can't find Black makeup artists." "That is just the most ridiculous statement ever," says Lucinda Martinez (2020), who leads Warner Media's Multicultural Marketing, Brand & Inclusion Strategy. Lucinda told me that once they gave Issa the show-runner job, she did what they couldn't. "People of color have no problem finding people of color," she says. "She hired Black makeup artists, creative services, you name it. When you hire more people of color, they open the door for others." And the product is better. Ava Duvernay's *Queen Sugar*, Shonda Rhimes' shows (all of them), and Issa Rae's *Insecure* are just a few examples of TV shows that have revolutionized the depiction of people of color on the screen. Queer cinematographer Ava Berkofsky is credited for using lighting practices in *Insecure* that embrace color with all skin tones, no longer using standard models defined by white skin. Berkofsky was brought in after previous cinematographers whose dated tactics just blasted light on Black talent. The result is Black images that are strikingly illuminated.

You have to welcome diverse candidates through the door. The hiring process suffers from the same lack of creativity and default bias. It makes my skin crawl when people say, "I want to hire more diverse talent, but I don't want to lower the hiring bar." That's biased and, frankly, insulting. That comment indicates that you assume that racially diverse talent lacks the same intellectual capacity or even work ethic as you. That comment also fails to consider that we have been reducing the standard of skill for years to hire well-connected yet mediocre white men, and no one is calling that "lowering the bar." It's a stain of thought when leaders such as Michael Moritz of Sequoia Capital talk about "not lowering their standards" when trying to hire more women (Guynn 2015). Improving diversity is not about lowering any bar. We can all raise the bar for fairness in our hiring practices.

Your Road Map to Revolution

Recruiting is all about finding the best talent, and there are many ways to open the door to a richly diverse applicant pool. First, confront your bias, which shuts that door often before you even realize it. Second, expand your talent pool: stop relying on the same employee referrals from the same Ivy League schools. And finally, launch an authentic marketing campaign for your jobs and company to encourage more people to take a chance on you.

- **Recognize bias when recruiting.** Question your first impressions when reading a résumé or meeting someone who doesn't look like you. Name bias exists. Let your awareness guide you to shut down your sneaky inner voice.
- **Stop relying on résumés as gatekeepers.** Instead, look to other less biased ways to assess talent, such as standardized interview questions, the use of cover letters, work sample tests, and more.
- **Stop the Friends and Family program** to limit recruiting from the same talent pools and referral sources. This will create more opportunities for more people. For accountability, set goals around employee referrals that help meet representational diversity goals. On the flip side, set limits to the number of "must-hires" allowed, particularly when hiring for interns.
- **Revamp your company website and marketing language to attract more candidates.** Show what DEI means to you and what it looks like in your organization from your job specs and career sites to your social media. Job seekers want to see themselves represented in the organization they wish to join.
- **Rewrite your job descriptions.** Beware of the "this is how we've always written it" organizational trap. Biased wording sends a subtle messaging and can influence some to not even consider applying.

We all tend to unconsciously conflate requirements and outcomes with our preferences and known approaches. Gain clarity on the must-have requirements for the role and what you're willing to flex on, and reword your job description inclusively. There's a reason why some job specs say "must-haves" and "nice-to-haves"—be consistent.

- **Expand your talent pool.** Go where the talent is, engage in targeted networking and pipeline building. Seek out diversity-focused organizations for referrals. If your industry is primarily white, start to widen the pool by recruiting and hiring from adjacent industries. Focus on transferable skills, rather than experience within your specific and homogenous industry.

4 | Make Better Hiring Decisions

We are often overworked, and when there's an open headcount the natural inclination is to fill it fast. I call this "the house is on fire" mentality. The minute someone quits, your instinct is to put out that fire by filling that seat. Who could possibly make a good decision under those circumstances? More help may lessen the load on your existing team members, but it's a short-term goal with temporary benefits. You rationalize yourself into shortcut decisions to lessen your teams' burdens. You recycle the old job description and follow the same patterns of recruitment that led you to your last hire. But here's the major flaw, you did not center on equity and inclusion with that hire, and you haven't yet with this one. Instead, pause and reflect on what core values and skills you need in all hires, what this new hire can contribute to your team's strategic growth and cultural transformation efforts, and how much wider a net you need to cast to ensure you have a diverse selection of talent from which to choose. Consider all the possibilities.

If I had a magic wand, I would slow down the hiring process. Rushing shuts down creativity in sourcing, pushes forth "safe" candidates, and, most damaging, increases bad hires. When I've pushed back on hiring managers' final candidate selections, sometimes they plead, "Just this once; I don't have time to interview for more diverse talent," or they simply respond, "Let's just hire him; he's 'a good fit,'" or he's "a transformative hire." Cue the eye roll.

Making a bad hire is both economically and culturally taxing. According to a study by Career Builder, 69% of employers said their companies were adversely affected by a bad hire last year. Forty-one percent of those businesses estimated the cost of a bad hire was over $25,000; 24% said it cost them more than $50,000 (Career Builder 2012). Bad hires can also lower morale and cause other people to leave.

Honestly, I've had my share of bad hiring decisions that, in hindsight, have caused heavier workloads and emotional distress. When I've reviewed my decision-making process, I've found the reasons inextricably tied to timing pressures, power differentials, uncertainty, and unwillingness to acknowledge my own biases. There were times when I let more senior leaders' biased opinions sway hiring decisions despite my reservations. There were times when I over-erred on the side of potential and did not partner with others to create the right conditions for the new hire's success. And there was a time when I hired someone rapidly without confirming feedback I had received from informal references. Indeed, this feedback referred to immature patterns of behavior and decision-making that came to light in their performance almost immediately. We handled it initially through coaching and eventually through a mutually agreed resignation but not without losing significant time, resources, and emotional energy.

We don't spend enough time thinking critically about the hiring micro-decisions we make every day (such as where we post roles and who we ask for referrals), the patterns of bias in decision making, and the outcomes and inefficiencies of our hiring processes. We tend to focus on the end result—who was hired—and not the many choices made along the way. We take for granted that hiring decisions, across organizations and boards alike, continue to be controlled by predominantly white men in power. We operate under the misguided notion that inserting a series of steps in the recruiting process will yield structure and fairness. Yet, when it comes to executive hiring, the roles that shape an organization's structural, operational, reputational, and talent strategies, we rarely question the impact of those decisions being mostly driven by the C-suite and handpicked from among a select and a few privileged sets.

We have to admit that determining someone's future output and competencies based on a series of interviews and other skills tests, no matter how well structured, is hard. And what makes it more complicated is a false claim of fairness when the hiring bar is raised and lowered at will, all the time. Even in a company that has built a structured recruiting method and introduced AI or other technology tools to cut against biases and reduce prejudice, the ultimate decision to make a hire or not will always rest with people crammed with biases and cultural blind spots. Paradigm, a DEI consulting company, has found that 98% of organizations already have a candidate pool more racially/ethnically diverse than their current workforce. The best candidate in the room doesn't necessarily fit the existing white professional mold, so the company misses out on diverse ideas and solutions because of a discriminatory caste system inherent in its culture.

Revamping your methods of assessing and interviewing candidates will reduce the abundance of bias and hasty hiring. You can level the playing field by ensuring traditionally underrepresented talent are fairly considered at every stage of the process. It may take more time, and you may have to address or help others confront uncomfortable truths. But it's worth it.

Once you commit to making better, less biased, and forward-thinking hiring decisions, we can begin to chip away against the imbalance of power that continues to replicate the same results.

The Right Hire or the White Hire?

Bias is everywhere—there's no question. Our brains make millions of assumptions daily based on past experiences or socialized ideas, which lead to bias. Implicit bias and pattern matching exists throughout the hiring process, leading to a leaky pipeline of highly competent, qualified, and diverse candidates. It continues throughout the employee lifecycle, influencing promotions, retention, and psychological safety. When you consciously or unconsciously penalize people for bringing their whole selves to work (or interviews), the clothes they wear, the way they talk, or for who they are, you perpetuate a cycle of discriminatory behavior.

At Google, we found that stripping out names in the screening process did move more female engineers through each stage of the hiring process—screens, onsite interviews, and offer acceptances. However, that was not the case for Black and Hispanic software engineers whose "pass-through rates" significantly lagged past the sourcing stage. When we experimented with taking out names in the early screening processes we found slight improvements but would again see the yield reduce at the later stages of the process when they came face-to-face or on the phone with interviewers. So why did white women get a lift from stripping information but BIPOC didn't? I believe it's because we couldn't eradicate the bias of listening to accents or affinity or any other racial bias present in those exchanges.

Consider someone who comes in for an interview with an accent that is difficult for you to understand. Research shows that we are extremely sensitive to cues of foreignness. Study subjects detected non-native speech in milliseconds, even in speech played backward (Giles and Rakic 2014). Why does that matter? Because it can be easy to disregard, pass up, or discriminate against a candidate because you deem their accent to indicate they are unintelligent or less educated. One of my favorite quotes from the movie *A Walk in the Clouds* is, "Just because I speak with an accent doesn't mean that I think with an accent." In this simple and elegant statement, the character of Alberto Alargón demands to be seen for his full self. We all deserve that. My grandmother is one of the smartest and most capable women I know. Her accent denotes her cultural and language heritage, not a limited intellectual capacity. Yet those considered stronger candidates are often those whose accents fit within a traditional white standard.

Iris Bohnet, author of *What Works*, has found 150 unconscious biases, from confirmation bias to familiarity bias (Bohnet 2018). Bias seeps into every aspect of life. Biases can profoundly disrupt the interview process, particularly considering race. If you are a white person who has no friends of color—a study by the Public Religion Research Institute found that found 75% of white people's social networks are entirely white (Cox, Navarro-Rivera, and Jones 2016)—how likely is it that your discomfort with a BIPOC candidate during the interview is a reflection of your segregated social connections? Furthermore, studies show that white people struggle to read emotions of Black people accurately and will perceive Black faces as automatically angrier than white faces. If you're shocked to hear this, you should be. It's essential to interrogate your biases and question yourself and others when BIPOC candidates are dismissed for being "cold," "angry," "loud," "fake," "awkward," and other racialized coded reasons. What is the factual basis for those interpretations?

"We can't eliminate bias, it exists," says Kenji Yoshino, author of *Covering*, and Chief Justice Earl Warren, professor of constitutional law at NYU School of Law. "But we can work to change our default behaviors in these moments of heightened awareness and shift from exclusive behavior to inclusive behavior. Focusing on what you can do as an individual can create new habits that lead to change. Look at the #metoo movement and how college students have shifted from sexual harassment bystanders to upstanders. Five years ago, if you saw someone leaving a party drunk, you probably would have just looked the other way, but now the default reaction is that if you see something, it's your responsibility to make sure that person is okay. Awareness leads to action" (Yoshino 2020).

Blind hiring, the process of removing identifying information from résumés, or sourcing from wider, untapped talent pools are useless practices if white hiring managers remain fearful and distrustful of BIPOC talent. For instance, in a study by Phoebe Chua and Melissa Mazamian (2020), they cite an example I've seen over and over in my career—Black candidates who are direct in their style of communication get pulled from the hiring slate for being too aggressive. In contrast, those who are white with a similar manner are moved forward in the hiring process without any reservations. I once questioned a colleague's assessment of a Black male executive for a top leadership role. We had a clear mandate to hire a diverse executive, and here was a highly credentialed leader who had served in multiple executive leadership roles. My colleague's reason for not moving this candidate forward: "I've heard that he's got sharp elbows." My response was: "He's a tall, Black man who has risen to the top ranks in predominantly white organizations. I'd be surprised if he hasn't turned off a few people. I could say the same about the other white men on the slate. Why are you not raising the same concerns about them?"

Unconscious bias training for everyone active in the hiring process is your first line of action (or defense). These training sessions are an opportunity to understand how subjective decisions are based on the decision maker's perceptions and to be more conscious of hiring bias. But I have led enough of these training sessions to know that a swift reversal in behavior is rarely an immediate outcome.

Prejudice doesn't disappear because you acknowledge it. It disappears when you are willing to combat your own, sneaky inner voices. That takes time and practice. Kenji has a formula to create new habits: trigger > routine > reward. The trigger is the awareness of your bias. The routine is what you do about it. And the reward comes when you do something positive about it. For example, a BIPOC team member tells you that they feel diminished by you because you constantly interrupt them (trigger). You set out to pause when you feel inclined to interrupt women and BIPOC in your next meeting (routine). Women and BIPOC team members share positive feedback about how much they enjoy your team meetings and can produce far more ideas and solutions (reward).

At VICE Media Group, we developed a hiring playbook providing hiring managers with a step-by-step road map for an inclusive and equitable hiring process to help our interviewers become more objective evaluators. We outlined the process and expectations at each stage of the hiring process, and in recognition that we needed to upskill everyone in the hiring process, tasked recruiters with reviewing the process and expectations with each search. Along the way we learned that bias existed at both the behavioral and structural level. That is, we had to get better at questioning our approach and decisions based on preconceived notions of what an ideal candidate should look like and test our processes and expected norms such as requiring college degrees and years of experience for roles for which those conditions are not necessary for success.

The most powerful action I know to combat bias is to call your perceptions and assumptions into question, again and again. After you receive a résumé, speak with a candidate, or interview someone, ask yourself objectively about your first impression. Write it down if it's helpful. If you thought the candidate is underqualified, ask yourself why. What was it that made you believe that? If you said intimidating, ask yourself why. Push yourself harder to see farther. That's what will get you in the right movement-making mindset.

Test Time

To help your team understand the impact of bias on brain patterns, ask them to take the Implicit Association Test (IAT) from Harvard's Project Implicit. The IAT is an online exercise that measures associations between concepts, stereotypes, and evaluations often reflecting attitudes and beliefs that we may be unaware of or unwilling to admit. Read: you can purport to be "woke" and try to behave without prejudice, but your automatic associations still associate Black people with violence and women with being in the home.

When I first took the test, I felt a deep sense of shame. Each test told me what I didn't want to hear, that I have a preference for younger people and light skinned people. This was an incredibly embarrassing result for me, but it shows that bias and stereotypes lie in all of us. Once you understand your baseline bias, you can begin to address it. For a more scalable approach, try Eskalera. This employee engagement platform has created an inclusion index and curriculum approach to make participants aware of their DEI strengths and development areas. It provides them with tools and activities to continue learning, growing, and training—much like any other skills-based practice.

Taking these tests won't save or heal you. They will help you come to terms with how these biases impact your day-to-day interactions and decisions, recognize situations where you are more prone to bias, and minimize its influence. "The problem is not seeing color; it's what you do once you see color," says Verna Myers (2014), chief diversity officer at Netflix.

Push for More . . . More Candidates, More Interview Prep, More Accountability

A series of experimental studies published by the *Harvard Business Review* found that the majority demographic group in the finalist pool (e.g. men vs. women, whites vs. BIPOC) indicated who would be most likely chosen as final candidates. If you have a finalist slate of two or three white candidates, a white candidate is significantly more likely to be selected. And if there's only one woman in your slate, she has no chance. Instead, the authors of that study found that when they added "just one more woman or minority candidate" to the pool of finalists, the chances of hiring slightly increased. For example, when a finalist pool of candidates consists of two or three Black or Hispanic candidates, you significantly increase the chances of selecting a Black or Hispanic candidate.

It makes sense—by increasing the commonality among candidates, you eliminate the "only" effect in the hiring process, which makes it nearly impossible for a candidate to be judged for criteria outside their control (such as ethnicity, sexual orientation, and gender). For real change, you need a critical mass of finalists from underrepresented groups to eliminate the psychological instinct that you're taking a risk or sacrificing for the sake of diversity.

Interviewing mandates—meaning you must interview a certain number of people who check a specific ethnicity or gender box—have risen in popularity. In 2003, the NFL established the Rooney rule, which required teams with head coaching vacancies to interview at least one BIPOC candidate. Since then, they've upped the requirement to two, and several tech companies, such as Amazon and Uber, have followed suit with diversity interview mandates. Like any goal you set, these can be effective but cannot be leaned on as the sole tools for increasing workplace diversity. What happens after the interview? Are you meeting this candidate just to hit your number? Or are you invested in the process?

If that's the former, revisit your motivations in Chapter 1. And know that creating equal opportunities for all genders, races, abilities, and identities should be the baseline, but it's also about the bottom line. The connection between financial performance and diversity is difficult to prove, as global research from Catalyst (2020b) has found, because research can only establish correlation between the two, not causation. But we can't deny the ample academic and industry reports stating that diverse organizations are more successful at recruiting and retaining exceptionally diverse talent and that teams that include different viewpoints, experiences, and cognitive styles boost creativity and innovation.

If you are invested in an inclusive hiring process, ensure that you and those who make hiring decisions—from screening to final selections—are equipped to evaluate a candidate's skills, knowledge, and lived experience fairly and objectively. At Greenhouse, a recruiting software developer, they focus on three areas for interview training: the rules, unconscious bias, and logistics. The rules cover what to ask and what not to ask (legally) and the best ways to respond to tough questions. They then cover bias, the need for a structured hiring process to tame these biases, and how these tendencies have shown up in past hiring decisions. And finally, they set expectations—what to expect throughout the process.

The more time you can prepare effectively for a successful interview and decision-making process, the more fair and just your hiring process.

> **Be disciplined.** Set aside time to prepare and debrief before and after the interview.
>
> **Prepare.** Review job description, candidate profile, and review key questions with a lens on the areas of importance to the role and team.
>
> **Put yourself in their shoes.** Make time to get to know the person, not just the candidate, ask about their expectations and be transparent about the process and discussion (as appropriate), and always test your biases.
>
> **Debrief while it is fresh.** If part of a panel, debrief immediately, even if just for five minutes. Separate intuitive feelings from objective data. Compare candidates against concrete, objective criteria (can't say this enough). Share your feedback with the recruitment team.

Ask for This: A Structured Hiring Approach

Use clear and consistent review criteria. A structured hiring approach is a step-by-step plan that applies a fair, consistent lens to hiring that begins when the role is first approved. It's a data-driven strategy that sets clear, objective criteria to evaluate all candidates, uses a deliberate process and an evaluation rubric applied consistently to all candidates, and ensures hiring decisions are based on evidence, not subjective assumptions. Here's a sample:

1. **Kick-off meeting:** Recruiters and hiring managers discuss team composition, aspirational mix, team culture, job responsibilities, and market outreach.

2. **Hiring rubric or scorecard criteria:** What technical or operational skills and capabilities do you need on the team? Other dimensions of success may be communication, collaboration, problem-solving, etc. Instead of open-ended questions that can be loosely interpreted, use a rating system on a standard three- to five-point scale to reduce bias.

3. **Interview planning:** Who is doing the interviews? How will you prepare them to ensure they are consistent? How will you intervene to lessen the impact of bias?

4. **Candidate evaluation:** Ensure everyone is clear on the hiring attributes you will use to make a final decision. Require explanations and specific examples that support decisions.

Structure is your friend. Unstructured and loose interviews risk introducing multiple biases without any checks and balances on the types of questions asked and how the interviewer evaluates answers and professional styles. In contrast, structured interviews with consistent parameters for what gets asked and how can significantly reduce biases.

Combat Bias with Consistency

Improving interviewing practices and decision-making across the board is crucial so that talented people are not being subtly shut out or excluded from the process. The subjective nature of the interview process makes it challenging to evaluate candidates without preconceived ideas, default perceptions, and subconscious expectations. Based on past interviewing and hiring experiences, our brain patterns influence our thoughts and predict future outcomes. For instance, thinking, "The last time I hired a Black video producer, he didn't turn out to be the rock star I thought he was" (judgment bias), or "I am so happy we hired Lana, who worked at Netflix, because I love talking about movies with her" (affinity bias). You can't fight these feelings—they exist—but you can establish protocols and strategies to thwart them from having too much hiring power.

One of the most successful ways to do this is to architect decision-making teams to allow for more diverse perspectives, robust feedback compilation, and richer candidate experiences. There should always be more than one person interviewing and evaluating a candidate. Final hiring decisions often come down to hiring managers and those who influence their decision-making. Some companies such as Google have transferred the power to hiring committees to introduce diverse perspectives and reach more objective decisions. Assembling an interview team with a diversity of experiences leads to less bias.

There are two ways I've seen this executed: One, where the people interview a candidate as a panel at once or in smaller groups throughout the interview process. I've seen this process work best when hiring for entry level talent or high-volume roles such as sales representatives and software engineers, and at small start-ups who need to hire fast. This practice is a time saver and will allow for a more fair evaluation by allowing everyone to hear the same questions and responses. To streamline the process, each interviewer is prepped and assigned a particular capability or question to ask. The benefits of this model is that it eliminates subjective circumstances (a distracted interviewer, an interviewee who was fatigued from six previous interviews). Still this interview process can be very overwhelming for a candidate. Be mindful that being the only person from an underrepresented or cultural group in a room or a Zoom with all eyes on you can be intimidating and lead to performance failures. The other method is sticking with a more traditional interview process where two to three finalists meet with three to five interviewers, with one being the hiring manager. Regardless of the interview process, ensuring the process is consistent, including asking each candidate similar questions, and that internal and external candidates are treated equally should be top priorities. That's the takeaway: consistency. Consistency can cut through institutional barriers for traditionally underrepresented talent.

In both situations, your interview team should reflect a diversity of skills and responsibilities to round out the panel's perspective and enhance the candidate's experience. You must assemble these interview teams with great care—regardless of seniority, status, or expertise, each interviewer must have an equal voice, and all must feel welcome to share their diverse opinions. You should also be intentional in selecting a mix of backgrounds for your panel—ideally, include two women or non-binary persons, or members of other underrepresented groups—especially if two interviewers are assessing against the same attributes.

To put together a solid interview team you should include:

- A direct peer;
- A cross-functional peer;
- A direct report; and
- The hiring manager.

Refinery29, owned by VICE Media Group, experienced a racial reckoning in the summer of 2020 when several current and previous employees raised claims about a toxic workplace culture for Black women. When my team was hiring for the editor in chief role, we designed a diverse interview panel that included the founder, the hiring manager, two peers (one cross-functional), two mid-level employees, and two junior level employees representing various perspectives. We set clear and shared expectations about the unique perspectives each would bring to decision-making. We also let the candidate know who would be interviewing them and why. The aim was not to misrepresent our representational diversity. We were honest and transparent about where we were as a company and what we aspired to be.

If you know it's critical for someone to meet a BIPOC in the process, make that happen, but be thoughtful of not overburdening or tokenizing your one Black engineer and requiring them to be on every interview team. At YouTube (owned by Google), Susan Wojcicki encouraged the recruitment team to think creatively and audaciously about hiring more Black and Hispanic software engineers. One of the recommendations was to ensure Black and Hispanic candidates would "see themselves" at YouTube by including a Black or Hispanic YouTuber in every interview process (Wojcicki 2016). Still, if you have less than 10 Black and Hispanic software engineers in the entire organization, and you're interviewing eight people a day, they won't have time to do the jobs you hired them to do. Plus, they didn't consider that only a portion of them were considered qualified interviewers, that is, received interview training and conducted a significant number of candidate interviews. Instead, the people ops (the term Google uses for HR) and business team tasked with diversity initiatives opted for a creative solution, whereby Black and Hispanic candidates would meet a YouTuber for lunch or coffee in the middle of their interview cycle.

Even small start-ups can systemize the hiring process and get everyone eager and excited to participate in the interview panel. When The Cru, a peer mentorship platform and community founded by Tiffany Dufu, was hiring for a director role, the COO enrolled a few members into the process. Here's the email she sent (Dufu 2020):

> Hi team,
>
> We've got a healthy candidate pipeline for the X role (thank you for spreading the word and sending in referrals!) and we're going to start scheduling interviews in the next few weeks.
>
> I've listed all of you as a part of the interview panel—candidates will always speak with me for at least a 30–45-minute phone screen before they make it to the next round with you all. As a part of this process, I've created a scorecard so that everyone is clear on what they'd be testing for in their time with candidates. This is all to make sure that we're getting different perspectives without asking redundant questions while also ensuring we're hiring the right person for this role who can get the job done. If you don't feel good about testing for what I have listed for you—no worries! Just talk to me about it so that I can ensure we're testing for each of these in one way, shape, or form.

At a start-up like The Cru, when you have less than 15 people on staff, every new hire is significant. I've often advised founders that they set the organizational DNA of their organization with their first 10–20 hires. Culture dynamics start at day 1 and get cemented over time with each new hire. Rightly so, Tiffany Dufu takes this process very seriously and recognizes that without new perspectives there is no innovation. Recently, when Tiffany shared her enthusiasm about hiring a new team member with a potential investor, the investor's first question was, "Where did they come from?" "I knew they were looking for the name of the company this person used to work for so that they could gauge the quality of the hire, but I decided to share what was far more important: 'They came from being an expert in the human condition. They came from grit, self-determination, and hustle'" she says. "If we're going to build new platforms that unite us and enable us to move our lives forward, we can't hire the same ole Silicon Valley prototypes who built the old ones. We'll have to do the work to recruit incredibly talented people who have a fresh lens on the world" (Dufu 2020).

Don't Interview for "Fit"; Interview for Function, Potential, and Culture Add

Tiffany's approach is a refreshing take on the more common practice of hiring people with a specific background like the investor was expecting (Ivy League, prestigious former company). Her attributes—grit, self-determination, and hustle—are much better indicators of success than one's arbitrary acceptance into a top-tier college. The conventional/traditional hire is not always the "safe" hire, and the person with a less name-brand background who went to a state school (which is the majority of the country) could be bringing in a wealth of skills that are missing from the company. That type of gatekeeping is a form of affinity bias.

Affinity bias, or "like" bias, is the concept that if you meet someone and identify with and thus like them, you might be more willing to push them through the process even if they don't score as high on key capabilities as another candidate. It is also the tendency for people to hire people like themselves ("mini-me's"). They figure that they fit the model of company success, and so they figure someone with a similar background (etc.) would fit. It's the most obvious way the hiring bar gets lowered or raised.

It's easy to connect with what looks familiar and to attribute positive qualities to that which feels comfortable. After all, in typical circumstances, these are the people you interact with most of your day. It's nearly impossible *not to* consider these questions during an interview: Will I get along with this person? Would I enjoy hanging out with them after work? Is this person going to have an easy time connecting with the other members on the team? We all want life to be easy, and no one wants to manage difficult employees or colleagues, but this line of risk-averting thinking is what creates a homogenous, anti-inclusive workplace. These are questions to ask yourself when evaluating a friendship, not a future employee. Too often this means folks make the mistake of hiring based on likability and affinity rather than proven skills and results.

Often masked as interviewing for culture fit, this dusty concept often leads to racial and other biases in the hiring process. Too often, BIPOC workers are denied a role or advancement because they are not seen as a good culture fit by white leadership. As Ellen Pao (2017) points out in *Reset*, a group of people with different backgrounds and worldviews may seem to be a bad culture fit, in that they may be slower to agree—but conflict is not always a bad thing. When different views test decisions, this strengthens decisions. If everyone is hired to have the same worldview, it's easy to create a disconnected bubble. Further, dismissing someone because they lack culture fit is often a coded way to suggest that a candidate has not assimilated into white culture or the white standards of professionalism of that particular workplace.

While every workplace has an organizational culture, you want to focus your hiring decisions more on your values and behavioral and strategic aspirations, and center equity and inclusion in your final choices. Instead, aim for "culture add," which helps assess whether a candidate will enhance your culture through explicit performance rather than implicitly biased cultural values. Hint: this also applies to existing employee evaluations. We'll discuss these in Chapter 8.

"Culture add" helps center each new hire's future contributions to your team. Consider these questions:

- What is our current culture, and how does it reflect our values and behavioral principles? What is missing?
- What core values, behavioral principles, and organizational practices do we need new hires to know about and match?
- What aspirations do we have for strategic growth and cultural transformation where a new hire could contribute?

Success is bringing on someone who is additive to your culture, someone who brings a different experience, different background while adding to your organization's values and behavioral expectations. Suppose there is something about a candidate that doesn't sit well with you. In that case, if there's a personality quirk that concerns you (e.g. he interrupts you in the interview or talks way too fast), that's not a reason to ding him immediately. I know you may think I'm crazy, but that's coachable. Consider the possibility that no manager has ever told him that he talks too fast. That's happened to me! I hired a direct report who in the interview process showed an affinity to interrupt, ever so politely, without letting me finish sentences. I caught it and asked the other interviewers if they noticed any patterns I should be aware of—two mentioned him being eager and engaged. I hired him, and he's been a terrific contributor. Barely two months into the role, I met with him to share my feedback about his performance, including the impact he had on me and others when he interrupted a conversation mid-sentence. He expressed immediate and genuine regret. I knew he had a good intent to be helpful and generative, but I also knew he could be far more influential if he paused, listened, and waited for an appropriate time before responding.

Background Check Q&A

Q. *Should companies be vetting folks before they are hired, for making public racist or sexist or homophobic comments on social media, if they have been sued for sexual harassment, etc.? Are online searches to check for these things legal and valuable?*

Yes, recruiters and hiring managers should conduct thorough due diligence on all candidates as part of their standard reference checks, specifically executive hires, to ensure they're not hiring serial harassers and abusers. It's tricky legally because it hasn't become common, but it's an issue that has come up specifically after #MeToo. In Hollywood, predatory execs would get fired for egregious behavior and then get picked up at another studio with an even bigger comp package (ugh!).

It can be complicated to police online searches. A freshly hired editor in chief got fired by Conde Nast before her start date because of racist tweets that surfaced from when she was a teenager. Does being a teenager give her a pass? Does it depend on what she said? You must establish real criteria for what you're looking for and what is considered a red flag. And then the interview panel should discuss this information collectively.

Ask Better Interview Questions

While it is hard to change how our brains are wired, it is possible to change the context of hiring decisions by training interviewers on how to shape their questions to get the information they need. Your best strategy against falling into the "fit" habit is to develop preset interview questions that speak to the candidates' abilities to perform consistently against predetermined performance metrics and organizational values. Accountability and analytics reduce bias, but there is a double-edged sword of data. You're still hiring human beings and should ask them better questions to understand who they are.

Research has shown that managers who conduct structured interviews with a combination of behavioral and situational questions have more successful outcomes than those who do unstructured interviewing. Google's reWork, among other similar resources, can provide you with great ideas for behavioral questions that can help you assess candidates' achievements in alignment with role expectations (i.e. "Tell me about a time . . . ?"). Another approach is to ask hypothetical questions (i.e. "What would you do if . . . ?").

Consider asking questions such as the following:

Describe a team project that you're proud of completing, and how you worked with other team members.

When you need to learn something new, how do you approach it? Where do your ideas come from?

Tell me about two people you have either managed or worked with whose lives you positively impacted? What would they say if I called them tomorrow?

Tell me how you build relationships. How do you make connections with people you have less in common with?

Help find the gems in your talent pool that do more than showcase the standard criteria of problem-solving abilities, intellectual curiosity, and self-awareness. Always remember to follow the story: What did you do? How did you do it? Why did you do that, and what were you thinking? What was the result/outcome? What did you do next? And after your interview, ask the receptionist, recruitment coordinator, or even security, "How was the candidate's interaction with you?" How people treat strangers speaks volumes about their capacity for compassion and respect.

These questions can help you assess what has shaped their career decisions, relationships, and openness to different perspectives. The goal is to create a conversation that leads to revelations about their character and competencies, especially those hard to track but valuable nonlinear trajectories, not a rehearsal. People no longer crave career paths. They want to grow where they are at, and beyond. Companies such as Kapor Capital have begun considering "distance traveled," where a job candidate came from and how many obstacles they had to overcome, as an essential measure of work ethic and resilience.

You don't want to fall into an assumption trap, believing that only those who have worked at a start-up are most qualified to work at yours because they know what it's like to work in that environment. That doesn't speak to potential. If you're interviewing for project management skills, ask how someone managed a project from start to finish. Those skills could have been developed at a previous role or through coaching or a personal project.

When you can take your time throughout the process and have the space to ask questions about a candidate's values, how they show up at work, their quirks, and talents, you can make better hiring decisions. "I want my team to develop relationships with people," says Keesha Jean-Baptiste, senior vice president and chief talent officer for Hearst Magazines. "They should meet them, get to know them, and go into the process with a full understanding of who these individuals, these multifaceted people are, so that you're coming from a place of support when you're hiring rather than thinking, 'Okay, I'm checking the box now'" (Jean-Baptiste 2020).

At Hearst, Keesha created a set of interview questions to help gauge mindset around DEI behaviors. The hiring manager, recruiter, and other interviewers would ask to hear the answer from multiple perspectives. For the mindset piece, they ask, "What have you done or put in place to augment diversity initiatives at your workplace?" She says, "It's a reality check to make sure that we're bringing in people whose values align with where we are trying to go." Note: This question should be asked of all hires, regardless of racial or other backgrounds, or role. This is how you ensure that DEI expectations are integrated in your hiring process.

Inclusion Q&A

Q. If I'm asked in an interview about our company's diversity or, more candidly, whether the candidate would be the "only," what should I say?

Legal teams get worried if you're considering hiring someone because of their demographic characteristics. It may sound obvious, but you shouldn't say we have a problem with hiring Black people so that's why you're here. Instead be honest about the state of diversity on your team and organization, and your aspirations to diversify. Say that this is my team's current demographic composition and I would like to change that to better align with our broader strategy, mission, and purpose. Be honest. I am always up front about our gaps and our opportunities; there is no way of sugarcoating it. I told a recent hire that she would be the first Black woman on the leadership team. As an executive of color, this was not her first rodeo. However, it was important to emphasize the weight and relevance of her position and what we were actively doing to hire more racially diverse talent across all levels. Candidates of color will understandably approach a job that specifies they are looking for diverse talent or where they will be the only BIPOC with a sense of trepidation. They worry about being tokenized ("the only") and the pressures that come from that experience. They are also naturally concerned that hiring managers may feel that they've checked the box and don't have to hire any more BIPOC team members. This can be immensely stressful.

Not speaking the truth they will encounter on their first day and beyond is a disservice to the individual and the mission you're trying to deliver on. Hiring managers should honestly share what candidates should expect as well as their aspirations for change. Perhaps most of the team is white, or they will be the only Black or BIPOC staff. In that case, share your genuine commitment to hiring many more BIPOC team members. The point is not to say we want to hire you for diversity but rather that we recognize we have had gaps and your skill set, voice, and lived experience would be additive to our organization. And that you see them for who they are and will ensure others do the same.

Standardize How You Debrief and Decide

Now it's time to compare notes. In an ideal world, if you're going through a structured process, you bring everyone on this job-filling journey together to determine if the candidate should move forward. In order to be effective at this stage of decision-making, each person must be comfortable actively and easily weighing in on decisions.

Ideally, the first review should focus on the role's core responsibilities: what are the must-have skills or talents. At Google, the hiring committee would review all the feedback and the skills tests and determine if the candidate was a pass or go. We would look for outliers: Why did someone give the candidate a low (or high) score on cognitive ability? Is that feedback valid or could it be attributed to bias? The hiring committee chair was responsible for holding us to unbiased evaluation criteria. Research from Lean In's 2020 report, "The State of Black Women in Corporate America," confirms that interviewers are less likely to lean on subjective, exclusive factors, such as culture fit or personality, when there is someone tasked with keeping an eye on biases (Lean In 2020).

Then, the review committee would push a little harder. In each set of conversations, we would aim to reset everyone, remind them what we are hiring for, what are the outcomes, and what biases we want to avoid. What could we be missing? Who are the people we are saying no to, and why? Are we looking at the candidate slate holistically? Is there recency bias—the memory bias that favors the candidate you interviewed yesterday versus the one you interviewed two weeks ago? Did we assess each person fairly?

Putting this structure in place and creating steadfast rules of assessment eliminates the personal pressure that is often felt in the hiring process. You must have a clear, consistent framework for decision-making, including determining who makes a final decision and whether those not involved in the full hiring process are allowed votes, vetoes, or recommendations. Be mindful of referrals. In many industries, most hiring is still coming through as referrals. I can't tell you how many times a white male senior colleague has vigorously fought for a candidate who did not meet the role's qualifications but was a referral from a friend. Then there's the founder or client who asks ever so graciously, Can you take a look at this person or can I add this person to the mix—as a favor for a friend? This structure protects you and empowers you to remind someone that their process and ask do not add value to your process.

Other questions we should ask regularly: "What perspectives are we missing by hiring for the same attributes? What backgrounds and viewpoints are we missing? Can we hire to fill those gaps, to ensure we break out of groupthink and build a diverse team who will bring in a broad range of ideas and perspectives?" Imagine adding, "If the final candidates across multiple slates remain disproportionately white, we will revisit decisions and always include a minimum of one or two BIPOC finalists. And, "If timing and budget pressures are affecting decisions, we will tap into a reserve budget to reduce limitations on our decision-making." Now you're putting measures to help you reach your goals.

At the end of the day, there is no perfect formula for hiring. Despite countless science-backed technical solutions that say otherwise, it is nearly impossible to make a 100% unbiased hiring decision that favors or not certain demographic characteristics. You can ensure fairness in your hiring by defining consistent and structured processes and encouraging your coworkers to follow these practices. Getting more underrepresented candidates through the door will require rethinking your applicant pool, job qualifications, bias in access to interviews and assessments, and hiring manager training. Change won't always happen fast, but the more aware you are of your perceptions and actions, both conscious and unconscious, and begin to take steps toward repairing them, the closer we will come to equity.

Try This: Self-Reflection Questions to Mitigate Bias

Proactively addressing biases is key to a more accurate assessment of future performance and function. Self-reflection and bias confrontation are hard, but they are essential tools for a hiring manager. After you meet with a candidate, jot down your answer to these questions:

- What skill sets does your team need? What do you have too much of?
- Why would you hire them? Why wouldn't you?
- Test whether you're having an intuitive feeling or judgment about this person. If you're having a negative reaction, what is it that this person is bringing up in you that makes you struggle? Are you under particular stress that may negatively affect your reactions? Does the candidate remind you of someone from your past?
- Have interviewers used coded language such as "cold," "opinionated," "bossy," "sharp elbowed," or "thick accent" disproportionately in reference to female or BIPOC candidates? Do these comments refer to the skills required for the role or instead reflect gendered and racialized biases interviewers may hold about these individuals?
- Will they be additive to your culture and actively support DEI? During interviews for the current UN secretary-general, male and female candidates were asked whether it was time for a female secretary-general. The final candidate was a man, but as part of the process he had to convince the interview panel that he was the feminist for the job.

Be honest with yourself and your answers.

Your Road Map to Revolution

Pay close attention to how your organization recruits and assesses talent at every step of the recruitment and hiring process. Ask yourself these questions: How can I influence who is hired at my organization? What role can I play in deciding which candidates are considered or how the process runs? If you help evaluate candidates, insist on reviewing a diverse slate. If we continue to make the same organizational mistakes of only hiring, listening to, and advancing people you know and with whom you feel comfortable with, you risk alienating your current team and your future one.

- **Continually examine bias throughout the hiring process.** There's no autopilot here! When you become aware of it, act. Call your perceptions and assumptions into question, again and again.

- **Require inclusive interviewing training for all.** Ensure those who make hiring decisions—from screening to final selections— objectively evaluate skills, experience, and potential. To be effective, this training should consist of relevant workplace scenarios where employees can quickly identify the impact of bias in decision-making and how they can prevent it.

- **Push for more candidates.** Everyone wants to get a new hire in the door quickly, but find the confidence to ask for more candidates, even when you're getting pressure to fill a seat. Don't accept excuses such as "But there's no qualified talent" or "Those are the only applicants we received." It's necessary to create a more diverse workforce.

- **Standardize the interviewing processes to keep assessments fair and balanced.** Consistency is key. Have a standard of questions to ask and a scorecard for all interviewers to use for review.

- **Designate a "selection criteria check."** Assign an HR colleague or other team member to keep everyone focused on the hiring benchmarks. Lean In research confirms that interviewers will be less likely to rely on traditionally exclusive notions of "culture fit" or personality when someone is watching out for these biases (Lean In n.d.).

- **Watch for affinity bias or the horn effect during interviews.** That's when you either connect with someone or like someone because they too went to your college or also love to play basketball or when something slightly off about the candidate grabs your attention and you can't move beyond it. You cannot let that guide your final impression of someone. Instead, explain why their skills or qualities would be additive to your team.

- **Shift your focus from culture fit to "culture add" when evaluating candidates.** Success is bringing someone who is additive to your culture. Aim for "culture add" by assessing whether a candidate enhances your culture.

- **Ask better interview questions.** Ask open-ended behavioral and hypothetical questions to understand a candidate's potential separate from their background. Talk about how they problem-solve and build relationships. Ask what their colleagues would say about them.
- **Standardize how you debrief and decide.** This is when you bring everyone together to compare notes and determine whether the candidate should move forward. Be ready to push back on feedback with thought-provoking questions (e.g. Why did you feel that way?).

5

Nurture a People-First Culture

Years ago at Disney, a new chief of staff, a young woman of color, was making the rounds getting to know leadership. When we met, I was immediately captivated by her curiosity and precision. Then she asked me one question that totally caught me off-guard: "Who is your best friend at work?" "I don't have one," I replied, disappointed in my answer. I had cultivated good relationships over the years, but I couldn't pick one "best friend" who I truly trusted, a colleague with whom I could freely share my concerns, doubts or fears, where I didn't need to feel on-guard as a woman of color or worried that my truths would cause them to run away, betray me to our managers, or ignore me.

My disappointment wasn't solely about not having a best friend at work but rather that question made me confront a deeply buried feeling that I had never felt fully welcomed, neither in my team nor in the broader organization.

Culture can mean a lot of different things. Culture is not ping pong tables or free lunch; it is how things get done. Its language is how people feel; it's whether they want to be at work, whether they want to engage with their colleagues, whether they feel safe, seen, and valued, whether they're encouraged and driven to create and contribute because they believe in what they're doing. Every single person on a team, from the most junior

85

individual contributor to a senior executive, contributes to a company's culture. And it's up to leaders to take it from being invisible to visible. What you say and do on a day-to-day basis creates culture—every comment you make, every uncomfortable moment that goes unaddressed, has a ripple effect. This is the energy you put forth and the substance of how people engage and interact.

Work culture is formative work—it doesn't just happen overnight. Severe, headline-making news about toxic workplaces typically reflect countless, individual racist interactions and microaggressions, e.g. "My manager touched my dreadlocks in a team meeting" or "I am constantly accused of being angry or animated when I'm simply making a point." These actions may not represent the totality of your culture, but they lead to a culture of mistrust, harmful work experiences, and systemic exclusion of whole swaths of people.

Managers are the linchpins in our organizations. They play a critical role in creating and sustaining inclusive workplace cultures.

"While I do believe that culture has to come from the top and it has to be centralized as a tenet of the company's mission, your lived experience is defined by your direct team and your direct leader," says Sherice Torres, vice president, marketing at Facebook. Even if your senior leadership demonstrates all six of the top traits of inclusive leadership according to Deloitte—curiosity, cultural intelligence, collaboration, commitment, courage, and cognizance (Dillon and Bourke 2016)—if you don't focus on what's happening in the middle, where the real sore spots reside, then the experience of underrepresented employees is going to be a disconnect from what you are claiming to be the culture of the company. And in the end, when there is complete inaction on the part of management to address these issues, employees feel that they have no choice but to leave.

As a manager, your success and capabilities are the primary indicators of growth within an organization. Yet I know you're consistently given myriad tasks without the necessary support to do your best—things such as being a leading expert in diversity and inclusion, acting as a therapist, and taking responsibility for the results of challenging industry conditions. To continue delivering at the pace of change, you need the right tools and personalized support to develop yourself first and then to do the same for others. We need to remember that we can't push an organization forward if we're not empowered to push ourselves forward.

This requires that you work toward creating workplaces characterized by safety, dignity, and respect of all workers and that you carve out time and space to reflect on your industry's culture and the ways workplace norms and habits have traditionally locked out or pushed out people of color. It further requires you to recognize your responsibility to respond to cultural conversations by stepping forward, not shrinking away, to advocate for change and that you rally your peers to push for change. This chapter helps you build your management skills with a lens on inclusion, belonging, psychological safety, and anti-racism.

Lead from the Beginning

A massive mistake leaders make is laboring over the hiring process and forgetting about what comes after the offer is accepted: what it's like for people to work here. When you understand your workplace's belonging gaps and the fractures in your culture and when you've done the work to create an inclusive workplace, you're less likely to have to hire someone from outside to lead a workshop to solve your "diversity dilemma." Setting up an inclusive culture first is the right thing to do for several reasons—including, it prevents having to course-correct after harm has been done. I've been called in to help with damage control too many times to count. The managers come to me asking for diversity training, and when I arrive I realize that there has been a precipitating blunder to bring about this desire to talk about corporate inclusion. An innocuous request for my talents is too often code for "We've been called out for our lack of diversity, toxic workplace culture, biased product campaigns, or all the above—and we need your help."

New hire onboarding is often an afterthought. This period is the essential introduction to a company's culture and one of the most critical parts of a DEI strategy. How you welcome new hires sets the tone for inclusion. Don't overlook this transition period. Eighty-six percent of new hires decide to stay with a company long-term within the first six months of employment, according to research from the Aberdeen Group (Willyerd 2014), a market research company.

Beyond handing out ID cards and filling out tax forms, onboarding is perhaps one of the best tools to help employees feel included from day 1. Think about when you've started at a new company and found yourself twiddling your fingers not knowing who to talk to or what to do. It's a horrible feeling, right? Your first day of work is one of the most disorienting experiences. It's like you're a foreigner walking into a place where you don't understand the language, the norms, the customs, the politics.

Your job is to decode it for your new hire so they feel an immediate sense of connection and belonging. What you do and say reduces the chances that your new hire will feel left out and disconnected and sets the tone for being at ease in a new space, feeling safe and welcomed to show up as the best version of themselves, and able to navigate in a new environment. Buffer, a social media engagement platform, starts the employee onboarding process as soon as a new hire officially accepts the position. The Buddy Program assigns two "buddies" to every new hire who help guide them through the first six weeks via regular communication and check-ins. This dream team consists of a role buddy (a peer who intimately understands the new hire's role and responsibilities) and a culture buddy (someone who can translate the company culture). The benefits are enormous: the new hire has clear points of contact and inside knowledge of the company, the buddies have an opportunity to network and increase their mentoring and leadership experience, and the company sees an increase in employee engagement and retention for all parties (Buffer staff communications 2020).

When I hired a Black male executive years ago, before him joining the company we spoke at length about the racialized tensions he would have to navigate on his team and across the organization. Throughout the hiring process, we built a strong rapport and trust, and I committed to clearing a path for him. We mutually agreed on what would be needed in terms of buy-in from colleagues to ensure he would be properly welcomed and set up for success. This bridging needs to be done with care and tailored to each new hire. Not all Black hires need or appreciate a path being paved on their behalf. Interventions must be tailored for each hire, and there has to be mutual trust all around that each hire is getting tailored support in addition to racially sensitive support. This is not about walking on eggshells around Black team members but rather about creating conditions for their success and the success of their teams and organizations.

I intentionally identified one of the most tenured white male executives as his "orientation buddy." In preparation for their engagement, I said this: "Here's what I need you to know. He is a very tall Black man being asked to lead a team of all-white females. During the recruitment process, I have found him to be one of the most pleasant individuals I know, but we must be prepared for the racial anxiety that his mere presence will cause many on this team. He is well aware of the imagined threat his mere presence poses in an all-white environment; this is not the first time he has been hired as the only executive of color. For far too long, he has had to make himself likable to reduce the anxiety of others. I know you want him to succeed just as I do. I will support him and engage in transparent conversations with his team about white fragility. My ask is that you, as his buddy and a skilled navigator of our organizational culture, provide him with the navigational tools he will need, internal credibility with leaders and his team that only you can provide, and serve as his leadership shield when some may question his ability to lead. Because it will likely happen. I'll partner with you throughout the entire process and ask that you let me know if you experience any discomfort in this process. It's better that we lay everything on the table now because, as James Baldwin has taught us, 'Nothing can be changed until it is faced.'"

His buddy was an exceptional partner. He immediately credentialed him across the organization by bringing him to senior meetings and amplifying his achievements. He shouldered the political and social risks when the Black executive's mistakes, common for new leaders learning to navigate new workplace cultures, were raised as red flags. While I did engage the leaders of his team in a conversation about white fragility, we never entirely shut down the racial anxiety of his predominantly white female team. In the end, the dominant culture rejected him, and he had a short tenure at Disney. In retrospect, we should have offered bespoke training or more intentional conversations about how to work together in a racially sensitive way. While we continued to excuse poor behavior of white male executives across the organization, his actions and failures were much more scrutinized than his white peers'. And it was a shame.

An emotional tax is levied on Black women and men throughout their careers. Catalyst's report found that when people feel psychologically unsafe, they are less likely to take professional risks and speak up at work. Only 56%

of Black employees were vocal about important or challenging issues in the workplace, compared with 74% of white employees (Dnika, Thorpe-Moscon, and McCluney 2016). The workplace has socially ostracized and silenced the ones who have the most to be vocal about. Having sponsors, allies, and buddies can help set you up for success and "clear your path," but sustaining a people-first culture will take an all-hands approach.

Building high trust in teams requires demonstrating respect and care for all of your team members. Before you offer inclusive team management programs, you may want to participate in racially sensitive management training. There's nothing more anxiety-inducing for a BIPOC employee than the thought of being one of a few people of color in an inclusion training. We worry that white people will talk about their whiteness in weird ways. That they will try to compensate for their discomfort by either ignoring us or making racially insensitive comments such as "I understand what you're saying, my wife is Asian" or "The way you've overcome racism is so inspiring."

Create an Inclusive Onboarding Experience

What's your company's onboarding process like? I remember my first day at Viacom when I was hired as head of talent acquisition. I had to attend the standard orientation program along with two other new hires. They played a video about Viacom, and honestly, it was uninspiring. It didn't match the energy I knew was symbolic of the organization; it didn't make me excited to work there. I wanted that moment to affirm my decision to join the organization—we all do. That's where you can step in.

To onboard your new hire into your systems and culture, ask yourself:

- What does this person need to succeed in their first 30, 60, and 90 days?
- What do I know about them that is vital to understanding how they work, and who else in the company should know those things?
- Who should be this person's point person for day-to-day questions, and who should be their buddy, an established or well-networked colleague, who can help them avoid missteps?
- Could my or the organization's idea of "professionalism" unintentionally make BIPOC employees feel uncomfortable or forced to

code-switch or downplay their differences? For example, are Black women being silently shamed for wearing their hair naturally)?

■ What can I decode about our organizational culture, language, and internal politics, to make it easier for this employee to feel like an insider?

Little details matter, too. I knew that one South Asian male executive was concerned that he would not have sufficient vacation days to visit his parents in India twice a year as had been his custom. When negotiating his compensation package, we added more vacation days to his employment contract and balanced it out by reducing the candidate's other less valuable fringe benefits.

Make a strong impression by customizing the pre-onboarding experience. Recruiters should pass on all relevant information to hiring managers and the teams responsible for onboarding to ensure all relevant considerations are considered for new hires. For example, if a candidate requires special accommodations such as wheelchair accessibility, ensure your orientation is set up to welcome that candidate seamlessly into your space and not as an add-on. Ask for your new hire's preferred workspace whether in the office or at home. Track religious holiday schedules so that if you're delivering orientations during Ramadan, for example, you do not offer those new hires water or other items commonly provided without consideration for cultural practices. Too often, people are left to their own devices to figure it out. And for those who may not have previous institutional knowledge or formal training in office politics, it's a sink-or-swim scenario.

Beyond getting administrative tasks out of the way, help facilitate a faster ramp time for your new hire by sending a personalized welcome email at least a week before they join. Curate a welcome package that speaks to how much you, your team, and the company are eager to welcome them. This can include a "new hire reading list" including HR documentation (handbook, benefits, etc.), glossary or example of company terms, current road map or strategy for the team, resources on how to get involved in DEI initiatives, and examples of how the team works together and across departments, including communication styles. If this looks like an exhaustive list of things to do, don't feel overwhelmed. You can space this out through their first week. The point is to provide them the navigational tools they will need to feel settled and informed.

Prepare your team, too, for the changing dynamics ahead. Clearly define the new hires' responsibilities, reporting lines, and handoff processes, if any. Set the expectation that everyone is responsible for building an inclusive and welcoming environment.

And when they arrive, communicate shared purpose and 90-day objectives, with check-in moments to receive and give feedback. In each check-in ask: What questions can I answer for you? What do you need to be successful? How can I support you?

Onboarding Exercises

I've found these team leader integration exercises to be effective in onboarding leaders and team members:

1. Create a team user manual. Bring the team together, and ask everyone to fill in a template that shares how each member of your team likes to work. For example, if someone needs quiet to think, they may decline your invitation to join you in the lobby. It's not about you; it's how they work. This can foster more robust communication and eliminate misguided assumptions and bias. These will require time to reflect on. You should also note that this exercise could be challenging for those who have previously felt sabotaged or undermined at work. It's not enough to ask the question; you have to be responsive and deliver your teammates the tailored support they need to do their best work. Some prompts:
   - How I like to work: (i.e. I need a quiet environment or I thrive in loud, open office layouts).
   - I'm most productive during these times/hours:
   - Best ways to communicate with me (i.e. chat over email will get you the quickest response; I prefer texts for emergencies only).
   - I like to receive feedback (i.e. face-to-face so I can work through it with you; via email so I have time to think and process before responding).

- Things I need to feel productive (i.e. time to reflect on new ideas, trust).
- Things that can hang me up (i.e. I need to understand the purpose and goals; it takes me a while to trust people).
- Things I love (i.e. brainstorming, socializing with colleagues, throwing out new ideas even if they're not fully thought through).
- Other things to know about me (i.e. I'm inspired by X, I'm allergic to dogs).

2. Team-building experience: Are there things you wish you knew about new team members but are too afraid to ask? Consider a facilitated session. To ensure anonymity, a facilitator asks team members to answer a few questions: Where do you want to grow this year as a manager or individual contributor? Where do you want to grow this year as a team? What's hanging you up right now? What is the thing that you just can't get to? How can your new leader support you?

3. The facilitator compiles the answers and shares them with the new leaders. The new leader privately reviews answers with the facilitator and reflects on responses. They agree to answer all questions and concerns of the team. Note that some questions or comments may not be answerable. For example, "Why were you selected for this role?" or "When will the organization be done with restructurings?" Sometimes the new leader's answers show points of connections that were not considered prior to this conversation. I've found these exercises to be successful in accelerating bonding and learning in a nonthreatening way in the early part of team forming, especially as they debunk the stories in our heads that keep us from honest relationship building.

4. Send a 30-60-90-day survey. It's never too early to assess how employees are integrating into their team and organization. A proper onboarding program will include a standard survey at key intervals, at least within the first month. Start as soon as someone begins the onboarding process, and then continue collecting information about your organization's engagement trends and

analyzing the data across demographic groups. This will serve as your starting point to identify strengths and areas of opportunity for your organization or team. To engender trust, you have to be committed to transparency and action. If team members don't experience the changes they may ask for in these surveys, they will not complete them. Head to Chapter 7 for more on transparency and accountability in surveys.

Facilitate Stronger Connections

Consider how your everyday actions (or inactions) affect the formation of your culture and your propensity for inclusion. While they may seem like small and inconsequential moments, having lunch with the same person every day or assuming that a BIPOC employee is an introvert when they're lonely all add up to longstanding systemic inequities in the workplace. Those are the barriers to inclusion.

A basic building block of nurturing an inclusive culture is to be willing to make room for others not like you. Think more consciously about how you connect and engage with your colleagues. When deciding whether to invite someone for coffee, to join your project, or represent the organization externally, try an exercise of substitution where you substitute the person you first considered for another and ask yourself: What made me choose the first person? What would be different?

Proximity and personal interactions lead to stronger social bonds, according to research from Lucille Nahemow and M. Powell Lawton (1975). Be intentional to break out of your bubble, for example, ensuring that your calendar reflects your stated priorities. How about inviting a Black colleague to coffee, finding out their interests, and then setting up an introduction to broaden their professional network? This can't just be about white people helping and educating themselves by being friendly with BIPOC staff—this is asking a BIPOC colleague for their time, time that could be used for promotable work. And if you're asking them for their time, make sure you're offering them something in return as a professional gain. How about seeking to mentor a young Hispanic colleague new to your organization?

Commit to attending one work event about a demographic group different than yours once a week, for example events hosted by employee resource groups or diversity-focused industry events, or schedule lunch with a coworker different than you. Whether you are a white or BIPOC manager, set aside time regularly to cultivate BIPOC staff, and ensure you are attuned to each staffer's unique needs so that you know you are clearing a path for their success and advancement. And then add it to your calendar as you would any recurring meeting. This also means creating a workplace environment where BIPOC colleagues have a sense of belonging, meaning tailoring the workplace to honor, and celebrate and embrace differences. If a team member is an observant Muslim, be considerate about their prayer times and fasting during Ramadan. Be mindful about office Christmas decorations when it comes to staff who aren't Christian.

As a manager, try to keep an eye on team interactions and workplace friendships. Social networks often develop into enablers for promotions and connections to professional opportunities, but BIPOC workers often feel socially isolated in predominantly white teams. Not surprisingly, a lack of strong social networks at work can sometimes lead them to pull back from attempting to build relationships with coworkers, attending social gatherings, or those optional meetings where exciting projects are doled out.

It's unfortunately common for BIPOC to have been undervalued, stalled, underpaid, held back for advancement, belittled, sabotaged, undermined, and pushed out of majority-white organizations. They often bring that added weight and trauma into a new workplace and may be coming in on edge, on guard, and slow to trust. If you suspect this is happening, speak privately with the person. Before you launch into solutions, ask directly about how they feel about the work environment. Then ask if they would be open to suggestions for more support, connecting them with an affinity group, a BIPOC mentor, or paid mental health services that can help unpack microaggressions.

Additionally, as their manager, be intentional about creating moments for idea sharing and cross-team socialization. Showcase the value of intersectional perspectives in processes, projects, and initiatives, and facilitate conversations that can help those not part of the dominant culture share their perspectives. Think about ways to promote collaboration across your team. It could be as simple as moving your desk structure and swapping seating or assigning different team members to projects. Or pairing up team members who would not normally work together as project leaders. Roanhorse Consulting, an indigenous women-led think tank, encourages co-leadership. "The idea that one person is supposed to know everything is antithetical to how my community grows up," says Vanessa Roanhorse. "So instead we have created a think trust or a group of people who share the responsibility of making choices, and lean on each other" (Roanhorse 2020). This type of nonhierarchical and untraditional (read: practices different from a white standard) structure could have profound benefits, such as allowing for more creative solutions from multiple perspectives and building vital team trust.

Create opportunities for social interaction that enable team members to connect in various settings, platforms, and time zones, and encourage all, regardless of level, to bring forth ideas or concerns (note: be prepared to act on those—that's Chapter 7).

To combat social isolation, Culture Amp experimented with a Slackbot called Donut that pairs up employees on a virtual coffee date. Participants receive an automated message every three weeks that starts a chat between two randomly selected employees. They also received conversation starters not tied to work. "The focus was to foster a sense of connectedness," says Stacey Nordwall (2020), people program lead at Culture Amp. It worked. After two years the program is still going strong. She says there are close to 100 people in the dedicated Slack channel at any given time, sharing photos of their meetings and a quick recap of what they talked about so everyone can learn more about each other.

That said, forced pairings can also go awry if they feel like a time waster. Maybe try a few rounds, and if people are clamoring for more, do more. But don't automate anything regularly just because people are afraid to tell their boss or peers something is wrong. It's important to think about how you structure pairings to build connections. For example, in a dinner party you would pair people with something in common—such as an interest or hobby. To avoid the awkwardness that is inevitable in forced pairings, I've found that offering prompts such as "Is there a specific moment in your career that has shaped how you think or go about work?" or "The biggest misconception people have about my role is . . . " can help break the ice and lead to meaningful conversations. For a broader set of questions, check out the Proust questionnaire, named for the French novelist who favored this type of game to understand the true nature of an individual. Some include: Which talent would you most like to have? What is the trait you most deplore in others? What is your idea of perfect happiness? (Carter and Servat 2005).

Beyond daily connections, learning about one another's racial identity, culture, and heritage leads to a stronger team community. One of my favorite team building questions is "What was your favorite childhood meal and why?" I love to see how often people who grew up in vastly different cultural and socioeconomic backgrounds can find an instant connection through foods of their past and present. It's important to normalize differences but not at the sake of those who bear the burden of being different.

Build Empathy Muscles

The best workplaces are built on trust and respect. Here's a basic formula for building trust adapted from Frances X. Frei and Anne Morris (2020): authenticity + consistency + empathy. You gain trust from others when they believe that you show up as your authentic self (authenticity), that you do so consistently and fairly (consistency), and when they believe you genuinely care about their feelings, needs and success (empathy). Miscommunication, assumptions, omissions, fear, bias, silence—this is what's destroying workplaces, and it's disproportionately harming BIPOC workers.

To fuel workplace connections, Dr. Brené Brown (2010) cites the four attributes of empathy from nursing scholar Theresa Wiseman:

Try to understand another's perspective.
Be nonjudgmental.
Try to identify another's feelings.
Communicate back the emotion you see.

The first step can be the most challenging when you can't fully understand what it's like to walk in another's shoes. Workplace exclusion is often unconscious, passive, and is fueled from a lack of knowledge about what someone else is dealing with. Do able bodied employees consider it difficult for a wheelchair-bound coworker to attend a rooftop lunch meeting when there are no accessible ramps? Probably not, and without understanding what it's like to live as another, those exclusionary practices get repeated. When you seek to know and connect with the people you work with and your consumers, you become more conscious about inclusion.

Privilege-exposing exercises can help. In *White Privilege: Unpacking the Invisible Knapsack*, Peggy McIntosh (1989) relies on situational context to present a deeper understanding of one's lived experience. To visualize your privilege, McIntosh lists a series of statements to agree or disagree with:

- If I should need to move, I can be pretty sure of renting or purchasing housing in an area which I can afford and in which I would want to live.
- I can be pretty sure that my neighbors in such a location will be neutral or pleasant to me.
- I can assume that I won't be perceived as angry, incompetent, childlike, or helpless because of my body.

This exercise can also reveal white privilege and norms in the workplace. Here are some additional examples:

- I'm not often interrupted or spoken over during a meeting.
- Coworkers don't confuse me with others of the same race or ethnicity.
- I've never been misgendered or had to correct my colleagues' assumptions about my personal life.
- I've never felt that I had to hide a central part of my identity at work, such as my sexuality, gender identity, disability, immigration status, or mental health status.
- My manager or my team members have navigated challenges similar to mine.
- I have family members or people in my network who I can ask for advice about my career goals or industry.
- In general, my performance reviews are focused on my work and not my personality, race, culture, or "style."
- I grew up participating in activities such as golfing or skiing that are common work outings.
- If I make a mistake, I can feel confident that my colleagues won't attribute it to my race.

- I have not been called in to state an opinion on behalf of my race.
- I can feel confident that when I walk into any business meeting I will be surrounded by people who look like me and who share my background.
- I don't worry that if I express my opinion strongly at work, my colleagues will assume I'm falling into a racial stereotype or that others may read it as "angry," "hysterical," or "emotional."

Your answers are important, but thinking about how other team members would answer these questions is even more vital. Who is agreeing with these statements? Who is not? What are the unseen advantages and disadvantages of gaining access and being visible in your workplace? When we give verbal feedback, are we focusing on the behavior, or are we labeling the person? What dictates those actions from setting the seats at a meeting to developing the agenda?

One commonly used approach to expose privilege at work is to organize a privilege walk, which is an exercise that physically illuminates the power of privilege and its effect on one's opportunity. The idea is simple in concept: All people start from the same line, but they have to take a step forward if they answer no to questions such as "Have your parents ever had to work more than one job to support your family?" or "Have you ever been the only person of your race in your department?" It's not only about seeing who ends up where at the end but rather the reflection process of discovering the many factors outside your control that define where you end up. The first time I did this at Google, I remember feeling a sense of discomfort when answering questions about my family's low socioeconomic status. It was also a chance to see how my family's immense sacrifices for my education had allowed me to leapfrog ahead of those from a similar background whose families couldn't provide the same educational opportunities.

Another activity that enables individuals to assess their privilege is "Privilege for sale": in this activity, individuals are given a specific amount of money and a list of privileges they can choose to purchase. For those with smaller amounts of money, decisions are often quickly made based on limited resources. For those with larger pots of money, I've seen teams wrestle with existential questions and real-life scenarios that can be humbling, jaw dropping, and eye opening. It can be a highly engaging way to examine what privileges you may have and take for granted.

A downside of these activities for BIPOC coworkers is that privilege is being exposed for white colleague's benefit and education but also at our cost. Many BIPOC have been pressured to code-switch and cover up their differences from their privileged white colleagues to make their coworkers feel more comfortable. Some BIPOC staff can be retraumatized by memories of past struggles that their colleagues are only now seeing. Before considering this or any other exercise in discussing racial privilege at work, ensure that you accommodate the feelings of BIPOC staff first. BIPOC staff and affinity groups should discuss and run these exercises, and if any BIPOC staff don't feel comfortable participating, that should be discussed beforehand.

I have worked with senior leaders (mostly white men) who, upon engaging in an exercise to write their own "outsider story," that is a moment when they have felt like an outsider and how that made them feel, have been brought to tears remembering moments when they felt the sting of exclusion. Perhaps they grew up with a lisp or stammer or were teased for being poor or fat. The outsider story technique is used to get majority leaders to shift perspective, build empathy and understanding about others, helping them shape their workplace inclusion narrative. It's important to note that "diversity" does not become a catchall for any kind of difference or hardship. If a company's definition of diversity is so broad that a "diverse slate" of candidates can, by their definition, still maintain a whites-only majority—that's a problematic definition of "diversity." This exercise aims to help us understand each other through our ability to tell our stories.

Empathy alone won't solve exclusionary practices, but it can help sensitize individuals to struggles that others around them may be facing, thus informing more considerate decision-making. For example, supporting remote work is a primary value of BetterUp, a personalized coaching platform (Fraser-Hill 2019). Yet, because all major meetings were held in the company's San Francisco office, all remote workers felt detached from the workplace culture and less included. To fix this and build empathy and understanding, CEO and founder Alexi Robichaux established remote weeks where the whole company worked remotely to understand what it's like to be the person on the video call. Now, post-Covid, we all understand what it's like to be on video calls all day, but at the time, there was a disconnect between the two teams. They now realized that certain activities that were mainstays during design meetings simply did not work in a remote experience. This test not only increased understanding and awareness of one another, but it also led to action to redesign the structure of meetings.

A day-in-the-life experience can also help bridge understanding. Ford Motor Company has an empathy training program where new engineers strap on a weighted suit to simulate the experience of a pregnant driver. They try to change the radio station, switch gears, while their bump bumps into the steering wheel. From this activity, the engineers physically understand the challenges of an eight-month-pregnant woman (Giang 2016).

You can also seek out a situation where you're the only one like you in the room (at a cultural event, place of worship, social gathering). This works in virtual spaces as well.

Cortney Harding, founder of Friends With Holograms, an award-winning VR/AR technology company, created a simulated VR experience to put viewers in the shoes of marginalized people at work. The scene was a typical meeting laden with microaggressions (getting talked down to), microinvalidations (being ignored), and bias and blind spots in action shown via thought bubbles. "One of the first people to see this was a white guy who was a manager at his family's business," Courtney says. "He came in skeptical and did the experience, and when he took off the headset, he said 'That wasn't a conversation, that was an emotional experience.' He then spent an hour unpacking the concept of privilege" (Harding 2020). The manager subsequently changed how he ran meetings (stopping interruptions, making sure he called on equal numbers of men and women) when he returned to the office the following week. This immersive storytelling and interactive experience is a powerful way to provide leaders with a safe space to experience workplace exclusion and practice emotionally charged conversations.

Take note of how it makes you feel (for some of you, this is your daily experience, so please skip this), and try to view ideas through different perspectives, insight, and authentic relationships.

These exercises are meant to help managers unpack how privilege works on a daily basis, why it's hard to see, and why it matters for effective allyship and sponsorship. When these aha moments happen through these exercises you can become empowered to leverage change not out of guilt but out of responsibility.

Raise Your Awareness

To truly absorb anti-racism learnings, people need to come to terms with their racial discomfort, racial missteps, and how they have been holding racism in place. This goes for white managers and BIPOC managers. I've seen BIPOC managers who manage BIPOC staff how they wished to be managed. And I've also experienced BIPOC managers who have been particularly cruel and abusive toward BIPOC employees, often replicating the same management mistreatments they incurred while moving up the corporate ladder. This can be particularly devastating for BIPOC employees who see themselves reflected in their manager.

Leaders can start by educating themselves about race as a sphere of identity, power, and privilege and how it impacts BIPOC employees emotionally, mentally, and physically. Admitting you don't know something is a sign of a confident, capable leader. Tap into that quest for knowledge, and continue searching for sources to help you better understand privilege and power and how to use that to inform your decisions. Make it your job to know how race, unconscious bias, and systemic inequities manifest in your workplace. Question how your experience might be different if you didn't hold the identities that give you privilege, such as your race, class, religion, ability, gender, or sexual orientation. That might mean noticing how often your colleagues use racially insensitive language or when biased language creeps into the promotion decision-making process.

Do your research—if you are white, don't lean on people of color to tell you what to say or do. It's not the traumatized person's job to teach you about their trauma. Think about how you would want someone to support you and what would you not want them to say or do. For BIPOC managers, while our education system rarely offers the resources and language we need to combat systemic racism, we can always do our research to back up our advocacy. BIPOC managers can also be better allies across communities of color. Black, Latinx, Asian, Middle East and North African, Indigenous, and other Black and Brown communities can learn more about each other's specific struggles and sensitivities to build stronger coalitions and collaboration. I know for me, vision and intent haven't always been enough. I've had to deepen my own knowledge and capacity for conflict management to better deal with workplace injustices.

In "Be a Better Ally" (Melaku, Breeman, Smith, et al. 2020) the authors offer suggestions for how to address the obstacles underrepresented colleagues face in the workplace. Always start a conversation by requesting permission; engage with curiosity and humility if granted. They further suggest you ask these reflection questions:

- I'm curious about what you find most challenging day-to-day—things that I may not notice or have overlooked before. Would you be comfortable sharing some of what you experience?
- If there was one thing you wish your white male colleagues would do more of to improve your experience, what would it be?
- If you were giving me advice on how to show up as an inclusive, fair, and welcoming colleague, what would you say?

Raising your level of awareness means that you have to recognize that not all members of an underrepresented group experience the workplace the same way. You need to learn more about and keep an eye out for your team's unique identity-based experiences and sometimes obstacles. For example, there is an increasing number of books now speaking about how women of color are marginalized and silenced in the workplace—read up. A white male manager once advised me to act with the same level of "swagger and attitude" that he brought to a meeting to be taken more seriously. He was convinced that he was offering me golden advice, but it was horrible. Instead of placing the burden on himself and the other white male team members to do a better job of listening and collaborating, he put it on me to act like him. I smiled sheepishly and nodded my head. For one, I thought his behavior was irritating and disrespectful—that would never fly in my Latino household. As a young Latina, I also knew that same behavior would read as overly confident and cocky coming from me. And while he was allowed to behave that way, I couldn't afford that risk. I didn't have the confidence then to tell him that, but you should know that is a truth many of us bear.

Try this: I've helped facilitate fishbowl activities, where groups are separated into an inner or outer circle to discuss ideas of identity, belonging, and shared experience. Those in the inner circle have a discussion; those in the outer ring listen. I've been part of powerful fishbowls where groups have been divided into BIPOC and white teams. There hasn't been a time when the white members in the middle circle haven't struggled with discussing their privilege and power. And when it's the white members' turn to listen, they often have emotional outbursts when they hear the harrowing stories of their BIPOC colleagues. I've heard a range of responses, including: "I've never realized that the language I take for granted in meetings causes you daily harm," "I have taken the privileges of being white for granted," "I didn't see that I had been inflicting harm on my colleagues," and "I'm just realizing now that I'm not the police here. I need to realize how to call people in, not shut them down." One thing to read about racism and another to listen to your peers speak about how they have to compartmentalize their identities in the workplace and in your presence. You must learn about and acknowledge the subtle and systemic discrimination that privileges white workers and impedes BIPOC workers if you intend to change those conditions.

Don't Be Afraid to Name It

Through our language, we have the power to reduce stigma, build accountability, and affirm our shared humanity. Fostering inclusive workplaces requires that we pay attention to the language we use. At the same time, we need to offer everyone the grace to make mistakes, learn, and do better.

As a DEI leader and consultant, I have been "advised" to use more palatable language. "Instead of racism or oppression, perhaps you could say 'implicit bias'?" "Could you just share the racial demographic data as white vs. other? We want to avoid litigation if we show the low representation counts." In this case, legal teams are concerned with offering any data that could be used against them in active lawsuits. And most recently, "Is it possible to not use the words 'systemic racism'? It causes an uncomfortable feeling that we believe will take away from your powerful message."

Really? Systemic racism, bias, and white male privilege are embedded deeply and widely in our society. A two-hour workshop or keynote won't stop the weaponization of white womanhood, the complicity of Latinx and Asian Americans in anti-Blackness, the disregard of indigenous, transgender, and disabled communities, or the persistent stereotypes and racial conflict that create a wedge between these groups. There is no quick fix, and ambiguous language does little to address the matters at hand.

Language matters. The words we use and the perceptions and images that they evoke have a profound impact on how we perceive each other. "Words carry weight and sometimes that is baggage—cultural, personal, historical," says Dr. Jennifer Sandoval (2020) of the University of Central Florida. As I've learned from Jennifer, Americans have a long history of using coded language, or race-neutral terms that describe racial identity, to disguise explicit or implicit racial bias, coded words such as "illegal immigrant" for people from Latin America, "bossy" to describe women who are assertive, or "thug" to describe men of color who aren't necessarily doing anything criminal or violent. This language fosters anxiety and dehumanizes BIPOC. It can also mask discomfort and disconnection. And in the workplace, discrediting a Black woman as "angry" or "challenging to manage" is another way to uphold white male standards of professionalism at the expense of anyone who doesn't fit that category. Subjective, coded language isn't just words. How people are perceived and their performance is reviewed affects who is selected for high profile assignments, promoted, or pushed out. Reflect on whether the language you are using has racist or derogatory connotations by asking yourself the following questions:

What words and phrases do I use that may inadvertently reinforce a group's immediate stereotype or negative image?

When describing a group of people, do I use coded language?

When I detect racially coded language, how can I sensitively address the hidden meaning?

We must name the root cause of the problem—racism—and be willing to reflect on what we downplay and why. We need to be intentional about the words we use to promote a space of belonging and inclusion for all. It requires us to address the deliberate and unconscious racist comments that BIPOC and other marginalized groups have to deal with on a daily basis. Predominately white workplace norms were built over decades—to preserve white culture and concentrate power in the hands of white males. These words are not fear-inducing when these terms are unpacked and debunked. They are just the truth.

Confronting our own privilege, access, and opportunity can be challenging, but it is necessary. One of the notable changes I've witnessed in the wake of the racial unrest following George Floyd's murder is that people now say the words "Black," "racism," and "white supremacy." They no longer whisper these terms.

Instead of what *not* to say, focus on what to say. One rabbi suggests an exercise in which white people start saying "white" when they talk about their day at home. Don't just say, I spoke to our son's teacher; say, I spoke to our white son's white teacher. Don't just say, I bumped into our neighbor/friend/colleague today; state, I bumped into our white neighbor/friend/colleague today. I saw a great movie/read a great book/heard a great song about a white couple coming to terms with their issues. Become conscious of whiteness as an everyday practice to better see how white supremacy and the exclusion and marginalization of BIPOC has been normalized.

Speaking the language of inclusion is important. As a cis-gendered, heterosexual woman, I've had to get thoughtful about language and the stigma and barriers faced by my LGBTQIA+ coworkers. I've made an active choice to ask people for their pronouns. (Note: please don't use the term "preferred pronouns'" when you ask for someone's pronouns. It makes it sound as if using someone's correct pronouns is optional, when it's about acknowledging a person's identity.) I've yet to find someone who finds it disrespectful. I've put Post-it notes on my speeches to remind myself to use my pronouns in my introductions, and I display she/her/*ella* in my social media to signal solidarity with transgender and non-binary people. I'm a fierce and imperfect ally who has to work at it, every day.

Do your research (the terms are constantly changing), and when in doubt, ask. Your intent as you enter emotionally complex conversations will have a much more substantial impact than whether or not you say Hispanic, Latina, or Latinx. Be ready to ask questions to learn the right words—and be open to being corrected. If you make a mistake, apologize and reflect on your error so you can correct it next time.

Along the way, you will discover that the inclusion revolution requires you break free from corporate speech and begin to recognize the racial systems that protect biased and inequitable language, actions, and behaviors. And if you're willing, you should challenge your peers to push for change alongside you. For white people, simply acknowledging you have benefitted from something that has seriously damaged someone sitting next to you is an excellent first move. What comes next is an ongoing process of building shared understanding, respect, and, hopefully, trust.

The Hidden Meaning of Language

One of my favorite sources of the hidden meaning of language is Rachel Cargle's Instagram page The Great Unlearn: @thegreatunlearn (Cargle n.d.). In it, she edits and dissects white people's comments that she receives to offer "some critical language and a more critical lens as you engage in these conversations in your own spaces." Here's an example:

The statement:

"Yes, systematic racism is real, but lots of white people who seem #blessed are dealing with their own childhood traumas and abuse."

The analysis:

"Yes/But," also known as "whataboutism," is a variant of the "tu quoque" logical fallacy that attempts to discredit an opponent's position by charging them with hypocrisy without directly refuting or disproving their argument (Zimmer 2017).

The statement:

"Although you are correct, I wish you would have not marked out her name. Her intentions don't seem to be malicious."

The analysis:

She is leaning on the idea that intentions hold more weight than the impact. I use what I was taught: if you accidentally step on someone's foot, you don't ever say, "Oh, stop crying, that wasn't my intention." You apologize, acknowledge the pain you caused, and walk more carefully and intentionally.

Your Road Map to Revolution

It's not enough to design and implement inclusive hiring practices. You will always struggle to attract, retain, and grow diverse talent unless you build a holistic inclusive talent strategy. Keep BIPOC candidates at the heart of everything you do, and lead with an unbiased, people-centered mindset. Increasing belonging is compelling—and complex to operationalize. Start by paying attention when the workplace might not work for others.

- **Assess your onboarding process.** What's the first impression you're making for a new hire? How can you customize the experience for each person to set them up for success? This is not about access to email but access to others who will be vital on their professional journey. A buddy system can be incredibly effective.
- **Personalize your onboarding process.** Beyond administrative tasks and personal preferences, are there cultural, religious, or ability needs that must be considered? What will help this person be most successful? Ask them!
- **Facilitate stronger connections.** Create stronger team bonds in an authentic and results-driven way, whether it's through structured conversations or spontaneous sharing moments. Look out for employees who may feel isolated from the team, and provide avenues of support.
- **Build empathy muscles to establish trust.** You can do this through privilege-exposing and day-in-the-life exercises to understand what the work environment is like for others. Also, consider

VR experiences that allow you to see what it's like for marginalized employees at work.

- **Recognize the impact of your words.** Understand that words come with meaning, that what you say is not always what you mean, and that you may be interpreted differently and held accountable for any harm. Normalize the use of pronouns, and notice when you use coded words. On your journey to conscious communication, you may make some slips. It's only natural. Don't let it stop your progress. Learn from it, and try again.

6 | Set Psychological Safety in Motion

What makes a perfect team? In 2012, Google set out to find the answer. Would it be bringing together the smartest people? Those who have similar work styles? A diverse mix of backgrounds? After months of research they concluded: "The 'who' part of the equation didn't seem to matter." The most successful teams, the ones who hit their goals and seemed to have the strongest bonds, shared key behaviors such as showing empathy for each other and taking turns in conversations. They all expressed a feeling of psychological safety, which allowed them to share more ideas, have constructive debates, and work together to achieve the best results (Duhigg 2016).

People on these successful teams lowered their walls and felt safe. That's the premise of psychological safety: you won't be punished for making a mistake or sharing your opinions, whatever they may be. That should be a given, right? Not quite.

In an ideal world, every one of your team members and colleagues feels safe and comfortable to share their truths, their personal experiences, and perceptions of your work environment, but that vulnerability doesn't always come easy—especially for BIPOC, junior employees, or those who are most risk averse and afraid of losing their jobs. The experience of women of color in the workplace, women like me, is like walking a shaky tightrope, every day. Daily decisions—which parts of myself do I bring forward, blend, or hide? How much space can I take? How many mistakes can I afford? Will I constantly have *"un pie aquí, y un pie allá"* (one foot in, and one foot out), while watching mediocrity be accepted and promoted?

You must prioritize creating a culture of psychological safety that empowers and encourages people to speak their truth. When you create safe workspaces at work where employees feel safe to speak up, they believe their voice is welcomed and that this is a company worth dedicating time and energy to. Amy Edmondson (1999), who identified the concept of psychological safety in teams in 1990, describes it as creating a space where new ideas and concepts are encouraged and accepted. In other words, psychological safety keeps people engaged, productive, and motivated.

Creating a culture of psychological safety starts with trust, and trust starts with you. Take a step back to rethink how you engage with your colleagues and teams and how you respond to their experiences in your daily interactions. Whether it's starting conversations about white fragility, or holding all-hands meetings calling out racially charged incidents when they happen, you can send a powerful message as an ally in a position of power and influence.

You can also make this more official and codify a new set of positive leadership skills that foster psychological safety, which will lead to solid business performance, suggests research by McKinsey (De Smet, Rubinstein, Schrah, et al. 2021). That is, skills training such as open dialogue, which allow leaders to explore disagreements and talk through tensions in their teams; cultural awareness to better understand norms in different cultures; situational awareness to develop a better understanding of what is going on around you and its implications for how people are treated; situational humility, my favorite, which encourages a growth mindset and curiosity; and sponsorship, to functionally equip leaders with tools and techniques to enable others' success.

Your Words Matter

If you educate yourself about common workplace microaggressions, you can be more vigilant and do more to support BIPOC colleagues. For example, Black women are often silenced through tone policing, where their comments are dismissed merely because of a white listener's feelings about how it was delivered. Comments such as "You're being too sensitive," "It was just a joke, calm down" or "I don't know why you're making such a big deal" make Black women doubt the legitimacy of their reactions, judgments, or feelings about racial slights. You can prevent this behavior in the moment, or later in private, by saying something such as "I love a good joke, but that was not funny" or "It may not have been your intent, but your comments were inappropriate and hurtful."

One of my superpowers is my depth of empathy and my willingness to be vulnerable with my teams and colleagues. That simply means leaning into my humanity and being able to tap into the human experiences of others. This plays out when I'm able to quell discord between team members, to discern subtle shifts in how team members interact, or to draw out the quieter team members. But these same leadership skills have also been dismissed as weak. Some find my methods of cultivating BIPOC talent as a threat to traditional workplace cultures. That is, cultures that have traditionally been skewed toward the success and dominance of white leaders.

Vulnerability doesn't diminish my capacity to lead—it enhances it. BIPOC staff are not a threat to white people's professional success. Finding ways to help BIPOC staff feel safe leads to the entire company's success—it makes no sense to isolate certain staff members to the point where they don't feel safe to make creative and meaningful contributions. The best teams trust each other, and to build trust a manager must allow for vulnerability and to create safety for everyone.

How can someone be candid and vulnerable with you if you're not vulnerable? Entering conversations about race, inequity, and exclusion as a white person can feel bewildering, scary, and antagonizing. Say so! And as a BIPOC manager, you must assert your boundaries. It's okay to pull a leader or workshop facilitator aside before a discussion and say, "I don't want to be called on to represent the Black experience during the discussion."

Share your experiences—the good and the not so good—honestly and vulnerably with your teams or colleagues. In my experience, they will be thankful for the opportunity to have an honest conversation where they, too, can become comfortable sharing the uncomfortable. You may start your conversations by admitting your nervousness or expressing your intentions. One past consulting client of mine, a white woman, did this when launching a diversity business council: "I want to begin by sharing that I'm an introvert, and these conversations make me really nervous. I mostly worry about disappointing you. My hope is that we can create a safe space for everyone. I also want to acknowledge that I'm sure that there is a lot that I don't know and ask for your grace as we navigate these uncertain waters together. Above all, please don't let me be narrow in what I expect or do."

Powerful, right? I could see everyone in that meeting, mostly BIPOC and junior employees, breathe a collective sigh of relief. I could see them put apprehensions or misgivings aside. She replaced criticism with curiosity, admitted her fears, and encouraged feedback. The group was ready and willing to listen and share. What followed was a productive, engaging, and illuminating conversation about the path forward where the employees could openly discuss and overcome the barriers they faced in building the workplace they deserved.

Vulnerability can lead to radical participation.

That was a winning moment, but I'm not going to sugarcoat how hard it is for people to drop the superficial office talk and have a real, honest conversation. What are the questions you need to ask? Start with: What is preventing you from feeling that you belong? How easy is it to discuss difficult issues or problems with your coworkers or with me? How often have you experienced bias or bullying? This can be painful to share and absorb.

Getting people to open up and talk is challenging when it's not anonymous. It's important to note that vulnerability can be more complex for BIPOC employees. Managers need to acknowledge racial imposter syndrome, which creates feelings of self-doubt and makes BIPOC employees afraid to reveal their vulnerabilities. Because these fears can also hurt their ability to learn and grow, you must find ways to draw them out and make them feel safe and supported when they make mistakes.

I get it. There are things I say now that I would never have blurted out 20 years ago. At a recent executive meeting of primarily white men, we discussed leadership models we believed were necessary to develop and grow the company. The group seemed to quickly form a consensus on a "benevolent dictatorship" leadership style for centralizing decision-making.

For me, this conversation was hugely uncomfortable. I grew up with grandparents and an entire community who suffered through a 30-year brutal dictatorship in the Dominican Republic, and it's taken some time and soul-searching to recognize that it wouldn't be a stretch to say I have an unhealthy relationship with power and people in authority. In that meeting, I felt safe enough to speak my truth. I said, "Most people don't know this about me, but I don't trust people in power, and it has taken me a long time to recognize that this language causes me emotional discomfort. Further, there is a racially systemic root to this. I don't think we should run this company like any kind of dictatorship." Hierarchies benefit white people, and the workplace is built hierarchically. If the executive ranks are all white and all the BIPOC are junior staffers, there is no way a "benevolent dictatorship" is going to be racially inclusive. A dictatorship is never a good business model when you acknowledge that good ideas can come from people at any seniority level. Now my boss and peers know my truth, and I created a space for others to speak their truth. I felt responsible to share a different point of view that could help us frame a more inclusive leadership approach. And I could do it because I felt safe at that moment—I didn't feel there was a risk of losing my colleagues' respect or my job.

Why did I feel that way? For one, I am in a top role at the company, but it was really about trust. I trusted everyone in that room and trusted that my boss would have my back. Fear and heaviness are real, but trust allows for conversations that build meaning and create connections. In her book *Conversational Intelligence: How Great Leaders Build Trust and Get Extraordinary Results*, author Judith Glaser (2016) shares that when we care about what others think and feel, our brain senses not only safety; the prefrontal cortex "reads" oxytocin as a signal to trust and open up. Our conversations feel freer and energizing, leading to better collaboration and a sense of belonging.

Another spark for conversations is to host panels, lunch and learns, speaker forums, and other event series centered on previously untouchable topics. The tech company Asana launched a Real Talk event series to share multiple lived experiences, including a panel of Latinx engineers across different tech backgrounds from Google, Slack, Airbnb, and Threadloom discussing the impact of cultural identity on their careers (Joel 2018). These events are becoming more common—I say, hold as many as your business will permit. The key is not letting the information fall flat but rather using them as an opportunity to launch additional conversations with your direct reports. What did they think about what they heard? Have they had similar experiences? What other topics would they rather talk about?

Keep these conversations going to build psychological safety.

Psychological Safety: Do You Have It?

In his book *Think Again*, Adam Grant (2021) notes that psychological safety begins with admitting our own mistakes and welcoming criticism from others. He goes on to further codify what it is and what it isn't:

When you have it:

See mistakes as opportunities to learn;
Willing to take risks and fail;
Speaking your mind in meetings;
Openly sharing your struggles;
Trust in your teammates and supervisors;
Sticking your neck out.

When you don't:

See mistakes as threats to your career;
Unwilling to rock the boat;
Keeping your ideas to yourself;
Only touting your strengths;
Fear of your teammates and supervisors;
Having your neck chopped off.

Foster Speak Up Culture

Psychological safety for BIPOC employees starts at the top of the organization. Treating all staff the same does not acknowledge the barriers BIPOC people have faced their whole lives before they joined their organizations. Suppose it's a norm for a white male executive team to use swear words, be crass, yell, and be combative and tease as a form of hazing and camaraderie. In that case, that needs to be reexamined when it comes to the psychological safety of women and BIPOC when they enter that team. In his recent memoir, Barack Obama (2020) said he found this specific behavior from his senior white male colleague to be invigorating. Still, he didn't realize that when he wasn't in the room, those same behaviors made women and BIPOC staff uncomfortable and recede in meetings. Valerie Jarret called Barack out on this, and he spoke privately to Rahm and other white male leaders to say they needed to knock it off; their work style intimidated their team members.

Start by role-modeling and reinforcing inclusive behaviors. Whenever you seek out and act on opinions from junior colleagues of color, others will see it's normal to listen to them. Whenever you publicly acknowledge a racialized misstep, such as calling one of your Black employees the wrong name by mistake, you signal to others that it is safe to do so. This further empowers and enables your senior leaders and managers to increase their self-awareness and improve conversations about race relations and underlying beliefs, assumptions, and emotions.

Employees are more likely to exhibit inclusive leadership if their managers exhibit these behaviors. For example, do leaders in your organization seek out opinions different from their own on a regular basis? Do your managers treat others with respect? When staff challenge a manager's ideas, how does the manager react—defensively, or do they listen and incorporate different ideas?

When kicking off a project, share your expectations about how you want the team to partner to achieve results, and remind them that how you get to the result matters as much as the outcome. Be respectful of other people's ideas and comments, even if you disagree. Say things such as "That's a helpful perspective" or "Thank you for bringing up that point" to prove that you welcome fresh ideas, challenging ideas, non-conformist ideas. Psychological safety is not about rewarding individuals and teams that only share what you want to hear. The goal is not to secure your comfort. It creates a climate where people can speak up and challenge ideas without fear. It's equally important to act on team members' good ideas, or corrective suggestions—don't just listen for show. If your teams don't believe you'll incorporate their ideas, they won't contribute to them.

It's time to welcome challenging conversations about power, privilege, access, and opportunity. White managers and BIPOC managers can become so afraid of making a mistake or saying the wrong thing that they don't say or do anything. This may be for different reasons. White leaders may have never been accustomed to talking about race and may have had bad experiences communicating their tensions in the past. I've often heard from white managers that they fear offering help because they feel that they will be slapped down when trying to be helpful. BIPOC managers may be afraid of deepening racial divisions between BIPOC and white staff and worry about their own job security if they raise racial tensions. Much too often, employees simply want to know that their managers care. Instead, they are often left with a void of recognition or unexplored shame about what they're experiencing at home or work.

The real enemy of inclusivity and equity is silence and inaction. Asking questions—of yourself and others—about power and privilege can help you reduce awkward silences and misunderstandings. And, I promise, you will come out of it more empowered, motivated, and inspired to start looking at your workplace, policies, and practices in a new light.

A speak-up culture doesn't happen by magic. A culture of fear exists because of well-founded worries of repercussions. Your job as a people manager is to create a supportive space because not every space is safe for all, where your team members will feel listened to and understood. This requires that you show real care and respect for your people and that you're willing to listen to raise your understanding not to solve and convince others of what you believe. It further requires you to keep quiet, let them speak, and open yourself to what they have to share by challenging your assumptions.

Show commitment to progress for each of your team members by not letting fear hold you back from creating an environment that everyone can access.

How much space do dominant voices take up in your organization? If your colleagues say they feel their voice is not being heard in meetings, amplify their ideas by using your own voice and privilege. Female aides adopted this amplification strategy in Obama's White House to avoid having their voices ignored by the predominantly male room. When a woman spoke up, other women would repeat her point or idea, giving back credit to the original speaker, according to *The Washington Post* (Eilperin 2019). This forced the men to listen and rendered them unable to steal credit for the idea. "We just started doing it, and made a purpose of doing it," one former Obama aide told *The Post.* "Obama noticed, and began calling more often on women and junior aides." Amplification pacts work. I've known colleagues to buddy up and commit to publicly backing each other so that if one of them spoke up against a microaggression in a meeting, they knew their buddy would amplify their words. Allyship can happen across genders and race; men can ensure that they repeat and credit women's ideas, and white people can commit to speaking up if a racist microaggression occurs in a meeting.

Ask yourself: How can I actively improve access to decision-making meetings? How do I challenge coded language and behavior when specific identities take up more space than others, physically or verbally? When was the last time I amplified the voice of an underrepresented or junior member of my team with a "+1" or "That's an important idea; let's hear more"? How do I decide who talks in a meeting?

As a manager, you never want to dominate the conversation but instead use your management platform to ensure that everyone who wants to can speak. I have become more mindful to make sure everyone on my team feels that their thoughts are being considered and contributing to the conversation even if I don't ultimately use their suggestion. I will say, "I haven't heard from Necca; did you have anything to add?" Some people don't like to speak up, and some are introverts, but those who have been systematically and consistently ignored in meetings, mansplained, or had their ideas stolen may need a supportive ally. An ally gives people the option.

"Early in my career, I had a hard time contributing in meetings," says Fran Hauser, author of *The Myth of the Nice Girl* (Hauser 2019). "I had a boss who would call me before a meeting and say, 'Fran, in today's meeting I am going to ask you to give everyone an update on the restructuring.' This gave me time to prepare my thoughts and contribute in a way that felt comfortable to me. Before long, it became natural to speak up and I didn't need a prompt." Tom Carmazzi, CEO of manufacturing corporation Tuthill, asks employees to write their thoughts on index cards and stick them to allow everyone to share their opinion without having to raise a hand. It was equitable anonymity and created safety for honest feedback (Carmazzi n.d.).

In the early part of my career, I was in a client meeting at Moody's, and as we were going around the table getting to know each other, sharing stories about our childhoods, a senior analyst turned to me and asked, "Daisy, answer me this, why do all Dominicans play baseball?" I instantly felt my stomach sink. I felt minimized by that cultural cliché and embarrassed that I needed to respond to it in front of my peers and clients. I stumbled for a bit and weakly said, "No; some of us become credit analysts." The table laughed and we moved on. Or so I thought.

A few days later, when I debriefed the meeting with Nicole Johnson, our team's manager, who happened to be an openly gay white woman, I mentioned the exchange as part of my report. I was worried at first, but to my surprise, she instantly expressed a deep sense of empathy and then jumped to action. She called for a full investigation by human resources, which I didn't even know was an available resource, and took immediate steps to ensure that senior analysts and all managers would never make insensitive and inappropriate comments like that again. Teams were trained on cultural sensitivity, and the senior analyst received coaching and offered a formal apology to me.

To be fair, it was awkward at first. But it was the jolt the team needed to focus more attention on power differentials and cultural insensitivities. It was a start and a positive model for me and others on what we should expect from our workplace. My boss Nicole modeled allyship by disrupting a seemingly harmless social exchange. By advocating for me and seeking a resolution that would not leave me feeling isolated and unsafe, she helped me see the agency I had to effect change for myself and others.

Not everyone is as courageous as Nicole, but we all can learn to be. Nicole's allyship came with solidarity and action.

The Four Stages of Psychological Safety

Another way to look at psychological safety is along a continuum of four stages developed by social scientist Timothy R. Clarke (2020) in which human beings feel (1) included, (2) safe to learn, (3) safe to contribute, and (4) safe to challenge the status quo—all without fear of being embarrassed, marginalized, or punished in some way. Moving through these four stages enables individuals and organizations to create higher levels of inclusion, collaboration, innovation, and belonging. If you and your teams feel all four, you will see a rise in confidence, engagement, happiness, and performance.

Stage 1: Inclusion Safety (Connect and Belong)

Inclusion safety allows us to operate without fear of rejection, embarrassment, or punishment, boosting confidence, resilience, and independence. When we create inclusion safety for others, regardless of our differences, we acknowledge our shared humanity and reject false theories of superiority.

Stage 2: Learner Safety (Learn and Grow)

Learner safety allows us to feel safe as we engage in all aspects of the learning process—asking questions, giving and receiving feedback, experimenting, and making mistakes. It's important to note here that BIPOC people have good reason to fear harsher punishment for making mistakes compared to their white colleagues. As novelist Celeste Ng (2020) put it, privilege is about who is allowed to make mistakes. When we sense learner safety, we're more willing to be vulnerable, take risks, make mistakes, and develop resilience in the learning process. Conversely, a lack of learner safety triggers the self-censoring instinct, causing us to shut down, retrench, and manage personal risk. Managers need to ensure that all staff, including BIPOC staff, know that there is a company commitment to their success and that, as appropriate, mistakes will be met with support, not punishment.

Stage 3: Contributor Safety (Be Heard and Make a Difference)

When contributor safety is present, we feel safe to contribute as a full team member, using our skills and abilities to participate in the value-creation process. We lean into what we're doing with energy and enthusiasm. We are encouraged to draw out our best efforts. What does this look like? A sense of autonomy, guidance, and encouragement in exchange for action and results.

Stage 4: Challenger Safety (Better Outcomes)

Challenger safety provides the support and confidence to ask questions such as "Why do we always do it this way?" "What could happen if we tried something else?" or "May I suggest a different approach?" It allows us to feel safe to challenge the status quo without retaliation or risk of damaging our personal standing or reputation. It allows us to overcome the pressure to conform and gives us a license to innovate and be creative. This includes safety for BIPOC to speak up when conventional wisdom or a traditional practice is biased or racist. As a manager, you should know that this might make them feel defensive and uncomfortable at first. Good managers will thank people for speaking up and course-correcting.

Thread Allyship

When Freada Kapor Klein was asked to be a judge on a VC panel for MIT, New Profit, and the Morgridge Family Foundation, she said, "Great, have you asked underrepresented people of color to be judges? Because if it's not a diverse team, I'm happy to give up my seat. I don't participate in events where it's all white anything" (Klein 2020). This is standard practice for Freada. Actions and statements like this from allies subtly shift behavior.

Being an ally means more than just recognizing your privilege and agreeing that people from traditionally underrepresented groups should be valued and accepted; it means normalizing speaking up against passive-aggressive racist statements, calling attention to the emotional and psychological labor of marginalized groups, and learning from your mistakes. Being an ally starts with empathy and seeking to understand the lived experience of others.

Allyship that doesn't come with solidarity and action is performative. Critical theorist bell hooks (1986) tells us that: "Solidarity is not the same as support. To experience solidarity, we must have a community of interests, shared beliefs and goals around which to unite [. . .]. Support can be occasional. It can be given and just as easily withdrawn. Solidarity requires sustained, ongoing commitment." It's about sacrificing your own comfort and convenience for that of others. If you see your non-Black team members (including other BIPOC) making racist, sexist, or ableist statements, overtly or subtly, shut it down. Stand up in those moments. You're in a position to create a safe space, and it is your responsibility—take that responsibility seriously.

The disconnect in what allyship means has led to a complicated feeling when it comes to the term: Research by leanin.org (2020) and Survey-Monkey shows more than 80% of white women and men say that they see themselves as allies to colleagues of other races and ethnicities. Still, less than half of Black women and only slightly more than half of Latinas feel they have strong allies at work. Allyship can look and feel like many different things based on your starting point and what you're trying to achieve. It's important to have a shared understanding of allyship because when there's not, it can add unintentional harm or insult to the groups we hope to support. This disconnect points to something fundamental: wanting to be an ally doesn't mean you are an ally. There are no certificates or capes for allies. If you have to name yourself an ally, you have to question why someone doesn't recognize you as one. It's easier to say you are an ally than to act like one.

Allyship means different things depending on what you're looking to accomplish:

- For some, it may be about being a good person who supports and acts on behalf of others.
- For others, it's about justice and correcting systems of mistreatment, abuse, and oppression.

This is how allies show up:

- Speak up: "I show support for . . . because . . . " "I use my privilege to help . . . "
- Learn: It takes more than reading a book or two to become an ally.
- Act: Challenge biased norms, stand up for injustice, bear witness.

An accomplice, a sister term to ally, takes risks and makes material sacrifices to actively challenge the status quo designed to benefit them. An accomplice will advance fairness and equity while working within and with organizational power structures. These terms are not interchangeable but are both key to understanding the role members of dominant groups can play in advancing inclusion.

My favorite word to use is upstander. Upstander refers to someone who speaks out and stands up for justice on behalf of others. It calls for reflection, compassion, understanding beyond oneself—and perhaps most importantly, courage. An upstander pays attention to news so that you're informed about what affects the lives of your colleagues.

There are slight differences between these terms, and you can choose to be an ally, accomplice, *and* upstander. Cultivating the role you choose, at the time you choose to exercise it, will help you build more racially inclusive and welcoming workplaces. Sometimes that means being willing to notice and interrupt racially charged behavior, such as constant interruptions or dismissive language in a meeting or workshop. It may also mean emailing someone's manager to let them know their team member is doing a great job or challenging bias during a performance review.

Mitigate Microaggressions

Great managers protect their employees from racial toxicity and enable them to do their best work. If you are a manager who acknowledges the need for greater diversity in your workplace, you also have to recognize your workplace's past harms regarding race. Perhaps the past status quo meant that most people who were hired were white; maybe the status quo meant that retention and upward movement of the few BIPOC staff was not a priority. If this description fits your workplace, white managers need to acknowledge your inherited traditional role in reproducing racial inequalities in the workplace and reflect on whether you have in the past actively or passively maintained a racially segregated norm in the workplace. BIPOC managers also have to consider whether they have, unintentionally or out of fear, prioritized white colleagues' comfort in ways that may make this more difficult for other BIPOC who are coming up in your company. If managers cannot be honest with themselves, they won't be able to help create and sustain a welcoming workplace for all.

Please unlock the courage to face the data and emotions you uncover throughout your reflection journey. The mirror may reveal that your language and behavior do not align with your espoused values. You may consider yourself liberal or social justice–oriented, but now your data may reveal contradictions. A natural tendency is to ignore, withdraw, or explain it away or deny it. But you need to face it. DeRay Mckesson (2018), civil rights activist, says, "Protest is telling the truth in public." Part of holding up a mirror is facing ourselves, doing something about it, and not letting that reflection fade away.

A microaggression is "the everyday slights, indignities, put-down, and insults that people of color, women, LGBTQIA+ populations, or those who are marginalized experience in their day-to-day interactions with people," according to Dr. Derald W. Sue (2010). They can be expressed verbally or through body language. Imagine a white woman clutching her bag when a Black man enters an elevator.

Have you ever wondered whether a comment at work is a lightly veiled expression of racism, sexism, or another ism? "Wait, did she ask about my ethnic heritage because she wants to get to know me or because she doesn't believe me to be American?" Statements such as "I'm not Black, but I know what feeling excluded feels like," "I don't see color," or "I can't believe this is still happening" can feel insulting and unhelpful. Being told that "we are all humans," or that "all lives matter," negates the unique discrimination and oppression of people of color.

These comments offend, upset, or hurt BIPOC colleagues and often leave them worrying that confronting them may lead to defensiveness or punishment. The sting of stigma wears heaviest when you're left to fend for yourself.

In "Racial Gaslighting and Microaggressions Can't be Ignored Any Longer," Evie Muir delineates degrees of intensity within microaggressions, "from microinvalidations (subtle denial of a persona's feeling, experience, or thoughts, 'I was only joking') to microinsults (comments which demean or discredit, 'She's so bossy') and microassaults (explicit attacks, 'That's so gay')" (Muir 2020). These can make a workplace feel hostile and toxic, affecting performance, relationships, retention, workplace culture, and morale.

Question yourself when you use such words, particularly jargon or commonly said phrases. What do you mean by that word or phrase? Does using that word share your meaning or does it hide your meaning? I have been guilty of hiding meaning through my choice of words in an effort to make something more "palatable," but true change cannot happen unless we say what we really mean.

Whenever I've been the target of a microaggression, my rule of thumb is to collect my thoughts before addressing the microaggression, to respond assertively and with "I" statements. "When you restated my comment in the meeting without giving me credit, I felt undermined." "When you referred to me as articulate, I felt as if you assumed that I shouldn't be." "When you confused me for the other Latinx in the room, I felt as if we were both invisible to you." This is the same principle if you've witnessed a microaggression and are not part of the group being marginalized by the comment or action, do not speak on their behalf. This could be unintentionally dehumanizing and belittling. Instead of saying, "You offended them," you may say, "Here's why I'm upset or hurt by your comments."

Let's be clear: It is not the responsibility of women, BIPOC, or members of marginalized communities to make workplaces microaggression free. But there are ways of responding that can lead to constructive conversations and outcomes, if both parties are willing.

Chanel Cathay's (2020) article "Racism Is Real in Corporate America—I Left Because I Had Enough" brought me to tears. She says, "Corporations must nurture Black talent while they have it, and employees must call out racist aggression when they see it. That is how to be an ally. Had even one of my colleagues spoken up about my treatment, I would not have felt so isolated." Her story is that of thousands of women of color stifled and diminished in the workplace. Speaking up is not enough. We must change the norms, systems, and processes that uphold discrimination and oppressive behaviors.

Proactive interventions and creative diversity training programs can help get ahead of toxic behavioral patterns and mitigate microaggressions. One company I know hired a vendor to train in-house diversity peer counselors who could volunteer to mediate conflict arising from microaggressions. This was meant as a safe place for positive change, outside of HR, when microaggressions need to be corrected but don't arise to HR levels (discipline and firing). BIPOC in a company may prefer using this option, as they may be fearful of reporting to HR. Often the BIPOCs in the company are junior staff, and the people micro-aggressing them are too often—sadly—their bosses. If you consider trying a peer counselor program like this, you should be sure to pay the peer counselors more for taking this responsibility beyond their standard job descriptions.

Even more effective is to tailor your training to the unique issues of each industry, organization, and team. One global law firm hired STEPS Consulting to design and deliver a program to ensure every partner understood how their behavior supported (or did not support) an inclusive environment. STEPS interviewed staff members of color, across all divisions and departments, and all seniority levels, to provide anonymous examples of microaggressions and systemic racism in the company. They then presented their findings in video, anonymizing the stories, and using actors to dramatize scenes. One scene showed a white partner struggling to have a conversation with a Black associate. The partner was well intended and wanted to be supportive, but the fear of doing or saying the wrong thing kept them from checking in with the associate and supporting them as needed.

Actors would stay in character after the scene, and the moderator would allow staff to question the actors about how they felt during the scene. The scenarios showed the kinds of interactions the company engaged in every day, to show how discrimination had in many cases crept in. It was also eye-opening and for many staff members, revelatory. "People have no idea of the impact of what they do and what they say," says Liz Jones (2020), USA Country Head of STEPS. "It's so often unconscious and unintentional. Most people don't come to work with the specific motive of making your day miserable. They come with a positive intent. These exercises are so powerful because you can see the impact of a wrongly placed word or tone. It makes you think: I wouldn't want anyone to feel that way."

Putting these company initiatives in place can encourage agency and action from people on all seniority levels. They alleviate the pressure on managers to design from scratch. They help leaders imagine what they can do to demonstrate equitable and inclusive leadership traits. And they help others hold the entire organization accountable for high performance in equity and inclusion.

Are your employees hungry for more ways to help but aren't sure where to start? That could be an opportunity for education, either building local team plans or curating a broader internal learning program to help employees and leaders explore their personal identity development, unconscious bias, and how to build empathetic cultural competence with others. My initial focus in designing inclusive learning programs at VICE Media Group was to increase management skills as the most immediate opportunity to influence teams.

Then, employees across the globe quickly started reaching out individually to ask for more DEI training. To help increase employee engagement despite limited resources (I couldn't train everyone all at once), we created a self-directed learning Inclusion Corner in our learning and development platform where employees at all levels across the globe could log in to take the latest DEI training, explore topics of interest, and share feedback on what worked or what they would like to learn. Over the first few months, we added courses on personal identity development, empathetic cultural competence, and Black History resources. All offerings aimed to apply in the workplace and their daily life. For example, we offered bespoke resources about how to talk about racism with your children and bystander intervention resources to stop anti–Asian American and xenophobic harassment. We encouraged teams and community groups to take the training together to help enhance the experience. We began to share team completion stats with leaders to give them a sense of what learning areas they could focus on with their teams. And we committed to expand our library to also include anti-Asian, LGBTQIA+, Indigenous, Middle Eastern, disability and accessibility modules. When you hear about a microaggression, whether it's someone being called a fiery Latina, deadnaming someone (calling a transgender person by their birth name, as opposed to how they identify now), or asking a Muslim woman if she ever takes off her Hijab, use that as an opportunity to educate. Tailor your courses to what's happening in your workplace.

One note: if you've committed a microaggression, pause and remind yourself that you're not a bad person, and that a good person would commit to making things right for the person harmed. Then, immediately acknowledge the other person's hurt, genuinely apologize, take responsibility to educate yourself, and take steps to make things right with the person harmed. This is not about pressuring the harmed person to forgive and forget so that you feel better—making real amends is key. It's important to note that managers of color can also make mistakes and inflict insults or invalidation on others, and this is equally unacceptable.

Perhaps the most important thing you can do is ensure the protection of the harmed party and commit to stopping the cycles of gaslighting that perpetuates these toxic norms. As Evie Muir (2020) shares, "If you can identify yourself in (any) examples, this is a time for radical self-reflection and committing to challenging your internalized biases and how they influence your interactions." Then, do the work to become a steady workplace ally, and challenge the racially harmful behaviors you see within your professional and social circles. You can prevent microaggressions and build workplaces of belonging.

Kick Covering to the Curb

In the early part of my career, as the only Latina and youngest person in most rooms, I can't tell you how many times a coworker, client, or other leader has said to me in a somewhat surprised tone, "You're so articulate!" or "Wow, you hold yourself so well." Why is this such a shock that a senior leader speaks and behaves professionally? The implication is that people who look like me aren't supposed to talk and hold space like an executive; the implication is that this corporate environment isn't designed for people who don't fit the white, "professional, polished" world. BIPOC are routinely called "unprofessional" whenever they make white colleagues uncomfortable. For BIPOC employees, there's always been an implicit understanding that predominantly white workplaces aren't designed for people like us.

It's easy to navigate a workplace where everyone looks like you, hangs out in the same places as you, speaks like you do, and considers how you dress and accessorize to be the right, "professional" way. Environments like this lead to what Kenji Yoshino (2006), an NYU law professor, has coined "covering," the practice of downplaying who you are to survive in a workplace. Covering is different from the closely related code-switching. As I explained earlier, code-switching is when a person quickly switches between different cultural and racial space and social situations with the appropriate language, style, tone, and level of formality; covering is hiding your differences in an attempt to fit in in a straight, white, male-dominated workplace culture.

I often fell prey to covering and have spent years unearthing the variety of ways I and other women of color like me have been professionally discouraged from bringing our full breadth of talents to work. I felt as if there were constant reminders from my white peers that a misstep could end my career—the margin of error was always slim—or that a misunderstanding would confirm negative stereotypes about other Latinx professionals. Covering is a sign of a non-inclusive culture, and it's felt deeply: more than 63% of all marginalized groups report covering (with 83% of LGBTQIA+ employees acknowledging it), while even 45% of straight white men do. Even straight white men have discussed how they feel that they can't speak up when colleagues make misogynistic comments, because this toxic form of male bonding was the predominant workplace social currency. Former hedge fund trader Sam Polk (2016) famously wrote about Wall Street's "culture of brutal conformity" to misogyny and the bro culture that forced the disrespect and exclusion of women. It makes you think, What mold are we all trying to fit? And isn't it a problem that no one feels that they have?

When Tiffany Dufu, the Black female author of *Drop the Ball* and founder of The Cru, was early in her career as a nonprofit fundraiser, she was frustrated over not having received a promotion she felt she deserved (Dufu 2020). To find out why, to learn and grow, she consulted one of her peers who offered this rationale: "She told me that I wore too much gold," Tiffany says. "I was dumbfounded and angry. Soon after, I went to a conference and noticed for the very first time that none of my nonprofit fundraising peers were wearing the amount of jewelry that I was. In fact, pretty much every woman was simply wearing studs in her ears, possibly a ring, and one piece of costume jewelry. I quickly recognized that I did not fit the norm, but I wished we could have had a meaningful conversation about it. The silence was cowardly. Here's what I wish she had said to me:

> Tiffany, you've chosen a career in which your primary role is to engender trust from high-net-worth individuals whose backgrounds are different from yours. Unfortunately, because of stereotypes that are not your fault, they'll make assumptions when they first encounter you, so how you present yourself matters. It's not fair and you shouldn't have to do this, but you might want to think about ways that you can show up less distracting so that they more quickly recognize your incredible intellect, storytelling, and passion for your cause.

"Soon after that conference, I decided that I would sacrifice my jewelry but that I would never sacrifice my natural hair. No matter how I'd need to evolve my professional look, my crown would always remain my glory."

Tiffany learned to adapt without losing herself, but she shouldn't have to. Talented women, BIPOC, people with disabilities, LGBTQIA+, religious minorities, and other marginalized groups are often pressured into sacrificing who they are to fit into organizations that have been designed exclusively for others (aka white heteronormative employees). Your gender, racial, religious, and cultural identity should not be considered a source of shame and something to be minimized. It is your magic! No one should have to spend all of their physical and emotional labor figuring out how to navigate workspaces so that they can survive.

And yet, here we are, trying our best to survive (and thrive) in workplaces that can suck the oxygen out of our capacity to grow and lead with joy in our chosen careers. Companies fail to focus on the root problem—the policies, systems, and processes that use a white standard of professionalism and measure everyone else negatively against it. You can't perform at your best when constantly modifying or playing down who you are, including your appearance, body language, abilities, and communication style. Yet we rarely consider the additional burdens we place on underrepresented talent in our organizations who have to hide parts of their identity to fit in at work. Too often, BIPOC staff have their judgment regularly questioned and have to hold back their true feelings, all because white workplace norms constantly signal to them that they don't really belong.

We tend to think of organizations as professional settings, yet the racialized norms that define professionalism at work are no longer apt for the modern workplace. You must assess who your company culture was designed to accommodate and who gets left out. You must create an inclusive culture where everyone is valued and diversity of perspectives, thoughts, and experience is welcomed, embraced, and celebrated. Ask yourself: What stories are we telling? Are we working with BIPOC, LGBTQIA+, and members of other marginalized communities and putting inclusion and equity at the heart of our work, publicly and privately?

First, have a candid conversation about covering at work. Covering is about minimizing authentic elements of your identity, personality, or circumstances to fit in, or seem to fit in. Some of us feel that we have to hide elements of our culture, class, health, tattoos, accents, and so on. We need to talk about this. Giving people—you, your leaders, and your team members—permission to share their real stories, the moments when they have kept a part of themselves, where they grew up, who they love, what they worry about, enables us to see each other through each other. A few tips: (1) check in with your team, and acknowledge that you are on this journey, (2) provide extra support for those who need it and especially those who may be afraid to ask for it, and (3) give folks a sense that you get it and care.

You can also launch policies encouraging people to show up as their authentic selves. As part of its benefits offerings, Capital One Financial Corporation began covering costly gender reassignment surgery, to signal to employees that they want them to bring their whole self to work every day (Hastwell 2019).

That said, no matter how well-intentioned your DEI efforts may be, white supremacy has a way of rearing its ugly head repeatedly. And what does white supremacy look like in the workplace? Let's talk about some of the unwritten rules that favor whiteness at work:

> *Tone policing.* Imagine presenting a solution for reducing bias in hiring and performance processes. The response you receive from a listener is: "Your points would resonate better if you sounded less emotional" or "I wish you would say that in a calmer way." I, like many women of color, have experienced tone policing. I have countless experiences of being tone policed as a woman, "Calm down," and as a Latina, "You sound angry." Who gets to define what is an "acceptable" or "professional" way to speak or write? The bias of white professional standards manifests in tone policing and harms women and people of color by making them feel uncomfortable or ashamed for raising valid concerns.
>
> To create a more powerful dialogue that prevents tone policing, ask yourself these questions: In what ways can I focus on what the

person is saying and not solely on how they are saying it? What else do I need to know to understand what the speaker is trying to communicate instead of dismissing or avoiding what they are saying? And before addressing someone's tone, ask yourself, "Am I responding to being shut down or silenced, or am I listening to understand?"

White comfort and white fragility: This can come in the form of "color blindness," or an avoidance of conversations about racial or gender inequality, bias, and injustice. When called out for saying or doing something racist, a white person might become defensive, blame the person for raising the issue, or justify what was said or done that caused harm. White people might deny that they might be part of the problem. Statements such as "I didn't mean that" or "You're overreacting" are not comforting—they invalidate the pain caused by careless comments. This response also prioritizes the white person's feelings over the person of color's feelings, even when the white person harmed the person of color.

Perfectionism: White people know that, for the most part, when they make mistakes, it won't be attributed to their race, it won't be assumed to reinforce a stereotype about their race, and won't be used as a reason to avoid hiring more people of their race. This is not true for BIPOC employees.

Inclusive leaders develop a culture of appreciation, reflection, and accountability. They empower team members to take risks and bring their professional authentic selves to work. These are not mutually exclusive.

A few months into joining Google, Danae Sterental, a young Latinx woman of Venezuelan descent asked me for coffee. When we met, it was instantly easy and comfortable. She had one of those bright, warm smiles that lit up a room. We connected over our shared heritage and experiences at Google. A few weeks later she shared a blog she wrote about our meeting. In it she mentioned being so consumed by emotion after we said our goodbyes that she cried the minute the elevator doors closed. She noted that I wore a white dress and heels, had long flowing hair, spoke Spanglish and greeted her with a warm hug and kiss. This was the first time that she saw herself reflected in a senior leader. Prior to meeting me, she wrote, she thought she needed to sacrifice her culture, her looks, and her identity to succeed in Silicon Valley. Meeting me changed that for her. She finally felt what it was like to belong—"You can be it, if you can see it"—and there was no going back. She has since received her MBA from Stanford and launched her own consultancy helping start-ups build thriving cultures. She's going to change the world by being her full authentic self and helping others do the same.

I wouldn't dare credit myself for her future success, but the impact of one positive encounter can be powerful and life changing—it gave Danae the surge to go higher.

Four Ways Covering Shows Up at Work

"Covering" describes how underrepresented groups go to great lengths to minimize the perceived stigmas of their identity in order to fit in. In "Uncovering Talent: A New Model of Inclusion," published by Deloitte, Dr. Christie Smith and Kenji Yoshino (2019) take a deep dive into the widespread occurrence of covering at work and the impacts on inclusion.

They identify four axes of covering:

1. Appearance-based: how employees alter the way they naturally present themselves in order to fit in;
2. Affiliation-based: how employees might go to extra lengths to avoid the stereotypical behaviors associated with their group;
3. Advocacy-based: how employees might avoid standing up for their group to fit in; and
4. Association-based: how employees might minimize association with others from their group to fit in.

Your Road Map to Revolution

Kind, thoughtful, and highly educated people often sit next to colleagues who face multiple barriers at work. Because navigating work is easy, they assume the same for others. Racially sensitive management demands rigor and courage to resist the urge to do things as they've always been done. Deepen your awareness, understanding, skills, and tools for listening and supporting your teams. Good managers will thank people for speaking up and course-correcting. Welcoming challenging conversations, admitting your own mistakes, and being willing to take risks can lead to radical employee engagement.

- **Set the right tone from the start.** Ask better questions and build an environment centered on trust. Start conversations that matter, but don't expect to hear all the answers. Vulnerability can lead to radical participation. It is the missing ingredient in workplaces—model that behavior.
- **Promote and model values of respect.** Model open dialogue and respect of others' ideas in meetings and among team members. When kicking off a project, share how you expect your team to work together. Be respectful of other people's ideas and comments, even if you disagree.
- **Foster speak up culture.** Be an ally and help amplify the voice of everyone on your team, especially those who feel the most silenced. Try amplification pacts, where meeting attendees agree ahead of time to support one another's ideas publicly.
- **Mitigate microaggressions.** Recognize the impact of microaggressions on your employees. Intervene when you see transgressions, and ask your peers to join you in intervening. Use "I" statements: I feel this; that comment made me feel that. If you were responsible for a painful comment, apologize.
- **Be sensitive and empathetic with your words.** Ensure that in difficult conversations, you focus on the message's content rather than the delivery. For example, go to BIPOC employees directly and privately with actionable, non-personality-based feedback.
- **Encourage a culture where covering isn't required.** You can't perform at your best when you're constantly modifying or playing down who you are, including your appearance, body language, abilities, and communication style. Stop using a white standard of professionalism.

- **Invite others on your journey.** Research shows that those around them influence people's mindsets, so you could catalyze those around you to do better and be better managers. Connect with peers to share ideas and resources, and hold each other accountable.

7

Tune into the Whispers and the Screams (and Everything in Between)

"Death by a thousand and one papercuts" is a term that comes from an ancient form of Chinese torture known as *lingchi*, where a person is subjected to hundreds of small cuts until the end. It's a dark but accurate metaphor for what happens in workplaces across America: the accumulation of seemingly small indignities. It's shutting up and shutting down to survive.

The truth about the lived experiences of people at your company often lies right beneath the surface. It floats in whispers and in knowing looks, and more recently, in raised voices demanding change through social media and within your companies. But the weighted feeling of having your power taken away from you over and over again remains. Over the course of my career, I've had to fight to be invited into leadership rooms by silencing my feelings, making myself smaller, and tiptoeing around dismissive behavior. I've had to make myself seem less threatening. It felt like carrying a five-ton weight. And I have not been alone. Our collective silence is deafening.

To build an inclusive and equitable workforce and get ahead of murmurs and exposés, tune into the whispers and assess what's happening in your workplace. Pay attention to what's happening behind closed doors and in the open in conference rooms or video meetings. To do that with a racial equity lens, you need to recognize that while racial inequity affects all people of color somewhat comparably, different racial and ethnic groups experience the workplace differently, and it's important to understand those differences. It's okay to seek understanding about the experience of Black, Latinx, and Asian employees on your team. The goal is to equip yourself to talk about and wrestle with the impact of race effectively—not in race-neutral ways.

I've worked in human resources for most of my career, and I can say with certainty that office gossip often bears some truth. Usually those rumors are spread off-handedly as happy hour chatter or light warnings—"Everyone knows he's a creep" or "She's totally racist"—without a more profound thought into how and where those sentiments were born. How do we know he's a creep? Did he harass someone? How do we know she's racist? Did she make a racial slur? And who is on the other end of these assaults? Whose responsibility is it to address the harm? Too often, as managers, we fail to follow up—and while this may be done to avoid conflict, this can result in a worsening toxic work culture.

Continue your inclusion revolution by checking in, being present, and listening to the real everyday experiences at your company for women, BIPOC, people with disabilities, LGBTQIA+, religious minorities, and other marginalized groups. You need this information to create an authentic culture of belonging. Do you know whether coworkers of less privileged groups feel they matter and are essential? What are their complaints? What goes unsaid in meetings? Where are the hot spots in employee resignations or patterns of dissatisfaction in your employee surveys? What are the retention and turnover rates for BIPOC in your company? Are you letting bad behavior slide because it comes from a team member you like?

Fundamentally, employees don't leave companies, they leave their managers. They walk away, sometimes flee, from best-in-class companies due to persistently bad experiences with their direct managers. Management, at its core, is about defining and assigning responsibilities, measuring on results, spotting inefficiencies, and identifying solutions. Management is also about leadership, which means inspiring teams, motivating them, supporting collaboration, and getting them to do more than they ever thought possible. That means being aware of your biases and taking in different views and perspectives that can enhance your decision-making. This also means having the courage to face the truth even when it is uncomfortable, admit your mistakes, and challenge the status quo. Some call those inclusive managerial skills. I just call it good management—to know your team, understand them, challenge them, and advocate for them. I'm betting you have hired someone from an underrepresented background before, so it's essential to ask yourself, Why aren't they sticking around? It's time to tune into what's going on.

Part of your responsibility as a leader is to deepen your understanding, listen to your teams, and support them. Many of us live in fear of shedding light on racially motivated incidents because we know it can be dangerous to do so. Instead, we give up small parts of ourselves, let our courage shrink, our voice diminish, and our contributions suffer. When someone shares their truth about a racialized incident ("I was called someone else's name in the middle of a client meeting"), listen, pay attention, and seek to understand their distress.

Good leadership is surrounding yourself with people of diverse perspectives who can disagree with you without fear of retaliation. You should care about building social bonds with your coworkers. Many are hurting, questioning whether they belong, whether they have rights that will be respected, whether their lives matter, how to express their feelings and process their questions. Listen to the pauses and the whispers, watch for the signs of discomfort—and acknowledge that the truth often starts quiet. Don't dismiss it as gossip or let it slide—when you hear something, ask for more information, more detail, more accountability.

Bottom line: take care of your people. When an issue is raised, act on it. When you see something, say something. Listen to your team, and encourage your team to listen to each other.

Be an Inclusion Truth Seeker

Ask questions before you provide answers. Listen to the lived experience of others and recognize the good, the bad, and the ugly about your culture. A truth seeker has an open mind and doesn't neglect or overlook information because it goes against what they believe to be true. Make it your mission to seek feedback and perspectives on how employees of different races and ethnicities experience work and how you and your organization can do better. That said, be careful that you don't force BIPOC to be problem solvers, when the responsibility for setting up an inclusive workplace culture is yours.

Expect to be uncomfortable. I have yet to engage in a conversation about racial equity where the simple use of words such as "racism," "whiteness," and "privilege" haven't made people feel visibly uneasy. For sustainable change, you will have to tolerate and push through discomfort and create opportunities for people to lean into these conversations in an honest and forthright way. And you will have to make it clear that you will not brush past or ignore conflict.

Embarking on a listening journey is a great way to start. I've led many listening sessions for the companies I've worked for—most have been designed as conversations where leaders have met with members of different employee resource groups to hear out their concerns. At VICE Media Group, our CEO Nancy Dubuc and I embarked on a seven-week Global Listening Series following allegations of negative experiences by Black and Brown former employees at Refinery 29, one of the company's recently acquired publications. We took the stories of these women very seriously.

To create brave spaces for conversation, we brought in a facilitator, a member of our internal communications team, to guide the discussion. In the welcoming remarks, the facilitator opened by explaining that Nancy and I were there to listen and not respond until the end, when we would offer closing remarks. It was important to have an impartial colleague whom the teams trusted to help facilitate the discussion. Alternatively, you can hire a third-party, neutral facilitator. The sessions were done on a video chat (this was during the pandemic), and were capped at 20 to provide everyone an opportunity to engage. They were explicitly framed to examine issues of inclusion, equity, and belonging across our teams. For those most afraid to speak up, we encouraged them to use our anonymous hotline to share their feedback. At the beginning of each session, we asked participants to reflect on these questions:

- What are the conditions (policies, programs) that may sustain white, male, hetero, cis, and/or able-bodied unequal power and dominant presence within our teams and work?
- In which situations have you felt things to be unfair and unsafe?

The dialogue was further framed in a three-pronged approach, allocating equal time for each section:

Stop: What are some things we should stop doing that are deterring the growth and presence of coworkers from marginalized groups?

Start: What are some things we should start doing to better support the growth and presence from coworkers from marginalized groups?

Continue: What are some things we should continue doing that currently support the growth and presence of coworkers from marginalized groups?

We witnessed an extraordinary level of transparency and bravery. Each group lifted up issues and concerns most relevant to their unique experience and geographic location. There were moments of levity such as when Nancy, whom I had not met in person since I was hired during quarantine, commented on not knowing how tall I was. When I shared that I was five feet two, her eyes went wide as she blurted, "No way!" She had assumed that my height would match my personality.

The conversations were insightful, raw, and often unsettling. Topics ranged from leadership accountability and management training to career advancement, pay equity, tone policing, and tokenism. Most subtly, employees wanted to understand the why. As in, Why are certain business decisions being made? We heard an appreciation for being asked to share their experiences. We also heard a desire for real change, action, not just a symbolic gesture of "Tell me your story." With each conversation, I witnessed Nancy stretch herself as she learned more about race and racism, honored the vulnerability of team members, and managed the discomfort with a genuine desire to change the culture at its deepest roots.

Part diagnostic, part conversations, these sessions helped dissolve interpersonal barriers, dispel some myths, and served as our source data for the most essential elements of our transformation plan. Every initiative we designed from that point on—from our second pay equity study to our learning programs and performance management processes—was informed by what we learned in those conversations. To keep the learning and engagement going, we launched additional versions of listening sessions with other leaders across the organization.

A note: to create a space for employees to share how they are truly doing, leaders need to be trained in listening skills and model vulnerability themselves by acknowledging what they know and don't know and committing to staying engaged through the stretch. This sends a powerful signal that "it's okay to not be okay with the status quo."

I often hear the stories of employees who feel ignored or misunderstood by their managers. By the time I hear about it, disproportionately from women and BIPOC employees, they either have one foot out the door or are too beaten down to care. A lot of listening with an anti-racist lens has to do with how you respond. Do you listen with the intent to build shared understanding (good), or do you focus on solving (bad)? Do your questions start with "Help me understand . . . ?" (good) or "Wouldn't you agree . . . ?" or "Don't you think . . . ?" (bad).

As a manager, it's important that you make yourself available so that your teams can access you when and if they need you. You need to show a willingness to talk.

You have to show "evidence of effort," a willingness to talk openly about thorny or uncomfortable issues, even when they differ from your own experiences, says corporate consultant and educator in his leadership trainings, Reggie Butler (2012, 2021). It's what your teams want and need from you. It's the opposite of what we have become accustomed to—an unemotional and distanced managerial standard that has long favored white men. Any variance is often dismissed and considered unprofessional. I don't need to intellectualize how I'm feeling. I know what it feels like to have my power taken away from me in daily interactions. It's an experience BIPOC employees are all too familiar with. How can you possibly help your teams overcome obstacles? Your teams just want to know that you care. Here's a simple approach:

- Hi, I have been awed and humbled by what this team has achieved during extraordinary circumstances.
- This training or conversation may surface some tough emotions . . .
- I want you to know that as your leader I'm not okay with how difficult this time is for you.
- I want to remind you to check in with your team members, and please know that I'm here to lean on at any time.
- Here are some helpful approaches and resources . . .

As a BIPOC leader, it's both important and challenging to advocate for yourself. It's okay to reply to emails asking for your advice with, "I'll get back to you." In the wake of the George Floyd murder, like many BIPOC and DEI professionals, I received countless emails asking for "advice." I would respond with a note and curated resource list: "Thank you for reaching out. These are important conversations that require much thought and reflection. I, like many other diversity, equity and inclusion practitioners of color, am managing my own health and well-being. Here is a list of diversity and anti-racist practitioners, some of whom I know and others who have been referred. I encourage you to reach out and learn about their offerings and how they may be helpful to you."

Being an ally, listener, and challenger of norms is a continuous process. Part of that process is examining our biases and educating ourselves about the experiences of people from vulnerable and marginalized identities. Another important part, perhaps most important, is building the muscle of listening, understanding, and reflecting, including the capacity to interpret new information. This may mean that, like Nancy and I, sometimes you will have to sit in ambiguity, conflict, and discomfort as you take in new information. Out of those moments can come real clarity on what we need to do next.

A Sample Discussion Guide

LISTENING SERIES—DISCUSSION GUIDE

Your role (leader):

- **Speak:** Set the stage and tone up top; summarize at end.
- **Listen:** Create a safe and brave space to share. Actively listen to participants.
- **Act:** Commit to an action by the end of the session. You can partner with your HR business partner and chief diversity officer to follow up on the session with action plans.

Conversation starters	We are here because XXX.
	I am interested in hearing firsthand from all of you.
	We know that XX can be a great place to work, but not everyone has the same experience. I want to hear from you what it's like to work here.
	I'm here to listen and won't have all the answers. Consider this the start of our conversation.
	I want to work with you to improve our overall culture and inclusivity.
Potential discussion themes	What should we start/stop/continue doing to improve our team culture?
	How does the way we work limit or enhance our work?
	How do you feel about your work-life balance?
Wrapping up	Thank them for their time.
	Summarize key themes you have heard.
	Remind them it is just the beginning of an ongoing conversation.
	Don't overpromise. Commit to things you are sure you can deliver.
	Let them know next steps (they will hear from you shortly).

After the session	You should plan on doing some follow-up with participants, through an email, summarizing the key themes that came from the session (what you heard—from the notes captured by HRBP) and your plan of action/next steps.
	It is critically important to follow through with anything committed to in the discussion.
Tips for inclusive conversations	Be ready to hear a variety of responses that you might not have expected.
	Repeat what you heard to them—the Oprah interview technique.
	While you may not understand or agree with all perspectives shared, practice empathetic listening. This is their experience—don't take that away from them by offering a counterpoint or rushing them to a point.
	Observe those who have not spoken, and create space for them to be heard.
	Look for opportunities to build trust and actively listen to encourage participant disclosure. Trust can be built through the setting of expectations, demonstrating vulnerability through personal risks, and being intentional about using inclusive language.
	Start with awareness of your default behaviors and how you are including, potentially excluding, or dismissing others.
	Questions to mitigate bias as you listen:

- Do I have an automatic feeling or judgment about this person?
- What may I have discounted and not heard in the right way?
- How can I consciously intervene to lessen the impact of this bias?

Get Smart with Surveys

Employee feedback is a golden resource for measuring inclusion. A well-crafted, anonymous engagement survey can help you gauge where specific hot spots or problems may exist within and across teams. They can further determine how these gaps affect your team's work and experience across different demographics (remember to track that) and where pockets of toxicity or exclusion may hide in the averages. I recommend that you incorporate DEI questions into your engagement surveys versus a stand-alone DEI survey to avoid survey fatigue and to continue to keep this work at the center.

Global research and advisory company Gartner created the Gartner Inclusion Index to help organizations get a holistic view of inclusion across their workforce. Employees are asked to respond to seven statements, and the greater degree to which they agree with the statements, the more inclusive the organization: fair treatment, integrating differences, decision-making, psychological safety, trust, belonging, and diversity.

Fair treatment: Employees at my organization who help the organization achieve its strategic objectives are rewarded and recognized fairly.

Integrating differences: Employees at my organization respect and value each other's opinions.

Decision-making: Members of my team fairly consider ideas and suggestions offered by other team members.

Psychological safety: I feel welcome to express my true feelings at work.

Trust: Communication we receive from the organization is honest and open.

Belonging: People in my organization care about me.

Diversity: Managers at my organization are as diverse as the broader workforce.

The most important element to gauge is whether your team members genuinely feel heard, accepted, and empowered to influence decision-making as it relates to their roles. Questions you can ask: Are your ideas listened to and acted on? Are issues handled, acknowledged, and solved in a racially and culturally sensitive manner? Do you feel that you can share aspects of yourself without shame or hindrance for career advancement? Tell me about a high point moment when you felt a sense of belonging with your team. With your company? If you had a magic wand and could grant three wishes so that everyone could feel a sense of belonging in the workplace, what would they be?

Or, you could try a multiple-choice approach as used by many organizations and survey providers:

What would make you feel like you belong?

- Being recognized for my accomplishments;
- Having opportunities to express my opinion freely;
- Having my contributions in team meetings recognized as valuable;
- Being comfortable with being myself at work;
- Feeling that my team/company cares about me as a person;
- Feedback on my personal growth;
- Working for a team/company whose values align with mine;
- Being invited to important company meetings;
- Seeing executives and co-workers who look like me.

And when you feel lost, confused, or stuck on how to approach these issues, just ask the open-ended question: What does working here feel like for you?

I feel I belong at company *x* is a true/false statement often found in engagement surveys and is intended to gauge employees' sense of belonging. I'm not convinced it's the right indicator for BIPOC and underrepresented employees. Why would we want to belong in organizations where we have been forced to leave large parts of ourselves outside so others can feel comfortable? Where we spend so much time shrinking ourselves to avoid standing out, swallowing our frustrations, or walking on eggshells to avoid making white people feel uncomfortable?

Instead, we should explicitly ask: What does it mean to be represented in your team and organization? How, if at all, are unconscious biases addressed in your workplaces? How comfortable do you feel asking for help to overcome work barriers or challenge the status quo? These questions can help you surface the root causes of racial disparities in your organization. It can also help you gauge whether leaders and managers are cultivating psychological safety, belonging, and inclusion by role modeling and reinforcing fair and inclusive behaviors.

At VICE Media Group, one of our digital leaders created an online form for his team to encourage everyone to raise questions, concerns, or issues. This was meant to create an additional channel for raising workplace issues, including microaggressions and racism, beyond what was already available via HR. In an email to his team he wrote, "This form allows you to raise your hand and say, 'I have a question' or 'I want to talk about something'—you can indicate you would like a response over email, or if you would like to arrange a 1:1 meeting with me and/or other members of the leadership team to discuss. There is an option to remain anonymous, and I will do my best to respond to those who choose to do so through group emails, or on an all-hands call going forward."

While employee engagement surveys are important tools for getting a pulse on an organization's cultural snapshot, there are pitfalls. Even when you create a safe space for people to speak up, there will be people on your team who have been betrayed and hurt too many times to trust you. I've found myself repeatedly emphasizing to employees that surveys are anonymous. I've stressed that the information we gather will never reflect on them individually and that we need their honest answers and appraisals because I can't fix what I don't know. But the fears of repercussions and judgment are real. People don't want to participate if there is no transparency in the survey analysis, even if they are anonymous.

When interpreting results, it's also important to look at the positive results as much as the lower-scoring results to also determine bright spot practices. We often jump to what is wrong but something that works well can be repurposed within other groups or potentially at scale.

You have to be cautious of survey fatigue. If you take too much time to share your findings and announce an action plan, people will not bother filling out surveys. Issues of bias, harassment, and discrimination at work often go unreported because the most marginalized employees either fear retaliation or don't know what options they have available to address grievances or concerns. Employees will only fill out surveys honestly if they believe in your willingness to listen to their opinions and recommendations and to use that information to deliver solutions.

Many corporate surveys are worded to prime positive responses (What's your favorite thing about working here? What does your boss do best?). If you want honest answers, you need immense internal trust, true assurances that there won't be backlash for negative responses, and a commitment to action results. Suppose staff respond that they want pay equity. In that case, you have to be committed to action and transparency, both in the responses and in a true and fair internal pay audit. The audit results have to be shared, and corrections must be made immediately as needed, including backpay. Or what if staff feel overstretched and understaffed, what if staff are asking for more hires to help lighten the load, to prevent requiring people from working on weekends, etc.? What if the team feels this is a toxic, racist, sexist workplace that they don't want to remain in, much less recruit women and BIPOC for? What if people complain about bad managers and high turnover and ask to know if exit interviews reveal patterns of bad behavior that have gone unaddressed? If your company is not willing to show that level of transparency or is not financially committed, then don't conduct surveys at all.

Allow for Anonymity and Maintain Multiple Reporting Systems

Confidentiality matters. Most companies also offer anonymous reporting hotlines for employees to speak up when they have legitimate concerns about misconduct. However, these are not stand-alone solutions for establishing an ethical and inclusive culture.

I've found that the most successful approach is to offer multiple channels of communication for raising concerns. If you're trying to get to the underlying issues of why underrepresented employees leave at a higher rate, for example, you may try independent, confidential platforms such as tEquitable. These platforms offer a sounding board for employees and insights for companies to be and do better. Furthermore, the agency they provide for employees to seek and effect solutions before issues of bias, discrimination, or harassment escalate may enable them to regain their confidence. One advantage that tEquitable has, by design, is that employees receive confidential advice and help to figure out what their next steps should be immediately. They're provided with in-the-moment coaching with actionable takeaways.

The cloud communications company Twilio used it to allow its employees to open up and anonymously share things that might be happening to them at work, without fear of retaliation. The data they received highlighted teams and functions with issues that needed to be addressed. These issues were previously hidden well under the surface. Now, management can enact more proactive solutions to help curb insidious behaviors before they take hold.

I'm often asked if it's worth it to go to human resources. Are they your friend or foe? There's a common perception that HR is an inefficient and sometimes corrupt "agent" of the organization, that claims of misconduct go to die once they are reported to HR, or worse, that those complaints become cause to penalize you. I'm not saying this doesn't happen—there are real stories and data to support those beliefs. I hear complaints all the time that "HR won't help me," "HR will make things worse," or "HR never did anything about it."

But, as someone who has been inside several of the largest HR teams on the planet, I can tell you that there are well-intentioned, capable HR leaders who are proactive, engaged, and concerned about your well-being. They want to provide support and promote a positive organizational climate. Sometimes they are handcuffed by confidentiality, but that shouldn't stop you from asking them to help defuse or solve complicated workplace situations.

And if you are an HR practitioner, here's what I say and recommend you to say: "This work requires that we remind ourselves of what our people and organizations need us to do and to pause and think about what type of HR leader we need to be for others. Sure, our role requires us to enforce workplace policies, conduct investigations, and sometimes reprimand or exit employees, which is unpleasant though necessary. But long gone are the days of simply policing bad behavior or serving as compliance officers. Our role is to help build more resilient, inclusive and responsive organizations." Managers shouldn't have to do this work alone. They're rarely equipped to do so.

Here's how to lean on HR:

Partner on difficult conversations: Everyone is too nervous about saying the wrong thing. HR can serve as a trusted and unbiased mediator. But know that having another person in the room, specifically from HR, can also raise anxiety levels. To tame those fears, say, "I have asked our HR partner to join us to help us avoid any misinterpretations and so that you can feel safe in your responses." And then make sure that that sense of safety is honored.

Facilitate listening sessions: I've always encouraged my team to serve as facilitators and notetakers during listening sessions. These experiences enable them to build closer ties to teams, glean insights they may not be privy to in their day-to-day, and learn to guide conversation safely and inclusively. Team members can also learn how to help support conversations between coworkers who may feel alone in what they are sharing and those who are hearing these stories for the first time.

Reaffirm a sense of fairness: Your HR teams can add fairness and transparency checks to processes across the entire employee journey— attraction, selection, development, promotion, and retention. They can help you identify gaps in those stages, develop rigorous methods for selecting and promoting members of your teams, and design compensation strategies and materials to ensure everyone on your teams understands your pay philosophy and approach.

Three Strategies for Better Truth-Seeking Conversations

During these conversations, it's important to listen and engage withhold judgment and not immediately launch into trying to solve things. Yes, you should respond to what you're hearing, but the goal should be to seek to understand what the other person is trying to convey and what is important to them. The listening portion is critical, rather than focusing on deciding where their story must go or how it must end. Three strategies are: acknowledge history; reduce defensiveness; and listen, do not debate.

Acknowledge history: If there has been an onslaught of reports and complaints about gender harassment, discrimination, or abusive conduct, don't try to pretend that you're unaware of the situation, even if you can't share specific and confidential details. You can paraphrase and reflect on what is being said or better yet, start the conversation with an acknowledgment of what you're there to discuss, admit what you can and can't share, and listen for content and emotion. Don't forget to ask: "How are you doing with all of this?"

Reduce defensiveness: Some people will be intimately familiar with what is happening, while others are just starting to join this work and conversation. Some are tired of (and maybe triggered by) talking about it, and others are eager to join the conversation. Some need rest and healing; others need action. Some may stay silent but have a lot to say. Don't discount, dismiss, or blame them. Even if something was not intended to offend, all attention should be on validating and apologizing for the offended person's pain, and your energy should be on making it right. No energy should be wasted on defending someone or a policy's intent. The intent is no longer relevant; the harmed person's pain is what's relevant. Honor whether they want to engage in the conversation or not. You can also offer another opportunity to speak if they don't want to do so in the moment.

Listen, do not debate: Your job here is to listen *if* your team members or coworkers want to talk to you about their experience. Do not debate them, rush to offer solutions to their experience, or extend "a different perspective." Be careful to separate intent from effect. You don't want to minimize your colleague's experience by focusing on defending a bad actor's intent. Instead, your act of listening can itself be a step toward their healing. Talking, for any trauma survivor, is a key way to work through emotions and understand their experience. Sometimes they may need to tell the same stories over and over again. Ask clarification questions, paraphrase what they are saying, and follow their lead. And always listen with the heart as well as with the mind.

Act on What You Hear

I'm often asked: What do you do with leaders who say they want to build diverse teams but are unaware of inequities within their teams? My answer is always the same because the answer *is* always the same: They know. They may not be aware of every detail or the extent of the exclusion people experience, but they likely have a sense of who the bad players are. They have heard the murmurs. And if they don't, one thing is sure, their inner circle are in the know.

Senior managers all know, but by and large, executive teams tend to be majority white and homogenous, and so they often all suffer from the same racial frailties and tensions. So when the stakes feel high, they all prefer to retreat, block, delay, or settle for a lesser goal. They lean on notions of "professionalism" and "appropriateness" as excuses to avoid or stifle challenging perspectives or conversations. The result is higher gaps of understanding between senior leadership and the lower ranks. The lower ranks suffer the most when the system isn't working. That's why white and BIPOC managers at all levels need to seek an understanding of your blind spots and the sore spots of those working under these conditions. If you can't overcome the silences and denials surrounding white fragility, privilege, and abuses of power in your workplace, you can't create conditions for change.

After you listen to the whispers and check in with your team, you must swiftly hold yourself accountable for acting on what you've heard. That's it. If there are no consequences for behaving in a manner that is not civil, then such behaviors will continue to disrupt the workplace and limit productivity. A company that wants civility as part of its culture must hold employees at every level accountable for behaving civilly.

As I was moving up the ranks in my career, I longed for leaders who would use their position of authority to challenge toxic behavior. As I grew into positions of leadership and power, I realized that it was up to me to model the behaviors I sought.

Anyone who has ever worked on my team knows that I have very little patience for disrespectful behavior. If I see or hear that someone is being belittled, misunderstood, or mistreated by a peer or manager, I bring the affected parties together to address conflict constructively and with care. I do so by naming what I saw or learned, as simple as stating, "I think this is what is happening right now," giving my team members license to express concerns or experiences, and making it clear that we can be respectful and kind while raising hard issues.

Following through and following up is the final act of creating a culture of belonging. When you do, that person feels they've been heard, supported, and that someone has their back. You have their back. They feel that they're part of a team. Instead, managers often try to avoid conflict and try to ignore issues. The people who raise racial issues at work are often blamed for raising them. For example, when an employee tells a manager they believe a colleague is mistreating Black employees in meetings, a manager might defend the bad actor and criticize the person who brought up the matter instead of empathizing with them and offering to investigate it. A manager might try to minimize the situation, all to avoid the discomfort of correcting a colleague's racist behavior. Whistleblowers are often shamed in companies, to the point where millions of workers fear that the professional costs are too high to speak up about harmful workplace behavior.

One of the toughest parts of this process is how you respond to what you're hearing from your employees and from your coworkers. It requires you to have the courage to speak up and act as an ally, to navigate minefield-laden, bureaucratic waters, and to push for changes that may be out of your power or pay grade. Instead of focusing on being polite and avoiding issues, try addressing those uncomfortable truths. I've found it helpful to role-play ways to handle conflict before a challenging conversation happens. It eases my conflict-adverse anxiety. It's a useful skill to build and one we can rarely be good at in the moment when we haven't built the muscles to do so. I write a script and practice in front of the mirror. When in doubt, remember that even tiny action steps are a step forward—the outcomes of small but mighty reflective acts create an opportunity to bake diversity, equity, inclusion, and belonging into your organizational DNA.

What does being reliable mean to you? Who is someone that you trust or can lean on? What do they do to create that feeling for you? For me, and most leaders I know, trust grows when you follow through on your word. When someone tells you that they're going to do something and they do it. It's about integrity—not morality, but the integrity of your word. Distrust grows when people feel that you're not doing anything to address their concerns or the truth does not lead to meaningful resolutions. When you create a gaping lag time in your response that void gets filled with panic, anger, frustration, you name it.

The formula is simple: listen, learn, respond, and do something about what you've learned.

But what if you don't know what to do? As a non-manager, this may look like being open to constructive feedback from peers or providing emotional support during difficult times. As a manager or leader this could mean ensuring your employees know that they will be heard, believed, and safe to raise concerns about inappropriate behavior.

While you must prioritize action, you also want to do it effectively and fairly. When, for example, a racial or LGBTQIA+-charged incident occurs, recognize the behavior and act on it swiftly—don't wait until the problematic behavior is repeated. Something as simple and direct as "I think what you said sounds biased" can be surprisingly effective. Effectively standing up to bias or a racial microaggression when you notice it will help you and your team push through change and work better together.

Organizational responses will range depending on the severity of the incident and behavior. You should have clearly defined grievance procedures—and you must follow them. Engage your HR partner and determine the best course of action to collect information, seek clarity from those who were involved, and determine what actions are necessary. In some cases it may make sense to engage an external investigator.

Sometimes the offender may be rehabilitable. In those cases, a private conversation, targeted coaching on inclusive and anti-racist competencies, and a personal apology can help heal trust and correct culture. In more egregious cases, the offender should be let go swiftly. Public apologies can sound trite and lessen trust if not tied to real action. In either case, it is up to leadership to commit to sustained steps over time to honor the vulnerability and courage employees bring to the process.

Even if solutions can't be implemented quickly, be transparent in your actions. If it's an issue requiring company support such as harassment charges, first, say something to show that you're not sitting in silence such as: "I've heard you, I reported it, and I am working with our HR or leadership team on next steps." While waiting for the resolution, which should ideally not take longer than a few weeks, all parties involved must maintain confidentiality. This is meant to protect everyone.

And if the company's response isn't what you know the employee is looking for, for example firing the offender, be honest about the process and what is in your control to change. You can say, "I went through all the channels (enumerate them). I appreciate that this is not the outcome you were hoping for, but here's what we plan to do as a leadership team (e.g. training in racially sensitive management, building inclusivity into management performance reviews)." Owning the decision and next steps, rather than leaving the blame on the organization, is how a leader shows up.

In 2018, Starbucks CEO Howard Shultz handled a racially charged incident in one of its Philadelphia chains quickly and decisively. He didn't try to sweep it under the rug or cross his fingers that the Twitterverse would move on to other things (as so many companies hope). He acknowledged what had happened on national TV, owned the mistake, said he was embarrassed and ashamed, issued an authentic apology, and shared a quick solution (shutting down all locations for racial bias training). The effectiveness of his proposed solution is debatable—one-day training doesn't always have long-term effects—but there was a genuine desire to shine a light on an uncomfortable truth. When leaders are transparent and act quickly to address a racist incident, they can help BIPOC staff feel safe, valued, and taken seriously.

Don't wait months to address an incident and waste time worrying over the perfect thing to say. While every situation is different and should be customized for your workplace, don't be afraid to look into it. This includes the offender who is a friend, a senior leader, or a high performer. If you hear reports that that person routinely bullies junior BIPOC staff, act quickly. Besides being the right thing to do, any bad manager is replaceable, and poor workplace morale has productivity consequences for the whole team. While you don't need a formal HR investigation to gather feedback from your team about their experiences with this manager, you should partner with them to ensure the data collection process is fair and consistent. You will gain the insights you need if you care to listen. Whether you learn that it is consistent abrasive behavior or a one-time experience, it is your responsibility to address it directly with the manager and HR.

We all have bad days but as managers and leaders, we set the tone from the top. I was once part of a group email in which a peer, a white male top executive in the company, chastised a junior BIPOC member of my team for making a mistake and not knowing how to do her job better. After checking in with my team member directly, I learned that it wasn't indeed her mistake—my team member had acted at the directive of another manager. She was mortified for being publicly flogged by a senior leader on a group email thread with peers and other managers. I reassured her that no negative action would be taken against her and that I would rectify the situation. I responded to the thread by listing the actions that had taken place, recognizing that the employee on my team followed the proper protocols, and thanking her and the team for resolving the issue. I then took my peer aside and let him know his actions devastated her. I said that if he had paused and done the same due diligence I had instead of attacking a weaker junior member of staff, we could have safeguarded her dignity and not modeled toxic behavior for others. He never apologized; I wish he did. Coming to her defense meant the world to my team member, but the damage was done. Still, even without the apology, it was important to correct the behavior publicly. If our teams believe humiliating junior team members is acceptable and unpunishable behavior, they will follow suit.

Repair Damage When It Happens

If only fixing workplace conflict were as easy as causing it. Recognizing and addressing conflict and misunderstanding is a significant first step reducing the impact of relationship- and career-damaging moments.

You've now learned to look for what's not always visible, especially the impact of your unconscious choices and behaviors that you model. But the most vital step comes next: what you do with this awareness.

Remember when we talked about a growth mindset? Our actions are guided by our inner beliefs, assumptions, and biases about how the world operates. Pay attention to your thinking when listening to the whispers: Are you focused on what they are saying and what they mean, or are you just thinking about what to say next? Are you more concerned with preserving peace and racial comfort than with grappling with how race matters? Establishing the right mindset won't happen overnight, but the important thing to know is that your internal dialogue influences your perception and behavior.

If you're a manager or leader who identifies as a woman, BIPOC, person with a disability, LGBTQIA+, religious minority, or other marginalized identities, you're not off the hook. Your lived experiences may make you more sensitive to exclusionary experiences but we still have to do the work. I've been guilty of making gendered assumptions when assigning job responsibilities. I've even scaled back inclusion programs when confronted by opposition from my white peers. Each time I've forced myself to face and admit my missteps but not before falling in the traps of my hidden blind spots.

"We all have a set of beliefs about our own racial identity, how we interact with other races based on our own individual lived experience, and our belief systems are being challenged right now," said Keesha Jean-Baptiste, Head of Talent at Hearst when I interviewed her (Jean-Baptiste 2020). "And when your belief system shifts you begin to see everything differently. Race is woven into your day-to-day, from where you choose to shop, who you choose to support, and other choices that may have been second nature." White people also have a race. They are not the invisible non-raced "norm." Race is not an issue that only Black and Brown people are responsible for dealing with (or solving). Instead, given that racism benefits white people, I'd argue that it is white people's responsibility to stop blindly allowing oppressive systems to exist.

This happens when you keep your rose-colored glasses on: When The Wing hired me following a racialized incident that seemed absurd on its face (a fight over a parking spot), I would come to learn that this was just the latest in a long string of incidents. Deeper issues of bias, power, and discrimination were routinely been skirted around and silenced. By the time this disagreement happened, there had been years of built-up racial tension, and this event became a headline-making, leadership-destroying upheaval.

When I was hired to help address the situation, I didn't know the full depth of what I was walking into. Yet my racism radar buzzed enough to know I couldn't just embark on future-looking diversity and inclusion initiatives for their membership. I first had to attend to the past experiences of staff—staff who I would soon learn was hurting from years of neglect and microaggressions. You can't take a step forward until you stand in the present, hold your company accountable, and start the healing process.

We had to elevate the whispers and have conversations about race and how racism shows up in the workplace today. I started our first session with the staff by saying:

We are here today to give voice to the experiences of people of color, especially Black women, who have been harmed—intentionally and unintentionally—by the practices, behaviors, norms, and expectations. We are here today because there is a gap . . . between the values we espoused and the experience of many in this room.

We first focused on hearing the voices and experiences of those who had been most harmed. Next, we shared with the staff how the status quo was harming Black women and encouraged everyone to be honest about their roles in supporting that status quo, knowingly or unknowingly. We used exercises designed to give every person the space and opportunity to speak their minds about the environment within the company and across their teams. This included group activities where the white women in the room were not allowed to speak first because we wanted to create conditions for everyone to share in being vulnerable. Much too often in cross-racial affinity groups, white women take up all the space. We tried to hold these sessions differently here—to hear from women of color first, and after, we would open the mic up to everyone else.

Inevitably, there would always be at least one white woman whom I'd have to remind, "It's not your turn. Not all the women of color have spoken yet." The purpose of these exercises is to give a voice to the voiceless, to allow those of marginalized communities to speak up and be heard without hindrances and obstacles. Inevitably, tensions arise for white participants. I can't tell you how many times I've heard someone erupt with, "You told me I can't defend myself! It's really hard. I wanna respond!"

In these sessions, if someone's harassing a person who is being silenced, the silenced person should be able to defend themselves first. These outbursts from silenced white participants are rarely about being harassed by BIPOC participants. It's about the fact that white people are supposed to be sitting there and simply listening—and listening to hard truths is difficult, especially if you've never done that before. But this is not the time to be defensive; this is the time to take it all in. I feel like reminding these white participants, "This is your mirror. Everything is coming at you, and it's everything that you have been unwilling to face up to this point. Everything that you have been unwilling to acknowledge. Tons of unwillingness being challenged all at once. And your anger is actively deflecting from the truth of the matter—that difficult and uncomfortable truth."

I was pleasantly taken aback in a few listening series at VICE Media Group when, to break the silence, the facilitator would randomly call on a white employee. On several occasions these employees would say, "I'd rather yield my time to a BIPOC colleague who hasn't spoken yet." On more than one occasion this was followed by, "I'm trying to put into practice what I'm learning." If you are a white person and these scenarios make you uncomfortable, ask yourself, why does it make me so uncomfortable to allow people of color to have an unconstrained voice? (Pro tip: If this is the first time you've engaged in these conversations, challenge your inclination to dismiss or trivialize because of any discomfort it may cause you. Instead be open to asking clarifying questions and considering what may have contributed to your reactions.)

We also used techniques for staff, particularly those adapted from Glenn Singleton's Courageous Conversation About Race model (Singleton n.d.). These exercises center on storytelling about race: How did race show up for you in the early parts of your life? How do you communicate that? How does it show up for you in the workplace? At every session, we would hear similar comments from white participants: This really hurts. This is really upsetting. I'm tired of talking about this. And during these sessions, we pushed into that anger to try to bring out where it was coming from. That anger came in the form of deflecting responsibility from the white employees and in the form of emotionally charged outbursts across the board.

The incident that caused The Wing to hire me wouldn't have exploded if they had gotten ahead of pay equity issues, exclusive cultures, and power abuses. The company leadership should have identified the right solutions early on. They would have been confident, comfortable, and prepared to bring this high emotion situation down to neutral by centering on equity and maintaining the safety of everyone affected while respecting the upset person's agency and humanity. Clarity on who you are and consistency in your behaviors, both on an individual and company-wide level, stops issues such as theirs from ever happening. With that preparation and confidence at hand, plus a well-designed risk management process, there would have been no news reporting, no damage to the brand, and most importantly, a reduction of the damage done, both emotionally and mentally, to their own people, members, and staff.

Deescalating a heated or tense situation at work is hard enough as it is. Adding in racial and gender identity dynamics can make work a daily battle for survival. You may choose to invest in conflict management training for your managers that enables them to recognize cognitive bias and how to reach an understanding through perspective taking. Suppose you can't invest in a formal training program that centers on anti-racism, belonging, and psychological safety. In that case, you can help create and join a diversity peer counseling program to help others learn what to do when they witness bias and unfairness in the workplace.

Whether you are white or a person of color, you create belonging and a place of safety by modeling inclusive behavior and creating a space of connection and understanding. I once coached two leaders of a creative team who had recently given a presentation to a big client. During the pitch, the client's chief marketing officer made several veiled racist comments that went unquestioned but not unnoticed. While no one mentioned anything during the pitch, they struggled with how to respond. Our creative team making the pitch was mostly BIPOC. They felt deeply triggered and wanted to call the whole thing off. At the same time, the risk of losing a big client during a financial downturn loomed large in everyone's minds.

When I met with the leaders of our creative team to work through how to address the situation, I encouraged them to schedule a follow-up meeting. Then they could seek understanding and clarity from the client team, who had seemed more welcoming and open to creative ideas. During the planning process for this follow-up meeting, the leaders and I discussed the importance of standing by our values and standing up for our team members, especially those with less privilege. I encouraged them to create a safe environment for sharing what they experienced in the previous meeting—and to seek to discover what perhaps they didn't know that they didn't know.

The follow-up meeting was a success. The CMO wasn't present, unfortunately, but the client team thanked us for being willing to have a "courageous conversation" where they could see and understand each other's perspectives. Our team leaders felt they had an opportunity to show up with clear and decisive leadership, and to reassert our organizational values of diversity, equity, and inclusion. They called it a "transformational moment" where they gained higher levels of wisdom, integrity, empathy, insight, and trust. They didn't win the pitch, but the creative team leaders gained the respect and trust of their creative peers and the client with whom they hoped to work in the future. In the end, the CMO never apologized, but that was not the aim. This was not the easy or risk-free route, but it was the right call to set context for understanding, speaking up, and challenging racist behavior and to model to our teams what courage, professionalism, and grace looks like in action.

Your Road Map to Revolution

We know from ample research that the culture and norms of a workplace significantly affect employees' sense of inclusion and belonging, job satisfaction, and performance. Management is about leadership, which means inspiring teams, motivating them, supporting collaboration, and getting them to do more than they ever thought possible. It also means protecting them when harm has been done. Tune in to what's happening, and do something about what you have learned—that's how you build trust and belonging.

- **Go on a listening tour.** Investigate and assess what work is like for everyone on your team. Listen carefully and purposefully to all members of your team. Resist the urge to present solutions, and wait until everyone is done speaking to offer your closing thoughts and ideas for what comes next.
- **Prove that you're open to tough conversations.** As a manager, you must make yourself available so that your teams can access you when and if they need you. You need to show a willingness to talk. Consider using outside agencies.
- **Offer anonymous ways to report what's going on.** Use surveys to understand trends on DEI in your workforce, tools that allow people to report wrongdoing, or hire an outside firm to summarize (and even dramatize) the insidious behavior that could be holding people back.

- **Follow through and follow up.** When you hear something, say something, do something. Listen, learn, respond, and act quickly. Even if it's not 100% the perfect action, doing something to show that you're taking it seriously counts—even just acknowledging that it happened

- **Lean on your HR team.** Engage your HR partner and decide the best course of action to collect information, seek clarity from those who were involved, and determine what actions are necessary. Ask them to sit in on difficult conversations.

- **Strengthen your emotional intelligence** to better discern whether a conversation or interaction is going the wrong way. Ask yourself: "Have I conducted myself in a way that would lead to inclusive outcomes? Or have I, in some small or large way, contributed to racial disparities or feelings of exclusions?"

- **Learn how to pause before critiquing how an issue is raised.** Don't be distracted if someone shares a problem in an angry manner that makes you uncomfortable—you should separate your fear of conflict from the need to listen to the wrongdoing that's being reported. Ask yourself: Do I require people to raise issues in an "acceptable" way because I'm scared of conflict? What can I do differently to ensure that all employees feel safe to raise racist incidents?

- **Make authentic apologies that demonstrate awareness of the impact of your words or actions on others.** But don't overdo it. Ask yourself: Should I apologize with, "Sorry I offended you," or "I'm sorry for what I just said. That was totally out of line, and based on my misinterpretation. My apologies again."

8

No Talent Left Behind

Leadership doesn't just happen; promotions don't fall from the sky. Biased performance reviews feed gender and racial disparities in the workplace because they determine how people get paid and who gets promoted. And we know from research that BIPOC employees, women of color in particular, receive less support and advancement opportunities. It is the responsibility of executive leadership to de-bias the inputs (i.e. performance evaluations) that determine who gets promoted, and provide managers with the tools to understand racial inequity dynamics across the employee lifecycle.

Managers, in turn, must develop the skills to coach their people into optimal performance and career growth. This means giving the people they manage as much attention as they give to creating products, platforms, or services. How do you do that? Ask good career questions, help individuals clarify their goals, offer coaching more than corrections on skills gaps, and prep all team members for their next role. We've all learned by now that talent is the lifeblood of an organization. Organizations that thrive ensure they have the right people doing the right jobs and nurtured with the right resources. Otherwise, you risk losing the talent you worked so hard to hire and need to retain.

Take Desiree Booker, a career strategist. She held two communication roles, with two different managers, and she shared how each person who managed her directly affected how long she stayed at each company. "In one, I had a manager who took the time to nurture and develop me, while the other manager wanted to fire me for every little mistake that I made," Desiree says. "The manager who took the time to develop me, he recognized my skills gaps when I was hired, but he saw my potential and was committed to helping me grow. That manager was a senior vice president. It's rare to find that level of investment in talent (especially junior talent) from a senior leader, and his guidance made a tremendous difference in the trajectory of my career."

Without intentional, supportive, and transparent growth and advancement practices, too many BIPOC employees aren't given a fair chance to succeed. A friend recently shared a story about a rock star Black woman he hired for his sales team. During the interview process, her talent, energy, and passion were undeniable, and they made her an offer without reservation. A year later he admitted he thought they made a mistake because she wasn't keeping up with her peers. I asked him, "Is she the only woman of color on your team? Is this the first time you're noticing this? Have you asked her what's going on and why she isn't meeting her goals or your expectations?" He said he checked in with her, and when it seemed that everything was fine, he let it go.

"You can't let it go," I told him. "Being the only woman of color on a team can feel lonely and challenging. As a manager of underrepresented talent, it is your job to provide critical, real-time advice and to show care for their growth and development. You have to dig deeper to build relationships and understand the obstacles she may be facing, especially because they're likely not part of your own repertoire of experiences. What are the barriers to her success that may be invisible to you? What, if anything, is preventing her from reaching her full capacity?"

We all need to know what's expected of us and how success will be measured; otherwise, you're left with career-damaging assumptions. Imagine if teachers told their students what contributed to their final grade at the *end* of the school year, and said, "Oh, by the way, all those test scores didn't matter. I'm grading you on how much you spoke up in class." When the rules of the game keep on changing, only those who have access to and the support from the game makers can succeed.

That's what's happening in the workplace. Many managers see performance as either meeting expectations or not—you're either great at what you do or you're missing the mark—but the truth is far from that. Factors such as microaggressions, double standards, and bias affect the sense of belonging and performance of BIPOC, women, LGBTQIA+, and other marginalized employees. Research has repeatedly shown that standard talent management practices such as performance reviews and promotional decisions remain stubbornly in favor of men in the workplace, with women of color receiving less support and more vague performance feedback.

Research has found that underrepresented employees often get passed over for promotion not because of lack of merit but because their managers failed to cultivate them. BIPOC are thwarted by ill-equipped, not necessarily ill-intentioned, managers who are often uncomfortable giving critical or constructive feedback across elements of difference (race, gender, nationality). There are those who either don't provide timely feedback, or when they do, it's so muddled in fear that it doesn't come across as feedback at all and those who fail to see barriers to equity for their team members and their responsibility to eliminate those barriers. More specifically, BIPOC employees' careers suffer from a:

- Lack of unbiased feedback from managers;
- Lack of performance management tools;
- Lack of individualized development opportunities;
- Lack of equal pay;
- Lack of internal support and confidants; and
- Lack of honest conversations.

There are always other forces at play. If my friend had probed more with his direct report, he may have discovered that the work might not be challenging enough for her or there might not be enough face-to-face interaction with customers. Or there could have been something else beneath the surface. Sales is very quantitative—she wasn't hitting her numbers—but she was one of the few, if only, Black women on the team. What was the story behind those numbers? Was she being assigned high-growth clients commensurate with those of her peers? Was she having a more challenging time closing clients because they didn't want to work with a Black person? Was something going on in her personal life prohibiting her from being fully present? Was she afraid to ask questions for fear of seeming incapable—a common challenge for Black employees who have long known that they have to "work twice as hard to get half as far" as their white counterparts?

But he didn't ask these questions, and this high-potential, Black, female rock star left the company. No, not just the company, she left because her manager and peers didn't recognize the systemic hurdles she was facing and did nothing to clear away those obstacles. In these situations "color-blind" management—or pretending that racism doesn't exist—pushes out BIPOC staff.

This happens everywhere. Despite all it has said, done, and invested, in the fall of 2020 Google again was the subject of public outrage over a racialized incident. Google had fired a prominent AI ethics researcher, Timnit Gebru, a Black woman who criticized the ethical and societal impacts of the technology and the company's lackluster DEI efforts. In an internal email to employees, CEO Sundar Pichai said, "We need to accept responsibility for the fact that a prominent Black, female leader with immense talent left Google unhappily. This loss has had a ripple effect through some of our least represented communities, who saw themselves and some of their experiences reflected in Dr. Gebru's" (Elias 2019).

To say this triggered me is an understatement. I was brought back to the months after I left Google, when a colleague called to say that she named me as a regrettable loss in a presentation about the high turnover of executives of color in the organization. To her surprise, one white male executive lifted his head up with a questioning look and said, "I didn't know Daisy left." I and so many others had left quietly. I can't speak to others' motives, but I chose not to answer the dozens of calls I received from journalists wanting to know why I "really left Google." I knew that if I spoke out, I would only be leaving a mess for the friends and colleagues, mostly BIPOC, who would be tasked with handling the repercussions and quieting everything down. I knew, at that time, it would only be a short-lived story that would weigh on the wrong people. The Latinx and Black employees in the company knew what I had done for our communities and felt my loss. But I was not ready to make a statement about why I left Google.

I am proud of Timnit for speaking up, and of the many Googlers who stood beside her. @GoogleWalkoutforRealChange circulated a petition calling on the company to strengthen its commitment to research integrity, stating, "Instead of being embraced by Google as an exceptionally talented and prolific contributor, Dr. Gebru has faced defensiveness, racism, gaslighting, research censorship, and now a retaliatory firing."

No public apologies were made. This wasn't a solo decision, and the world needed to hear from the entire organization. Following an internal investigation, the company announced that it would increase resources for retaining and promoting employees, addressing disputes among workers and managers, and evaluating the performance of vice presidents on diversity and inclusion goals. These bare minimum changes were already in effect or had been advocated for years, albeit poorly managed. Like many organizations, Google has lost immensely talented BIPOC professionals and leaders repeatedly. The difference now was the public outcry and moment of global reckoning.

It's a basic premise: when an employee doesn't see a future at their company and doesn't feel that they belong there—for a myriad of reasons from lack of promotions to everyday exclusions—they will look for opportunities elsewhere. More than 93% of millennials of all races left their employers the last time they changed roles, noting only 7% took a new position within the same company, according to a Gallup study, and Black employees in general are 30% more likely to leave than white employees. Here are the factors that lead to flight:

- Lack of opportunities to learn and grow;
- Poor quality of manager;
- Poor quality of management;
- Lack of interest in the type of work;
- Lack of opportunities for advancement;
- Lack of access to senior leadership; and
- Racial prejudice and microaggressions.

As a manager, it's your job to eliminate these barriers, help people see their future, and help them get there. It's not a pipeline issue, it's a progression issue. Because the workplace is not equal for everyone and the everyday experiences and opportunities can be drastically different based on who you are, where you came from, and what you look like, it's the combination of providing the right runway for each person and nurturing talent along the way that will lead to an inclusion revolution.

So where to begin? First, look deeper into the factors that lead to racial disparities on your teams and work toward reducing them. You'll have to master the dance between the macro and the micro. The mark of a great leader is understanding people in their infinite complexity, challenging them with a bolder vision of what is possible, and inspiring the best work of their lives. Additionally, great managers help their team members overcome obstacles and sometimes address uncertainty at work and in their personal lives. It's creating a culture of transparent performance assessment, fair and equitable treatment, meaningful compensation philosophies, and effective communication. Phew! I know that's a lot, so let's break down how to revolutionize your performance management and be that great boss people will be talking about for years to come:

Step 1: Get to know your team.
Step 2: Remove bias from performance evaluations.
Step 3: Ensure transparency in the goal-setting and promotion process.
Step 4: Create individual growth plans.
Step 5: Provide ongoing performance feedback.
Step 6: Pay fairly.

Step 1: Get to Know Your Team

Growing leaders can't start early enough. Who are they? What makes them tick? What are their strengths? What are their derailers? The foundation of performance management is understanding the nuances of the individuals on your team! It's about the people, people. Advice on being a good manager is ubiquitous. Still it often fails to specify that women on your team may need help taking credit for their ideas, or that BIPOC may not feel comfortable sharing their ideas in a meeting unless encouraged. Strengths are often obvious; it's figuring out what's holding someone back that has the potential to unleash real magic.

What do you know about the people on your team? And I mean, what do you really know about their intellectual curiosity and their state of well-being and mental health? Do you know what charges them up, what drains them, and what's important to them? At your next one-on-one, or even better, at a lunch, coffee, or tea break, start by asking one of these questions: What are your favorite things to work on? What would you like to learn if you had more time? Tell me about a time that you went to work and shared an experience from work with a friend or family member.

Think of these conversation starters: What would you do if you had a free day to spend on anything you would like? What do you usually do for lunch or when you get a rare break in the day? You'll be surprised by how much you help your team members feel at ease. What they share can be very telling about what they value, what holds them back, what they appreciate, and what they fear or dislike about work, all leading to a stronger sense of trust and belonging.

I often start my leadership meetings with a prompt to enhance our sense of community and to help everyone bring joy to our work. I've asked everything from: What is one thing that brought you joy this past week? What is the thing that you just can't get to now that is causing you angst? Tell us a short story about who you were at age 10? The creative-minded on my team always jump to it. The more introverted labor over their response. But they all join at the right pace for them, often sharing laughter and a sense of discovery when we learn things about each other.

That sense of psychological safety has taken time to build. People have a hard time being vulnerable and sharing what they believe is potentially harmful information. In many organizations, let's call them "bobblehead" organizations, everyone bobs their head all day. No one is going to share their innermost fears and dreams unless they're safe to do so. If bobblehead behavior is what's rewarded in your organization, that's what you'll get. You'll miss out on taking worthwhile risks, getting creative, and finding opportunities to grow. The best thing you can do, whether from the very beginning or if you're going to start now, is to genuinely demonstrate interest in your people, to share with them what you're asking them to share with you—your wishes, vulnerabilities—and to be consistent with what you promise and how you honor their frankness.

Regular check-ins prevent workers from checking out, says the EY Belonging Barometer report, which found that 39% of respondents, across gender and age, say that when colleagues check in with them about how they are doing, both personally and professionally, they feel a greatest sense of belonging at work. Across all generations, the check-in took priority over actions such as: public recognition (23%), being invited to out-of-office events (20%), being asked to join a meeting with senior leaders (14%), and being included on emails with senior leaders (9%) (Twaronite 2019).

There's no fixed equation for how much time you should spend with your team members, but it should be a significant portion of your week, every week, consistently. Not surprisingly, employees who regularly meet with their managers are more likely to feel informed and engaged. "It's your job to build your people," says Sherice Torres, vice president, marketing, Facebook. "When people say to me, 'Oh, this coaching and HR stuff is taking too much of my time,' guess what? That is your job now. To me, the best managers are only spending 20 to 30 percent of their time as an individual contributor or creating deliverables. The vast majority of your time is coaching and building your people and coaching and building your competencies to better coach and build your people" (Torres 2020).

Beyond rote agenda items and to-dos, check-ins should incorporate a feeling assessment, too. At Sprinklr, a customer experience management platform, managers focus on happiness questions in their one-on-ones: How happy are you, and what would it take to make you happier? To quantify it, they use a happiness scale to level set the data: employees are asked to rate their happiness level on a scale of one to ten, and then to discuss what it would take to make it a ten. Additionally, managers have daily "heartbeat calls" with team members. They also use an employee engagement tool that they developed to track employee satisfaction with their programs (*Authority Magazine* 2021).

You also want to better understand each team member's career aspirations and goals, and acknowledge that your BIPOC employees may face different hurdles. According to Gallup, employees who work with their managers to discuss performance development goals are four times as likely to be engaged in the job. Besides the vital one-on-one time, every employee on your team should do a self-review. Employee self-assessments are a great way to start and to codify mutually agreed-upon goals. What do you want to do? How do you want to feel? Where do you want to grow? How can we make your work goals more connected to your personal and professional aspirations?

Step 2: Remove Bias from Performance Evaluations

Dismantling racial bias is a critical factor in the fight for workplace equality. Racial bias is often the most damaging in the growth and development of employees. Many companies have invested in impressive leadership development programs for good reason—it's key to their competitive growth and adaptability in fast-changing markets. It increases engagement and commitment when employees see pathways for growth. But what happens when future leaders' development plans or road maps laden with racial bias? We get the outcomes we currently see in organizations.

Katica Roy, Founder of Pipeline Equity, has found in her research that for every 100 men promoted or hired to a managerial position, only 72 women are promoted or hired (Roy 2020). The gap widens when intersected with race and ethnicity. Only 58 Black women are promoted to manager for every 100 men, and only 68 Latinas are promoted to manager for every 100 men. The big picture is that almost 90% of the Fortune 500 CEOs are still white males. They held 96.4% of the Fortune 500 CEO positions in 2000. Today, only 1% of the Fortune 500 CEOs are African Americans, 2.4% are East Asians or South Asians, and 3.4% are Latinx.

Organizations such as Management Leadership for Tomorrow (MLT), Code 2040, Girls Who Code, the Emma Bowen Foundation, among many others, have long provided a playbook for underrepresented talent to ascend from high school, college, or graduate school to the professional ranks. Their theory of change is predicated on surrounding BIPOC talent with support networks of peers and mentors who can provide the professional experience and social capital necessary for success. These programs do a wonderful job harnessing talent, but they don't always change the hearts and minds of the people they will be interacting with on a daily basis in the institutions where they study, train, and work.

Managers influence their employee's motivations, morale, and career path perhaps most powerfully during the performance review cycle. More than half of a performance rating reflects the rater's own characteristics, not those of the person being rated, according to *Harvard Business Review* (Buckingham and Goodall 2021). This well-studied phenomenon is called the idiosyncratic rater effect. Katica also shared that only 46% of women (vs. 51% of men) believe promotion criteria are fair and objective. While 42% of companies check for bias in reviews and promotions by gender, only 18% track outcomes for the compounding bias of race *and* gender.

Be aware of personal or institutional biases on expectations of performance. Because even if you're not keeping track, those who work for you are. Understand that how people approach their work varies based on their influences, experiences and education or training. Did the person meet the performance expectations but just in a different way than you anticipated or would have done it yourself? It's imperative to monitor performance at the same level and standard, regardless of racial or gender identity, and to monitor your own performance in managing others. For example, ask yourself:

- Who are the people on your team whom you regularly offer an extra helping hand?
- Which team members do you grant the benefit of the doubt when mistakes are made?
- Who do you push to meet with on a regular basis?

If you're not answering everyone (or no one), bias may be at play.

To ensure BIPOC talent is not left behind, understand and address these four common biases that can sneak up in performance reviews as shared in Culture Amp's "Performance Management Post-Covid-19: Biases to Consider" (Dorniak-Wall 2020):

Recency Bias: "What have you done for me lately?" It's true; most of us are more likely to remember things that have happened recently than things that have occurred throughout the entire year or quarter, i.e. your performance cycle.

Do this: Gather your notes on what they achieved and how they achieved it throughout the year. To better track their deliverables, you may ask an employee to fill out a form highlighting their achievements and areas of development or use a platform like Lattice that helps you track performance reviews, goals, and one-on-one meeting agendas.

And if you further want to ensure your manager fairly tracks your performance, create your own tracking tool. For my one-on-ones with my boss, I draft an update that covers the following: a personal check-in, top outcomes for the week, and items for discussion (tasks/projects to discuss/shared updates on). I use a Google doc that we both track so that she and I can revisit updates throughout the year. During my last performance review, she commented on how useful it was to revisit my progress through this tool. These tools can also provide a forum for celebrating success, asking for help when needed, and temperature checks on how people feel.

Proximity bias: We tend to favor what is familiar to us. And if you work remotely or with a geographically dispersed team, it's easy to discount work and people you do not regularly see.

Do this: I'll repeat it, managers should regularly schedule check-ins with their direct reports to keep a close eye on their productivity and well-being.

Confirmation bias: This bias is based on our perception of others. In "Four Unconscious Biases That Distort Performance Reviews," Steffen Maier (2016) shares that a white male manager may assume that white male employees are more assertive. "This could cause them to more easily recall instances in which they asserted their position during a meeting. On the other hand, they may perceive their Asian female team members to be less assertive, predisposing them to forget when they suggested an effective strategy or were successful in a tough negotiation."

Do this: Conduct frequent one-on-ones (yes, I've said it again, weekly check-ins are necessary), consider and integrate 360 feedback from cross-team collaborators, and consider self-evaluations.

Gender and intersectional bias: We know from intersectional studies that bias isn't binary to race or gender. So how does it show up in performance reviews? A woman can experience compounded biases across multiple aspects of their identity, including race, sexual orientation, age, and disability. In a study by Catalyst, a respondent, who is African American, was once told in a performance review that her hair was "too fun" and that it made people question her maturity (Catalyst 2020b). Through analyzing more than 25,000 pieces of peer feedback, Culture Amp has found that feedback about women tends to focus more on their personality and behavioral attitudes and for men on their accomplishments (Culture Amp n.d.).

If you're tempted to use the words "compassionate," "helpful," or "organized" to describe a woman or BIPOC member of your team, reflect a bit more. What kind of leadership skills have they demonstrated? If Jewel mentored new hires whose performance was significantly accelerated, instead of saying, "She's incredibly accommodating," you could say she "leads by example," or "is an ingenious leader."

Managers should keep in mind: The best leaders inspire leadership in others. Hierarchies and white male supremacy both create unfair and low expectations on women and BIPOC staff. White men are groomed for leadership by our culture, from birth. Women and BIPOC are gaslighted into being grateful for being begrudgingly allowed into spaces where white men assume they don't belong and are rarely groomed for leadership.

Do this: Ensure that you're training managers to deliver fair and constructive feedback. Help your managers consistently approach each review by defining specific, measurable goals for their teams. How well and how often did this employee produce expected deliveries, or went beyond expectations? Did this employee achieve their goals, projects, and priorities this year? If they didn't, why not? What could be standing in their way? When you concentrate on performance, accomplishments, and "the how," your behaviors, you diminish potential biases inherent in racial, ethnic or personality perceptions.

In 2021, The National Center for State Courts embarked on a research project to better understand implicit bias among judges and how it affected court decisions. They found that biased judgments were more likely when the basis for judgment is somewhat vague or subjective—situations without much precedent or involved new laws (Elek and Miller 2021).

The triggers that affected the judges' performance and led to bias included: stress (a heavy backlog, threats to safety, political pressure, loud construction noise), fatigue (long hours, lack of support), and time pressure. It's hard to make complex decisions quickly when you can't process all the incoming information fairly. "Decision makers who are rushed, stressed, distracted, or pressured are more likely to apply stereotypes—recalling facts in ways biased by stereotypes and making more stereotypic judgments—than decision makers whose cognitive abilities are not similarly constrained," the report stated.

To counteract this widespread problem, beyond the obvious factors of getting more sleep, trying to slow down, and be more present, there was a call for judges to articulate their reasoning process. When judges took the time to write down why they were making a decision before announcing it, they could assess the validity of the ruling with an eye for implicit bias. Taking that extra step to check your response or decision, handwriting or typing your reasoning, and then evaluating the decision can mitigate rash moves driven by bias. Could you imagine writing this: "I passed Tiffany Dufu over for a promotion because I don't deem her professional enough because of her wardrobe and accessories." I'm betting you won't be that brutally honest with yourself, but if you want to dismantle long-standing inequities in your workplace, you should.

Here's a mindful exercise to try in your daily life. Before you make a decision at work—whether it's asking someone to step in as a hand model for a video shoot or deciding who to nominate to speak at a conference—pause to reflect on any assumptions you may have made. Try to evaluate the perception and intention in your decision: Would I have made this same decision if this person were a man, a woman, BIPOC, white, straight, LGBTQIA+, a mom, someone who lived in the suburbs, someone from the South?

For instance, people assumed Tiffany Dufu wasn't professional enough because of her jewelry, and managers constantly assume a new mother would not want to travel to a conference because she has a young child at home. Inaccurate, biased, and preconceived notions that businesses started by Black founders fail have led to a tremendous lack of funding for Black venture capitalists (1% out of the $150 billion in US venture investment in 2020) and a high rate of loan rejection.

Assumptions do not lead to diverse, equitable, and inclusive workplaces. Assumptions based on stereotypes will only come back to bite you. You need to recognize and outsmart assumptions that close the door on people's ambitions, innovation, and careers.

Step 3: Ensure Transparency in the Goal-Setting and Promotion Process.

Too often, I've seen raises, discretionary incentives, and promotions were dependent on who the boss liked, related to, identified with, and socialized with. This is bias. Or I've seen the promotion go to the team member with the most recent wins versus those who steadily deliver over the year without fanfare. Or sometimes, the promotion went to the most demanding person. That is, the white male employee who is more often lauded as ambitious versus BIPOC female-identifying employees who are more prone to being accused of not being a team player or not willing to wait their turn. That's lazy leadership. To most employees, the promotion process is too obscure: Is it based on timing? Simply asking for it? Budget? Actual merit?

This subjectivity and bias must stop. When it comes to career advancement, there must be well-defined, clear pathways for career progression and benchmarks for promotions, pay raises, and other incentives; otherwise, you can fall into the same "favoring those I like" anti-inclusive habits. No one should feel that they're being passed over for a promotion—they should understand what is necessary to be considered for the next level.

Higher education is notoriously transparent about what it takes to get to be eligible for a promotion for administrative positions. Purdue University, for example, posts clearly on its website that: "Staff promotions take place twice a year. Approved promotions go into effect January 1 and July 1. January 1 promotions must be submitted to the VP of Human Resources by November 1 and July 1 promotions must be submitted by March 31" (Purdue University HR n.d.) Most companies aren't this routine, but you can let your team know that promotion reviews happen in X month because that's when budgets are decided and you have to put forth any promotion proposals by X date.

Then, be clear about what it takes. To assess promotion readiness, Purdue presents this evaluation criteria:

- Skill set (ensuring their skill set matches the requirements of the position);
- Sustained performance (high performance levels in at least the two most recent review cycles);

- Demonstrated steps taken to gain new skills and continue to grow in their career; and
- Personal motivation and willingness for an increase in level and responsibility.

These organizational guidelines are a great start, but even better is to sit down with each employee on your team and clearly define specifics under each bullet; otherwise, it's still subjective and ripe for interpretation. Which skills are required? What does high performance mean? What does it mean to champion culture? How do you expect someone to demonstrate willingness to learn and grow? How are you measuring motivation? Setting your employees up for success with opportunities to grow their skills takes time, effort, and budget. This is how you transform workplace culture and business outcomes. Consistent measurement around established performance criteria enables you to equitably disseminate information about what is expected of all employees to get a raise, get promoted, or develop their skills. Then, there are no surprises.

At Endeavor, a global talent management company, as part of their talent management practices, they established a promotion process whereby they look at each role and show what is required to be promoted. "This allows for equity, eliminates the unwritten rules of success at companies, and what that might mean for an individual in their career trajectory," says Alicin Reidy Williamson, Endeavor's senior vice president and chief inclusion officer (Williamson 2020).

To create a fair promotion and performance management process, you have to (1) establish transparent, measurable, and time-bound goals and (2) assess each individual against these metrics—what they achieve and how they do so. That's it! But, unsurprisingly, it's not that simple. How you assess the individuals is where ambiguity creeps in. It might be tempting to think we can just trust our instincts. But we've learned about where that can lead us with recruitment processes, haven't we? The hard truth is that implicit bias is masterful at creeping in all the time, and it's really difficult to see and therefore stop it in its tracks. The secret weapon: data. Using well-developed, engaging, and flexible performance management tools and processes help bypass imperfect and often compromised impressions—and enable you to be in lockstep with your teams and deliver on your aspirations of fairness.

Fortune 500 companies largely have formalized performance management processes, but many suffer flaws from collecting data that place too much weight on opaque, arbitrary, and biased ratings. Too often, fuzzy reasoning for evaluation is used to excuse ongoing advancement gaps regarding race, gender, and other marginalized identities.

Performance management platforms such as Culture Amp and 15five offer useful guides and tools for delivering structured performance conversations and capturing the data. Try asking: How did you produce quality and powerful results in your day-to-day life? How have you demonstrated key characteristics or company values (insert: teamwork and collaboration, inclusion, and belonging)? What, if anything, is hanging you up right now?

Tools such as Factorial can help you evaluate employee performance through customized questionnaires. To improve manager effectiveness and inclusivity, you can also use Employment Hero, which uses peer-to-peer recognition and user happiness surveys to help you communicate with your team. GE has seen the benefit of ceasing year-end performance reviews to establish a continuous dialogue around goals and accountability. They launched an internal app that allows for a constant exchange of feedback through voice memos, quick text notes, and attached documents between all members of a team—not just the traditional boss-subordinate relationships. Think of it like a 24/7 Evernote job tracker. This tremendous amount of data collection helps to inform and inspire GE's annual goal-setting conversations, which make them more meaningful, engaging, robust, and collaborative.

Step 4: Create Individual Growth Plans

Take the time to figure out what your employees need to be ready, and what you as a manager can offer your team to help them achieve to their fullest capacity. That will help you develop strong leaders who find meaning in their work. How you manage the complexity of different experiences, backgrounds, thinking, and communication styles in a team will be the key to creating a trusting, inclusive environment required to unlock the full potential of your teams. Good performance management is developing a personalized plan: What will it take for *this person* to advance, grow, and get promoted? And how do we achieve that together?

Thought starters:

- What talent is needed for growth, and how do we best use our talent?
- What emotional and tactical skills and training do our managers, leaders, and teams need to better support our business and culture strategy?
- How are we developing these skills across our teams?

Then, consider leadership potential versus readiness. Those who are deemed "ready" are most often granted the promotion, access, opportunity. Being "twice as good" is only half the battle. The other half is overcoming the unmerited success of mostly white men whose potential is assumed and not questioned nearly as much as it is for BIPOC employees. To address bias in the velocity and rate at which BIPOC, women, LGBTQIA+ and other traditionally underrepresented employees are hired and promoted versus their peers, you must also examine your assumptions in their potential and readiness to succeed. I have never hired an executive who had all the competencies desired for their role. Beyond making a bet based on their past experiences and qualifications, I've pushed hiring managers to consider the unintended consequences of BIPOC and female candidates not having the same access and opportunities as their white male counterparts. This is where clarity on developing future competence in leadership roles comes in.

Leadership potential may not automatically or necessarily develop into leadership growth. In a study about leadership potential versus readiness, Frances Jackson and Emma Hansen (2016) note that an employee's potential is judged on their motivations, development orientation, and their ability to master complexity, among other attributes needed for strategic and executive roles.

Leadership readiness is focused on the here and now—tomorrow, next week, or maybe next year as a stretch goal to reach. Readiness requires a willingness to lead and deliver results, ability to bring others along and navigate ambiguity, and qualities such as authenticity, confidence, learning agility, and flexibility.

To close the gap for those on your team between having leadership potential and being ready to be promoted:

- Encourage your employees to move toward readiness. Some of your employees may already have well-defined ambitions but may not know how to get started or what supporting mechanisms may be available to them. Other employees may need more encouragement and a "Hey, I've been impressed with your professional growth this past year, and I'm curious, what would you like to do next?"
- Offer those exciting stretch roles that help employees see themselves beyond their current boundaries. This is not just about adding more work, although sometimes that's what it feels like, but about enabling them to expand their networks, skill sets, and organizational knowledge.
- Facilitate coaching. At Culture Amp, each employee has access to a professional coach through the Coaching for Everyone program. Coaches help assess where a person is and wants to be and then guide each person through a strategy to reach their goals. As a manager, you can also be your team member's best coach in key developmental moments.
- Do a gut check. Ask your boss or whomever is in charge of approving promotions for feedback on your employee: What are their initial impressions? Do they think he or she is ready and has potential? If not, why? When you have that knowledge, you can help your team members fix it.
- Be wary of the "prove-it-again" bias. Women of color, especially in male dominated fields such as science and technology, continually report that they have to provide more evidence of competence than their white male peers. We give more weight to a man's potential than his actual performance. This is especially true for BIPOC employees. To reduce this bias, focus on potential and detail their accomplishments.

To continually check for biases that creep in when determining someone's trajectory, start with the facts. For each person on your team, identify the top skill/attribute that could make them leadership ready. Pinpoint either something that would have a significant impact on this person's career trajectory or something they are motivated to work on. Based on what you learned, offer opportunities for training and coaching. Be proactive in your approach to make that happen—research has shown that 40% of employees who receive poor job training leave their positions within the first year. If you're fortunate enough to have an HR business partner and a learning and development department at your company, reach out and partner with them to deliver programs for your team members. If not, you can design your own development planning approach based on the growth aspirations of your team members.

Most established companies already offer training and professional development classes internally or budget for external courses. Encourage your team to take advantage of these—you should, too! Pixar University offers required training and optional classes for different disciplines to ensure learning is part of the company culture; "Etsy School" offers classes such as navigating a difficult conversation. When I worked at Google courses varied from coding 101 to enhancing managerial effectiveness (Culture Amp n.d. b).

That's the easy part. More often, someone needs not just raw skills to succeed. There are always invisible promotion requirements: no one will write, "Having a senior level sponsor or advocate will seal the deal for your career path." As a manager, if you know that visibility is essential, what are the next steps to secure cross-department support or mentorship? That's where individual coaching can identify leadership opportunities and performance derailers. Slack, for instance, has a program called Rising Tides, a six-month sponsorship program for a diverse group of emerging leaders who have historically lacked support. Program participants receive career development training, executive coaching, and one-on-one sponsorship with a Slack executive team member, focusing on building a supportive community of peers (Slack Blog 2019).

I have personally benefited from coaching throughout my career. Some coaches were assigned for a discrete period as part of a leadership development program. Some coaches were folks I had sought out myself, to accelerate my growth and development. They have helped me understand my derailers, internal bullies, beasts, or burdens—those that exist and those that I made up. I learned that corporate coaching could be critical to the long-term success of your team members and to your company as a whole.

You can address disparities in how resources and opportunities are distributed in your organization. If you bring a race consciousness lens to common assumptions about leadership and professional development, you can avoid falling into unconscious stereotyping. Once you educate yourself on the unique obstacles your diverse colleagues are facing, you can become a better manager at working to erase historic and systemic barriers. In some cases, your diverse colleagues may have lacked learning opportunities, or experienced an anti-inclusive workplace earlier in their careers. It's imperative to ask more profound questions and to look closer to understand underlying issues. For example, historically, Black women don't like to ask for help at the risk of seeming weak, so as a manager, it's up to you to say, "What are the barriers to your success here, and how can I help you?" Or, more broadly, "No one on this team needs to suffer in silence . . . my door is always open for any question, and you will never be judged for asking one."

Step 5: Provide Feedback—Always

When I think back to that rock star employee on my friend's sales team, without throwing my friend under the bus, it seemed that she wasn't receiving consistent feedback. And it didn't seem as if she was offered support until after her annual sales tanked. She was blindsided.

She's not alone. It won't surprise you that giving feedback is high on a manager's "don't want to do it" list, and so they tend to skip it entirely. Dr. Carla Jefferies of the University of Southern Queensland discovered that people fail to give constructive feedback to protect themselves, not others (Jarrett 2012). It's natural to want to avoid an uncomfortable conversation or hurt another person's feelings, but the ramifications of feedback avoidance are too high. That person sitting in ignorant bliss will never have the chance to understand what they could be doing better until it's often way too late—they get passed over for a promotion or even are the first on the list to be let go. I had to let go of a seasoned Black manager once whose look of surprise still haunts me. When he asked, "What can I do differently?" I said, "I'm afraid there's not much you can do now. Your story here has already been written, and it's too late to change the narrative. My hope is that in your next role, you are given a fair chance to shine and that you ask for and are provided with the feedback you deserve, when it matters."

While it may feel easier at the moment to cut your losses, it's imperative to work with someone to grow and develop them—I can't say it enough, talent is the most important resource of any organization. In 2014, Jack Zenger and Joseph Folkman (2018) surveyed workers, and 92% of the respondents agreed with the assertion, "Negative (redirecting) feedback, *if delivered appropriately*, is effective at improving performance." Only 8% didn't want to hear it. When managers fear that giving feedback to someone that doesn't look like you will be misinterpreted as racist or sexist, it perpetuates an even greater cycle of avoidance. In HR, too often, I see managers fail to be honest with their BIPOC and female team members on what their strengths are and—crucially—where they need to fill gaps or build their skills.

Performance management conversations tend to raise the anxiety level of both manager and employees, but if properly carried out, they can make all the difference. For instance, I once worked with someone who was very stubborn and often argued with his colleagues. My job as his manager was to call it out and address it in a manner that would be well received on his end. In situations such as these, always think bigger: What is the goal of improving a skill? It's not about softening the blow but instead focusing on your core message and what you hope he takes away from the conversation. What do you want to happen next? Focus on the behavior or the action, not feelings, and give examples. "I noticed you didn't want to incorporate Breanna's changes into the proposal, which created tension in the meeting" would be likelier to get the results we'd want, versus, "You are being stubborn."

There's always a chance that someone won't take feedback well, but it shouldn't stop you from having the conversation—it's your job. The kindest thing to do is to give someone the right feedback at the right time, even if it unleashes a whole wealth of emotions. I've seen this too, the bias of kindness, when you enable people in your organization to wander from role to role, often failing miserably in each, because you simply won't come face-to-face with the discomfort of telling them the truth about their performance. I've seen this happen to BIPOC employees, where a white manager can't bear the social risk of being the one to let them go but won't offer the genuine kindness of constructive feedback. All around them, their colleagues often complain quietly that they do not pull their weight in team projects, but no one is willing to give them the feedback BIPOC staff deserve. Least of all, their managers.

At VICE Media Group, the source of many employee complaints was the inability to give and receive effective feedback. We know from neuroscience that receiving negative feedback can instigate a fight-or-flight response. We also know that managers are not generally effective at providing performance feedback, much less with a lens on interpersonal bias. So we offered feedback training, which included concrete tools to de-bias feedback.

We sent periodic nudges, sought out the "social influencers" in teams to sell the value of good feedback, and our own CEO acknowledged publicly her efforts to improve on her feedback. And then we reported on ourselves whenever we missed the mark. At one point we were transparent about our struggles, telling our teams, "Do you know that only 20% of managers have downloaded our Effective Feedback learning module? Come on. We can do better than that."

It comes down to authenticity and preplanning. If this person believes that you're coming from a genuine place of care and that your core message is aligned with the goals for career growth you've outlined together, the feedback should be taken more positively. Doing this work ahead of time helps you build purpose into what you're saying—this is not a gotcha moment or cause for reproach. There's so much mistrust and apprehension, and it's not wrong. But what's wrong is assuming every action is against us, and from a management perspective, not addressing that elephant in the room. If you notice someone getting defensive, call them in, especially if you're their manager. Say, "I understand this may have been your experience, but I am talking to you from a genuine place of care because I want to see you thrive."

Two tips: First, feedback is always best given in the moment. Second, find out how each member of your team likes to receive feedback. I know people eager for feedback and others who recoil over the slightest criticism. I have eight direct reports, and each needs to receive feedback differently based on their lived experiences, identities, and professional journeys. It took me months to get to know them and build trust with them so they knew my feedback was coming from a place of care, not just authority.

Ask for permission to kick off the conversations ("Is it okay if we talk about your performance, or a recent project, and share some feedback?")

Or turn the tables, and ask, "What do you think is going well? What do you think you could improve on in your relationships with your colleagues? Where do you think this is holding you back?" And always have a follow-up plan. Ask how you can be helpful, and decide when to revisit the topic. Keep checking in with the person to continue to garner trust and make sharing feedback even easier next time.

Trust is vital in any relationship, especially when delivering and receiving performance feedback. Women, BIPOC, LGBTQIA+, and members of other underrepresented groups often carry added pressure to prove their worth and value. Trust has not always been a two-way street for them. It has historically been weaponized against them. This often shows up when a woman or BIPOC is more quickly or harshly punished or criticized for making a mistake, especially compared to white males. That tiny margin of error is so punitive that they are barely able to make peace with their mistakes. They haven't experienced feedback that felt fair. As a manager, you are responsible to understand what is behind a team member's reluctance to share their weaknesses with you or explain a dip in performance versus jumping to their deficiencies. Get curious and ask: "Where did you feel you delivered the best results? What made that possible? Where did you most need support? Where do you think you'll need support moving forward? What does that look like?"

Prioritize purpose and meaning when having these conversations. Traditional performance management puts ratings evaluations at the center. Still, purpose and meaning are far more powerful in motivating employees than money and ratings, says talent management advisor Alan Colquitt, the former director of global assessment, workforce research, and organizational effectiveness at Eli Lilly (Galli 2017). When Alan worked at the company, monthly pulse surveys revealed a significant drop in engagement for 80% of employees following the annual performance review process. Worse, that drop stayed down for nearly half the year. So in 2017 Eli Lilly transformed its performance management process by eliminating an annual review and ratings system and shifted toward a model of ongoing check-ins on goals with a focus on learning and growth.

A cautionary word: there is a difference between intention and action, between thoughtful responses and performative acts of "kindness." White men and women have courted me for jobs, created roles for me, hired me, made important introductions, paraded me across organizations, mentored and sponsored me, but also held back when their support would have truly mattered. This made me feel like their support was performative—meant to make them feel like a "good" white person, but not meant to significantly advance my career.

For example, years ago, I was offered a role managing two functions and offered a barely 5% increase in salary. When I asked for an increase based on market rates for similar dual leadership roles, my white female manager rejected my request. Her patience wore thin with my reluctance to accept the offer and instead of meeting me halfway, she reprimanded me by saying, "You know how to play the game but refuse to do so. Why can't you just take this now and wait until your next turn." This was my turn! What else did I need to prove?

I had another white male boss who genuinely believed he was my biggest advocate and champion. Yet he hoarded data about how women and people of color were being mistreated across the organization, the information that I needed to create fairer working conditions for these employees.

I've also worked for BIPOC managers who at first seemed supportive, but in the end did not advocate for me as an act of self-preservation. They may have thought they were doing the right thing, but their actions told a different story.

Three Ways to Shake Up the Performance Review

A manager's role is to enable and amplify employee contributions that are of value to the organization, and those values and traits necessary for 21st century leadership are shifting. Humility, empathy, inclusivity, accountability, resiliency, transparency—that's what matters in today's economy! Build that in your development plans and performance review metrics.

1. **Gather feedback from multiple sources versus just one manager.** You can increase transparency and diversity of opinions by allowing employees to nominate who should provide feedback as part of their performance review. This can be within

their immediate team or cross-functionally. Note: We are all biased. Having more people evaluate performance doesn't make opinions less biased. But it does help you balance your own perspective.

2. **Use artificial intelligence (AI) tools to detect, mitigate, and remove bias from performance reviews.** AI-enabled solutions such as adverse impact analysis tools can detect potential discrimination across different employee stages. These insights can, in turn, help organizations take steps to address any demographic discrepancies. Note: Despite the great promise of AI, concerns remain that it can perpetuate or even increase biases in talent processes given it relies on data collected and developed by humans and is trained by machine learning created by humans. We must continuously test for weaknesses in the process of the tools that claim to eradicate bias and make adjustments as necessary.

3. **Emphasize allyship.** Author Kenji Yoshino (2020) shared in an interview that he has been working with one pharmaceutical company that wants to evaluate allyship as part of their performance review. Together, they are trying to determine the metrics of being a good ally in assessing performance outcomes. I have a hunch that their findings will show that allies who provide support, surface issues, or push for changes significantly reduce barriers to advancement and recognition for underrepresented employees.

Tips for Mitigating Bias in Performance Evaluations

Access resources to help you think through and manage your biases before launching into a performance management conversation. Google gives managers an unbiasing checklist to use during performance management. You can adapt this easily, and the key is ensuring consistency across all of your performance conversations. Here's how to do that based on The Management Center's (2021) "Three Ways to Mitigate Bias in Performance Evaluations":

1. **Use a performance management rubric.** These guides outline clear and consistent evaluation criteria that help you judge what matters. An effective rubric defines the standards against which the employee's performance (goals and results achieved, including supporting core values and behavioral expectations) will be assessed.

2. **Collect proof points and feedback to inform your assessment.** Avoid confirmation bias by filling out your review based on the information you gather about whether they did or did not meet expectations. Examples include project deliverables, how you've experienced their collaboration with others, and other key achievements. Seek out different perspectives from peers and others who generally interact with your team members to balance your own perspective.

3. **Be specific in your feedback.** There's nothing worse than receiving unclear feedback about your developmental opportunities. As I've noted in the previous chapter, men tend to receive more detailed feedback on competencies and technical skills. Women receive feedback about their relational skills, communication styles, and teamwork. It's no surprise, then, that men have far better chances to improve their outcomes and speed up their opportunities for advancement. Unbiased feedback reflects on results and the how of your achievements and not matters related to how someone identifies.

Step 6: Pay Fairly

We can't discuss performance management without talking about money. Communication about pay is the most critical element of compensation management, yet it is usually the weakest skill in a manager's tool kit. Although many companies have compensation philosophies in place, employees don't often receive communication about the details of these plans from those beyond top management and HR. Pay equity analysis, also called pay parity audits, are not yet standard across all organizations. Even in companies with clearly defined compensation practices, managers are not often trained on how to talk to employees about how compensation is determined.

Pay perception matters more than what is actually paid. Everyone just wants to know how their pay is determined, if it is fair and at or above market rates, and if their peers are earning the same. There is too much smoke and mirrors around compensation structures, which can lead employees to feel undervalued and underappreciated. Coupled with well-publicized stats about equal pay, employees often wonder, Am I being paid fairly?

Sometimes managers don't even know the complete compensation plans of their teams! First, you have to know your data—how much your people are being paid and if there are any differences in pay relative to age, race, gender, job levels, and other relevant criteria.

Next, get smart on your pay guidelines (pay ranges or pay grades) and how to communicate them to your teams. If you're a new manager, you may have inherited the salary structure for your team. Ask why are people paid the way they are. You're always going to compensate your top performers well, but who is determining who are your top performers? Who negotiated more? Who is delivering the most impact on your team?

Also, make sure your team has a clear understanding of the business fundamentals and company metrics. Does your company need to operate with a profit to consider pay increases? It seems obvious, but financial conditions of organizations are not always the same. The more you can do to demystify the pay process, the more you will build trust among your team.

Then, conduct a pay equity audit to close any wage gaps. You should aim to examine the factors of why someone is paid more or less than another. In the purest of cases, pay inequity is due to market competition and where you are coming from (and how much they paid you). For instance, a company may pay engineers in Silicon Valley more than in other cities because of the local competitive rates driven by Apple and Google.

More often, unequal pay arises when women and BIPOC are often punished for asking for raises and promotions, in part due to the bias of "you don't really belong here, so you should just be happy to have any job here."

When they ask for pay equity, they are often viewed as ungrateful. They can't always use the same strategies and affinity bias boost to get the same treatment as white men. This contributes to the systemic undervaluing of women and BIPOC in raises and promotions. In 2021, compared to each $1 earned by a white, non-Hispanic man, on average:

- Asian-American women earned $0.87;
- All women earned $0.82;
- African and Black American women earned $0.62;
- Native American women earned $0.60; and
- Latinas earned $0.55.

At Reddit, Ellen Pao (2019) reviewed all the pay bands for every position and then automatically highballed everyone—everyone got the max salary for each position. This eliminated inequality in salary by race and gender; however, some critics said that it deprived staff of chances to sharpen their negotiating skills (to which I respond, you should offer staff universal training on how to negotiate through companies such as Wager and then ensure that your managers apply fair practices when budgeting merit raises and promotions). Salesforce has notoriously done the same, as should all companies to ensure that BIPOC and women are paid the same as white men for the same positions.

Be clear with your teams: Say, "We are reviewing pay equity in our company, or how you compare against your peers in similar roles. We are hoping to create more fair and equal systems of compensation." You may not always be able to fix it. Maybe you don't have enough money in the bank to exceed market rates. Tell them that. Have the conversation. People want to know that their concerns are heard and that there is a plan to course-correct when possible. That's inclusion, that's fairness, that's leadership.

Your Road Map for Revolution

Managers are curators and stewards of an organization's shared purpose, climate, and culture. Ensure that your core talent processes, including performance management and promotions, support your DEI journey, especially your commitment to anti-racism. What will it take for BIPOC employees to succeed at your company? How can they get a promotion? Share that info. Be aware of the racial dynamics at your organization, and understand how this may be affecting a team member's performance or perceptions about their performance.

- **Get to know your team.** What are their goals? Aspirations? What do they need to learn? What could be holding them back? The better you understand how each team member works, the more you can create an environment where they can thrive.
- **Look for bias in performance reviews.** As we've discussed throughout the book, bias is unavoidable. Sharpen your awareness to know when you're making assumptions about someone's work or desire for new opportunities.
- **Define paths to advancement.** When it comes to career advancement, there must be well-defined, clear pathways for career progression and benchmarks for promotions, pay raises, and other incentives; otherwise, you can fall into "favoring those I like" anti-inclusive habits. Everyone should understand what is necessary to be considered for their next professional level.
- **Create individualized learning plans.** What will it take to get someone ready for the next level? Encourage BIPOC employees to take stretch opportunities. Don't penalize them for learning.
- **Don't be afraid to give feedback, especially for BIPOC employees who receive less support at work.** Without candid performance reviews, people don't have a chance to succeed. Confront your fear of feedback; otherwise, you could be holding someone back. Establish trust and explain that your feedback comes from a place of support and growth.
- **Run pay audits regularly.** Create an action plan to eliminate racial or gender inequity and have up-front and honest conversations when you cannot give someone the pay they expect.

9 | Build Support Scaffolding

Success is not a solo sport. Everyone needs support along their career path. Without it, you're operating at a deficit. Too often, marginalized folks lack support, while their white peers seem to have an unlimited safety net and crew of champions and cheerleaders. In the 1970s, Pope Consulting conducted a study at a pharmaceutical company where Black engineers were falling behind in their progress and deliverables compared to white engineers (Pope Consulting 2020). Well ahead of the times, rather than push out underperforming engineers, the staff hired a consultant to study the issue. Turns out, the closed social networks prevented Black engineers from getting the mentorship, peer advice, and support they needed to succeed. White managers were uncomfortable mentoring (or befriending) Black staff. Perhaps these managers tended to hire and cultivate staff that reminded them of themselves—that's affinity bias. And white peers were uncomfortable extending friendship to Black staff.

This social unease, lack of support, and sense of inequality profoundly affected performance. When new white engineers had questions, they just asked other white engineers and got on track immediately. Yet Black new hires were afraid of revealing what they didn't know and so went to the library to study what to do—losing valuable time and dramatically slowing their onboarding process and productivity. "Black employees told us that they were fearful of asking too many questions because it could reinforce a stereotype that they were less intelligent than their white counterparts," Pat Pope, CEO of Pope Consulting said. "After our study, it was clear that the informal systems of learning and development collapsed, so we told the company that they needed to formalize for their Black employees what the others get informally."

To address this, company leadership created a complete curriculum program for all employees and an onboarding training program for all hires that addressed the unique needs of new employees. Within a year they had permanently closed the achievement gap between Black and white engineers. "It was never an issue of talent, it was an issue of development and structural support," says Pope.

Not having a decoder ring was damaging their career future.

"Your counterpart will get opportunities, and you get a chance," says Lucinda Martinez, former EVP, Multicultural Marketing, Brand and Inclusion Strategy at Warner Media. "An opportunity comes with support. It's saying, 'Look, I want you to meet Maria, Maria is amazing. Give her insight into the culture. I'm about to give her a stretch role, but she could benefit from your help.' A chance is when you throw the person out there and hope that they make it, no phone calls are made. When you get a chance, it comes with no support, and if you make a mistake you're counted out. That's why people of color don't make it to the end. Your counterpart gets a pat on the back, you get a pat on the head" (Martinez 2020).

Your support system can make or break your career, from leading you to a new job to helping you succeed once you've entered the doors. Research from Professors Jennifer Merluzzi and Adina Sterling (2017a) found that Black employees are more likely to be promoted when referred by another employee by a factor of 1.2 compared to Black employees without a referral. That internal assurance—that willingness for someone to vouch for another—was required to deem a BIPOC employee promotable. Interestingly, they found that women received no benefit from being referred. The women at the firm they studied did receive statistically fewer regular promotions than men, but there was no difference in the data if a woman was referred. This could be because those referrals may come from people with less positional privilege or clout in the organization, a common finding in studies about mentoring women.

I'm curious about the organizational clout that these referrers may have compared to those referring male candidates. Was it a valid referral? Was someone bullishly advocating for them or merely giving a meh-recommendation? Were these women part of formal mentorship programs where senior leaders outside their direct management chain could credibly vouch on their behalf? The 2019 report "Being Black in Corporate America: An Intersectional Exploration" by Coqual (2021), formerly the Center for Talent Innovation, found that Black women were less likely to have access to the same support and advocacy as white women. The 2019 McKinsey "Women in the Workplace Report" found that for every 100 men who were promoted, only 72 women were promoted, only 68 Latina women, and only 58 Black women (Lean In and McKinsey & Company 2020). These numbers haven't changed for years. This lack of promotion compounds into poor retention rates, and thus your compositional diversity takes a hit—again.

So what can you do about it? First, think about the career support you have in your own life. I've found that workplace guidance comes in many forms or roles:

Your decoder ring: Learned knowledge of office politics, situational awareness;

Peer support: A career community that understands and guides you;

Connections: The people you know who lead you to opportunities and advice;

Mentorship and sponsorship: A Mentor is someone who provides career advice, guidance or coaching, while a sponsor is someone who advocates for you;

External advisors: Internal and external experts and leaders who help influence company culture for the better.

Think about which of these types of support you have personally and how they have been valuable to you. Next, as a manager, consider who on your team has relationships that check all these categories. Who has had access to fair and just opportunities for professional exposure and growth? Who is provided with coaching, mentorship, sponsorship, and other avenues of support to reach their career goals? From these questions, you can begin to figure out your biggest inclusion breakdowns and think about ways to solve them. If you're not sure, ask them. I often start my one-on-ones with, "How can I be of help to you?"

The unique struggles BIPOC and other marginalized employees experience run the gamut from having your presence, seniority, or expertise questioned to struggling with defining how to show up or speak up without seeming threatening or becoming overly exposed. Negative stereotyping and overt discrimination are part of the identity threats they face every day. And not seeing yourself represented in the organization or departments that you aspire to be in, well, that can be discouraging.

There are two types of action you can take. First, your contribution as a manager can facilitate these connections and set the tone for your team by participating or sponsoring events, mentoring someone different than you, communicating regularly with teams on the importance of DEI, and being a vocal supporter of professional development and inclusion of marginalized communities. There have been times I reflexively agreed to speak on a panel or in a company AMA (ask me anything) without thinking about who else on my team or network could benefit from the exposure. Assumptions and omissions can only come back to bite you.

Second, leverage your leadership to help establish and advocate for programs and policies that can build this scaffolding. This can come in the form of employee resource groups (ERGs), DEI councils, and mentorship programs. This is allyship on a broader scale—creating connections and opportunities that create a more positive work experience. Here's how you can help build more effective support systems.

1. Give Out Decoder Rings

As I progressed throughout my career, I was invited to join numerous leadership programs designed for women and BIPOC yet not as often considered for the traditional leadership grooming programs that seemed readily available for white men. When I would join these conventional leadership programs, it was as if I were entering these elite, social spaces with secret handshakes and codes. I was invited, but I didn't always feel welcomed. I appeased their progressive leanings and "savior" mentalities, but I was "bro'ed" out when it came to being "one of them." Invited to join but kept a comfortable distance. Why is that? Is it racism? Is it sexism? Did my presence cause anxiety because they had no clue how to engage with me? Why wasn't I asked to join before? Was it because my performance and potential was not deemed "high potential" enough, and by whom? Is it because of the dreaded Friends and Family program that keeps the same individuals in the same circles and jobs? I've often wondered how my career, and those of others like me considered "high potential diverse talent," could have been different should we have been routed through those programs and fully welcomed from the start?

It's no secret that every workplace has its own version of office politics, and you will be at a deficit if you don't have access to that nuanced "how to succeed at work" playbook that has been passed down for generations of white people. What we deem as succeeding, surviving really, requires navigational tools that we're often unaware exist, or are even available to us. As my friend Minda Harts says in her book, *The Memo*, "For so long I tried to fight the fact that there are rules to this getting ahead thing. No one sat me down and said, 'Hey girl, this is how you play the game. This is how *they* do it, and this is how *they* win" (Harts 2019). When I joined Time Warner, I called it a decoder ring. It was as if my white male and female colleagues were given a decoder to all things across the enterprise, and I was blindly making my way without a compass. You may not even recognize how well you navigate office politics because it comes so naturally to you—it's a subtle systemic challenge against equity in the workplace.

For many white professionals, career advice comes early from their parents and professionals in their networks. It continues through the connections made at coveted internships, personal relationships (remember the Friends and Family program), and exclusive social groups. I remember my mentor and thought leader on women in the workplace, Dr. Ella Bell, framing this for me. She said, "Daisy, it's quite simple. Many of us (referring to BIPOC) didn't grow up with a family for whom dinner table conversations were a time to discuss how to navigate workplace politics. Your colleagues did, and that's why they're far more confident in what to say, when to say it and to whom. You're just playing catch-up." Those relationships, that shorthand, facilitates mentorships and sponsorships, and opportunities.

For others, who may have been the first member of their family to go to a private college (raises hand), or who had parents without experience in the corporate world (raises hand again), they had to find their own way, often facing headwinds invisible to others.

On the come up: BIPOC managers and leaders have been building our own corporate equity for quite some time and are now in positions to call the shots, change the conditions, and create access and opportunity for those coming behind us. We know what it's like to be the first, and the mix of pride, pressure, and responsibility that comes with that. We are helping decode for others what took us years to figure out. How to bring our perspectives to the table while not having to carry the weight of being the only. How to hold a multiplicity of perspectives while acknowledging the shared experience of belonging to our communities. But we still conduct the same calculus very quickly—is it safe or not to have this conversation? Constantly worrying about raising "the race card" or speaking about how these things affect me because of my race. We are not as alone as when we started, but we're still battling systemic racism and all the isms.

As I mentioned in Chapter 5, buddy programs have proven to be beneficial for smoothing the onboarding process. But they rely on human capital and time, often at a premium. And if there is only one Black "vulture buddy," that person won't have time to think, let alone help someone else. You need a scalable option.

How to Be More Supportive: Revolutionize Your Employee Handbook

I know, you're probably thinking, Who reads the employee handbook? Isn't it a collection of mundane legalese about vacation policies, ethics, and other codes of conduct? Yes, that's true, but you also have an opportunity to create a document that offers the keys to success at your organization and helps your team understand the unwritten rules of your organization.

When I conducted founder training for Kapor Capital, I was promoting the power of an employee handbook, but their founding partner Freada Kapor was dubious. "Employee handbooks are terrible, no one reads them," she said. I agreed, but said that they only remain unread and dusty if you don't bring them to life. As shared in Project Include, an employee handbook sets out policies and practices as well as benefits. It can be an important tool for ensuring inclusion and belonging in the workplace. They shouldn't be simply about the legal implications, but more about the behavioral expectations. Project Include further advises transparency in expectations from the employee (behavior, norms, work product) and what employees should expect from their employer (culture, benefits, performance management). From a start-up to a Fortune 500, employee handbooks set expectations, allow you to reinforce why employees should work for you, and share the company's values and behavioral principles.

When done well, an employee handbook makes the implicit explicit. It lays out expected behavioral principles and best practices and decodes the cultural nuances. This means that you're not only explicitly sharing your codes of conduct, anti-discrimination, and anti-harassment policies, for example, but also referring to these in ongoing conversations with your team members. At VICE, we prioritized updating our employee handbook by creating "code of conduct and respect in the workplace" policies in my first year to clearly outline what it takes to succeed in the organization and the specific behaviors we wanted to encourage and discourage. We intentionally included a section on microaggressions with instructions on how to address or combat them, guidance on gender pronouns, and shared multiple channels for raising concerns. It states what's expected of employees regarding behaviors of decency and respect. It's not just what you're saying but how you're saying it.

One of the best examples I've seen comes from the tech and gaming company Valve, which shares everything from company philosophy and onboarding to performance and hiring principles. What stands out is the way they talk about the company and expectations. The opening page reads: "A fearless adventure in knowing what to do when no one's there telling you what to do." And later goes on to say, "This handbook is about the choices you're going to be making and how to think about them. Mainly, it's about how not to freak out now that you're here." They break down "Advancement versus Growth," and there's even a chapter on risks ("What if I screw up? But what if we ALL screw up?"). My favorite part may be the fun illustrations that illuminate cultural nuance. For example, there's Fig. 3-1: Method to working without a boss.

Step 1. Come up with a bright idea
Step 2. Tell a coworker about it
Step 3. Work on it together
Step 4. Ship it!

In this clever four-part illustration, the company underscores the importance of collaboration. They didn't say, "Collaboration is key to our success!" They simply showed you how to do it.

If your company has a traditional (read: boring) handbook, reach out to your HR team and suggest helping rework it. And take it upon yourself to review it with your own team to decode its language. Have a team meeting where you discuss what success looks like at your company, break it down for them. What are the unspoken rules? What are leadership expectations? How long does advancement take? What could be the reasons why some advance faster than others? How important is it to be seen, known? Is yours a culture where partnership is earned versus granted?

Now, I'm fully aware that every workplace has unspoken norms that could never be printed in an employee handbook. If you want to get approval on a project, you must get John's buy-in, or visibility on this team is the key to promotion. They're unwritten, but they're not unseen. Use examples from your own life. Say, "Here's what helped me when I was trying to get approval for a new headcount, or here's how I learned to navigate this place." Know it's not going to be the same for everyone. A white guy may advise me to walk into the CEO's office with the bravado of, well, a white man and demand we push forward with a long delayed project, but that might not work for this Latina who has to battle the lingering perceptions of the "fiery Latina." Address that: say, "Let's think of how we can dissolve stereotypes and find ways for your team members to embrace their power with organizational awareness, confidence, and authenticity." The more you can share these shortcuts and prime them for office life (and politics), the more primed they will be to succeed.

2. Foster Peer Relationships

Tiffany Dufu, founder of The Cru, a peer mentorship platform, credits her own group of "badass peer mentors" for blazing her path forward. She says they embrace her vulnerability and allow her to share her greatest triumphs and worst fears without judgment. And they hold her accountable. They check in on her goals, help devise plans, and give her the encouragement and cheerleading she may need. "I do all of this for them as well," she says. "It's like we're all climbing a mountain together, tethered to one another to ensure that all of us reach the summit" (Dufu 2020) I'm proud to be a member of Tiffany's Cru. These close, trusting relationships have helped catalyze my potential—a place where social capital is offered and exchanged.

Relationships like these are the cornerstone of belonging, and when you can create an environment of psychological safety, close social interactions result in strong social bonds. Researchers Wilder and Thompson (1980) found that people form favorable views toward people they spend time with regularly, even if they previously disliked them.

So imagine if you're surrounded by people you like and aren't showing bias! Gallup has consistently found that having a best friend at work leads to better engagement, happiness, and performance (Marken 2019). It's not surprising when you consider that we spend more time with our coworkers than our families on any given day. The people around you strongly influence you and your potential success, but it can be difficult for women and BIPOC to make connections at work when they constantly receive social signals that set them apart. Social belonging is a fundamental human need, yet 40% of people say they feel isolated at work.

How to Be More Supportive: Champion ERGs (Employee Resource Groups)

At every company in which I've worked, I've seen ERGs run the gamut in structure and style from committees filled with junior employees who use them as a place to connect and navigate the ways of work to incredibly influential groups that shape company culture, products, and DEI practices. At their essence, ERGs have been created to respond to the lack of representation and community for women, BIPOC, LGBTQIA+, and other underrepresented groups. They are typically employee-led groups formed around common backgrounds, such as gender, race, ethnicity, and sexual orientation. When run well, they offer employees community, camaraderie, and connections throughout the organization, a sense of belonging. ERGs can be key organizational enablers in attracting, retaining, and advancing underrepresented communities, but they need structure and support. ERGs have a voice but don't always have a strong voice.

Affinity groups, another term for ERGs, can often devolve into social groups or book clubs rather than action-oriented reform organizations. In some ways, they can have the unintended effect of encouraging people to self-segregate (again). There are plenty of pitfalls, but you need to diversify the mix to get it right. When junior BIPOC make up the majority composition of an affinity group, they do not have the power and positional privilege to speak up to reform white male leadership. You need engagement from the top and mid-level leaders who can help garner support for new programs and ideas.

An ERG should welcome everyone of all levels. Still, it would be ideal to invite company stakeholders to the table who are willing to help shape vision, policy, and an operational road map. Ideally, that would include: an executive sponsor, two to three middle-level managers, an HR representative, and a rich cross-section of all races and identities. ERGs should remain safe spaces for employees, so consider extending the invitation to one key meeting or event. Think back to the story of CEO Brian O'Kelley in Chapter 2. It was an invitation to a female-focused ERG that provided the insight that the women of his workplace were feeling seriously excluded.

Here's how you can help an ERG achieve their goals:

Volunteer to be an executive sponsor. Senior leaders can help to both accelerate progress and remove blockers. You need to be willing to spend your political and financial capital. You don't need to be a member of the ERG's identity group. Still, you must advocate for them within your senior circles, including securing budget and other resources which may not come easily to the more junior members of the group.

Reward ERG leaders. Not every organization is in a place where they can pay all ERG members. Still, they should be mindful of providing meaningful rewards such as integrating a goal in performance management reviews that focuses on leadership contributions to ERGs and creating opportunities for ERG leaders to amplify their messaging across the company, connect with senior leadership, and share best practices across groups. Authors Minda Harts, Sarah Lacy, and Eve Rodsky (2020) persuasively lay out the case for paying ERG leaders (disproportionately women and BIPOC) in *Fast Company*: "ERGs are very real networks that require skilled internal champions. Yet many researchers still argue it's a net drain on women's careers, even potentially hurting their ability to get promoted because it takes time away from the job they're getting evaluated on." Some can follow the lead of Twitter, which announced a new compensation program for its ERG leaders. "This work is essential to Twitter's success—it is not a 'side hustle' or 'volunteer activity,'" said Dalana Brand, Twitter's vice president of People Experience and head of Inclusion and Diversity (Hilgers 2021). It's not possible for every company, this I know, but finding ways to compensate ERG leaders creatively, even just a small bonus at the end of the year demonstrates respect for their work and contributions.

Listen in and act. I've been asked, "Hey, if I am white, can I attend an ERG meeting? I want to be an ally, but I also don't want to encroach on their safe space." The answer is yes, if you're invited. Successful ERGs recognize that they need outside support to take action. Just in the last year alone, ERGs have had a 60% decrease in how many Black people are leading them, doing less lifting for the company, says Aubrey Blanche, global head of Equitable Design & Impact at Culture Amp (Blanche 2020).

That alleviates the least privileged people from taking on the most work. If you're a white man, spend an equal amount of unpaid time thinking about how to change the systemic unfairness and bias, going to conferences about diversity and inclusion, and then taking action. Then talk to other white peers in the company about the work. Measure the difference and share your results.

3. Widen Your Network, Expand Others'

Ah, networking. The necessary evil. As a manager, you should encourage and facilitate networking opportunities, while looking at your own network and your connections at work. It's worth analyzing your circle: Who's in there? Who is sitting just outside your social circles? Who you surround yourself with, whose input you seek, and whose information you frequently validate is how you build a sense of community for some and not others. This is where bias tends to be reinforced. It also creates a whisper network of opportunity. Every move you make has a ripple effect whether you realize it or not. It's the go-to on your team when you have to assign a last-minute task, to the person you most often text when you're curious about something. There's a difference between those you instinctively welcome and those from whom you keep a vast distance. These involuntary behaviors create connections, networks, opportunities, and a feeling (or lack) of belonging.

Take a moment to think about and write down answers to the following questions:

Who do you have breakfast or lunch with on most days?
Who is your first call when you need help with a project?
Whose ideas do you question more often or have less patience for?
Who do you prioritize when building out a project team?

The answers may not jump out at you immediately, but if you take time to take stock of your daily routines, you may start to see some patterns emerge. The good news is that you have the power to change your answers and behavior. In her book *The Person You Mean to Be: How Good People Fight Bias*, Dolly Chugh (2021) explains the metaphor of headwinds and tailwinds, as coined by Shai Davidai and Thomas Gilovich, to explain the invisibility of systemic differences. Similarly, use headwinds and tailwinds as a metaphor to explain our perception of our advantages and disadvantages. Headwinds, says Chugh, are the challenges, big or small, visible or invisible, that make life harder for some but not all people. Tailwinds are the forces that propel you forward that are easily unnoticed or forgotten. Because these headwinds and tailwinds are often invisible to us, we frequently miss how much we dismiss those facing headwinds and ignore the advantages of others.

During Women's History Month in 2020, Jennifer DaSilva, president of WPP creative agency Berlin Cameron, publicly announced her personal goal of connecting four women every weekday throughout the month (DaSilva 2020). She set aside one night a week after her kids went to bed to make connections. She became so passionate about it, she started an event series to open dialogues and foster more vulnerable connections. Eventually, she challenged her social followers to take on the same goal—to connect four women a week—and help support one another.

We won't truly expand our networks and communities until we begin to have honest and informed conversations about the intersections of race and gender. I love the spirit of Jennifer's Connect4Women initiative. Taking ownership of networking, opening doors for others, and helping support others on their career paths is an integral part of creating a more diverse workforce. But here's where the real opportunity lies: Who are you connecting with? Do they all look the same? How many connections are you making that are cross-cultural, cross-generational, cross-identity? Those are the questions I asked Jennifer when she asked me to join—and I'm so glad I did. Jennifer has recalled that conversation as an opportunity to reflect on her intentions and outcomes.

Here's an exercise for you: List two or three people on your team and outside of the workplace who you would go to if you had an issue to discuss. Next, categorize them by their demographics: race, gender, religion, abilities, sexual orientation, gender identity, age, etc. What does that look like? The list likely looks very much like you and probably thinks like you. Look at your social media profiles: Who are you connected to on LinkedIn? If your followers are 98% white and male, that's your story, and that needs to change. You must broaden your network.

But please don't start blindly connecting with all the BIPOC on your LinkedIn search. Expanding your networks takes time, thought, and care. Reach out with a note that speaks about what you value about their experience or profile. Ask to be connected through a mutual friend, and allow the other person to decline. Seek out differences while recognizing that the emotional vigilance of those you wish to widen your circle may be rightfully high. Or focus on people in your company—seek out the perspective of someone different from you, even if that just means grabbing a coffee or tea with someone you don't ordinarily talk to on your team or outside of your team.

Your company is no different. If you were to ask those same who-do-you-lunch-with questions of your CEO, or board members, what do you think they would say? Who holds power across the organization? How is that power distributed or abused? Whose behavior is consistently excused? What harms are downplayed? Whose voice or what perspective is missing from decision-making? You can take responsibility for your own learning as a leader by digging deeper into this simple exercise.

How to Be More Supportive: Create Valuable Connections

Start internally. Expanding your networks and communities is not simply the result of fabricated social interactions. How you initiate conversations about race with employees or bring up dialogue about the experiences of majority and minority cultures in your workplace can also help enhance your own networks and connections. Hopefully there's a relationship there to start a one-on-one or collective team conversation about matters that affect their communities with each other and yourself. Try encouraging dialogue, not debate. Model to others what being an empathetic listener looks like by doing just that, creating a space for sharing and listening. Remember you learn by listening, not talking. Begin by honestly acknowledging why you're even having the conversation: "I haven't acknowledged this before because I haven't known how to start the conversation. I want to be a resource. I want to enhance our relationships. I'm not saying I'm an expert but that I care." However you start the conversation, it's about acknowledging conversation and opening the door.

You can also engage in ongoing check-ins. Natural connection points to check in with your team: performance management conversations or goal setting in the talent process. You can begin by saying, "I want to check in to make sure things are okay and that I'm not missing anything. Do you think you have the right resources for your career or projects? Do you feel that your work makes sense? What has been going on since the last time we talked that could be affecting your performance?" Look for those natural points along the way to continue this dialogue. This makes it easier to build relationships and broaden your networks. It's not just this conversation but every conversation.

4. Mentorship and Sponsorship

Having a personal team of advisors is not just having access to a life jacket; it's getting a ticket on the speed boat. This is particularly true for women, BIPOC, LGBTQIA+, and members of underrepresented communities in the workplace who face systemic obstacles throughout their careers. Sponsorship and mentorship are slightly different entities. Mentorship is about upskilling, and sponsorship is about putting your professional equity at stake to help someone succeed. With mentorship, you're advising someone; with sponsorship, you're sharing your access and privilege. For some that may mean hard-earned political influence and power. Professor Herminia Ibarra argues for these kinds of relationships to flourish, both executives and their organizations must be clear about what steps they might take to ensure women have the sponsorship support they need. She says, "While a mentor is someone who has knowledge and will share it with you, a sponsor is a person who has power and will use it for you" (Ibarra et al. 2010).

It's a bigger play and it's what has been documented as the missing piece for the proper advancement of women and BIPOC into leadership. "In general, women are over-mentored and under-sponsored, and female founders are over-mentored and underfunded," says Katica Roy (2020), CEO and founder of Pipeline, a software as a service (Saas) company that uses artificial intelligence to identify and take action against intersectional organizational gender bias. While there is equal merit in both relationships, mentors stand beside you, while a sponsor stands before you, clearing the path ahead. Sometimes they can be one and the same!

My mentors and sponsors have offered me different kinds and degrees of support. They have offered insider knowledge that is often invisible to those without access to leadership, introductions to influential people, advocated for promotions before I even thought I was ready, and opened up doors for opportunities I may have never been considered for. They have also checked me when I've grown impatient, made me face my development gaps, and have shared vulnerable mistakes of their own to help me avoid making the same missteps. And I, in turn, have also honored the relationship by sharing insights and resources not on their radar, prioritizing their asks, and honoring their contributions to my career every chance I get. The most effective mentor relationships happen naturally, but when only 37% of professionals say they have a mentor, managers have to step in to open up access.

How to Be More Supportive: Start Mentoring

Pledge to mentor someone who needs it the most, doesn't look like you, or didn't have the same experiences and upbringing as you. "I stopped mentoring men," says Brian O'Kelley, founder and CEO of Waybridge. "And once I did, the women I mentored gained more opportunities and access to special projects because of my capital at the company" (O'Kelley 2020). A formula for mentoring success: Have a clear idea of what you both hope to gain; commit to regular meetings; and listen to learn about each other. Ask your mentee your own business and career questions, too, for a fresh point of view.

Mentor relationships can be mutually beneficial. Don't look at mentorship as an opportunity to simply pass on your knowledge; think of it as a chance to gain insight into a different perspective or trends and to help you hone your intergenerational and cross-cultural communication and leadership style. "Every once in a while I come across a woman who will tell me that she doesn't have time to mentor," says The Cru founder Tiffany Dufu. "She'll actually complain about all of the requests she gets from young women in her organization. While I do understand the overwhelm of a full inbox, it's important to recognize that Mentees are a critical part of our success ecosystem. They help me more than they probably realize. My Mentees keep me grounded and relevant, and they've helped me to advance my leadership in countless ways. From childcare to fashion emergencies, to editorial advice and research, there's just no way I'd be where I am without their support" (Dufu 2020).

How to Be More Supportive: Stick Your Neck Out for Your Team

A sponsorship relationship is grounded on trust, loyalty, and confidence. A sponsor must feel confident that the person they're putting up for an opportunity will deliver. As in the case of access to critical roles in an organization, the playing field remains uneven. We must overcome the natural tendency only to build sponsorship-type relationships with those who we are most comfortable with, whether because they match our social identities or because of closer proximity.

Here's a secret: you already are a sponsor! "A lot of times we talk about these coveted sponsorship relationships, but actually your first sponsor is going to be your manager," says Cindy Pace, vice president, Global Chief Diversity & Inclusion Officer at MetLife (Pace 2020). That's your role as a manager! To be there for your team. Lean into sponsorship to promote underrepresented groups. Cindy is an excellent example of a manager who not only seeks to advocate high-potential employees on her team but who also actively designs organizational programs that seek to ensure all leaders do the same. Speak up for people! Introduce them to someone on your network who can make further connections for them. Be a coach, a cheerleader, a sage all wrapped in one. If you're doing your job well, your rate of internal promotions will increase. Internal mobility is an untapped opportunity.

Internal research at Deutsche Bank revealed that female managing directors who left the firm to work for competitors were not doing so to improve their work-life balance. Instead, they'd left the company for bigger jobs they hadn't even been considered for previously. Deutsche Bank created a sponsorship program to generate more exposure and assignments for women that could lead to advancement. The program secured advocates for promotion within the executive committee through intentional pairings. A year later, one third of the participants were in more prominent roles, and another third were considered ready to take on broader responsibilities (Ibarra et al. 2010).

How to Be More Supportive: Launch a Mentorship Program Focused on Specific Pain Points

According to Catalyst, 71% of Fortune 500 companies have mentoring programs, but these relationships rarely evolve to stronger advocate relationships, the space where sponsorship thrives (Catalyst 2020b). Most of the time—based on poor matches, unengaged participants, and a lack of goals—these relationships fizzle. Participants are more apt to have a successful relationship when there is a clearly stated strategy and shared mission.

Unilever, for example, created programs to advance women into management in critical areas. Its Supply Chain Female Mentoring program matched more than 45 senior leaders at the vice president level and above to mentor and coach more than 90 women directors in departments with low advancement rates for women. Recognizing a leak in their internal pipeline, they set up a mentorship program to fix it. A tactical and achievable goal—ensuring that women advance in these departments—gave mentors a mission they could rally behind, creating a more effective and impactful program (Pace 2020).

Likewise, in 2012, MetLife recognized that high-potential women hit a barrier and were not promoted to officer level roles at the same pace as high potential men. A year later, they launched the Developing Women's Career Experience (DWCE), a 14-month program that included peer coaching, leadership presence guidance, and laser mentoring provided by a senior leader. They didn't leave the success of the mentor-mentee relationship up to chance but rather coached the participants on being a more effective mentor with training on creating developmental assignments, giving more effective feedback, and providing training on the raw skills needed for advancement. The results were clear: since DWCE's inception in 2013, more than 26% of the 250 women who have completed the program have been promoted into officer roles (Pace 2020).

"That's three times more than the average in the company," says Cindy, who was involved with the program's creation and launch. "People started asking me, What's going on? How does this work? And I said, 'It's what you focus on. If you focus on it and measure it, it usually gets done.'"

How to Be More Supportive: Build Mentorship Programs That Can Evolve into Sponsorships

You cannot force relationships or demand that someone spend their hard-earned capital for someone they may not be enthusiastic about. An automatic mentor/sponsor program would allow BIPOC staff access to senior leaders who have the influence and access to help advance the way. Mentors of color who saw themselves reflected in me were crucial to me as I rose up the ranks—yet there are often few senior staff of color at companies, and they are often overtaxed when asked to meet the needs of all junior BIPOC.

White male leaders need to be part of the solution. Or pay BIPOC mentors for these extra duties. And if you do that, the BIPOC person should be allotted additional space—more personal days and flex time and additional time to achieve annual performance goals, etc., since all that additional support takes time away from high-visibility, promotable work.

The best program I've seen to date was the SAGE program at Google. Sages (mentors) and Sagees (mentees) were paired up in traditional methods based on personal and professional interests. I participated as Sage and my Sagee, Adrianna Samaniego, selected me because of our shared ethnic background. In our monthly meetings, many of which we had over a meal near my home, I played several supporting roles—offered advice about tough choices I had faced myself, helped her strategize to be more effective in her role, and made connections that helped her gain admittance into the MBA program of choice.

What made this program unique is that all had to attend a mandatory one-day training in which Sages, often white managers, participated in cultural sensitivity training designed to develop and nurture skills, tools, self-awareness, and gain confidence in navigating cultural and racial differences. I, along with my white peers, fellow Sages, left the program far better equipped to mentor our Sagees and manage more inclusively. Adrianna and I have remained close as our relationship has evolved from a mentor providing career advice to a sponsor making critical introductions for MBA programs and new career opportunities. Through various career transitions and even cross-country moves, we remain each other's advocates.

5. External Advisors

A few years ago, VICE Media Group, under the leadership of CEO Nancy Dubuc, created an external diversity and inclusion advisory committee that focused on gender-equality efforts at the company. Gloria Steinen, Michelle Obama's former chief of staff Tina Tchen, Roberta Kaplan (who argued against the Defense of Marriage Act before the Supreme Court), among others, sat on this council. They were tasked with holding VICE Media Group executives and decision makers accountable to improve company policies and procedures to improve its gender diversity, parity, and to curb what was widely characterized as a "boys club." It worked. As of 2020, of their new employees, 56% are women and 50% are people of color. We must follow this model and improve our efforts for even more racial diversity.

An external DEI council or advisory board should be compensated for their services. They play a key role in holding leaders accountable and provide strategic advice and counsel. An active council or board can do so much more than simply track quarterly progress. They can be game changers by doing exactly what exceptional leaders do: challenge leaders with a bolder vision of what is possible and leverage their wisdom and influence to help achieve outstanding results. When they get intimate with employees, that is to offer office hours or speak at internal events, they can better understand the experience on the ground, where people are stumbling and where progress is achievable. In many companies such as Comcast and Sodexo, having an external board is a requirement ensuring strategies and practices are not created and tracked in an internal silo.

Many companies already have many of the building blocks of a strong DEI initiative. They've created affinity groups, ERGs, and other councils. I've sat in on my fair share of employee resource group meetings that discuss and workshop systemic challenges. I've personally made presentations on how to improve recruitment and retention rates. Still, these conversations are a lot of talk and little action when you don't have a sponsor who can ensure that the ERG has the support they need to make their vision a reality.

There's always value having external voices that question what you're doing and don't have the unspoken pressures to maintain the company culture within the current status quo. Workplace culture is often difficult to see on the inside; it's the water you're swimming in, so it can be hard for insiders to change it, or even see the need for change. External voices can be excellent sources of knowledge and credibility, constantly reflecting on what you need, and helping build the suitable support structures. Emily Best, of Seed & Spark, values the candor of her advisory board. "They have to be people who would call you on your BS, especially if you're a white manager like me," she says. "You don't want to build an advisory board who is just there to make you feel good about yourself. You want them to challenge you" (Best 2020).

Internal advisory boards can also use pressure to get things done. When the meditation app Headspace announced the creation of an internal diversity council, more than 60 people immediately volunteered. That action results in more diversity-minded events plus a budget for a dedicated head count to run the council. Alicin Williamson of Endeavor created an internal Diversity and Inclusion (D&I) group of the leaders from various departments across the company. "I asked them what success looked like in specific business areas to gain insight and create buy-in from each individual department. That is how we were able to cross-collaborate across a commitment to D&I," she says (Williamson 2020).

Years ago I helped launch a women's initiative at Disney. As I looked around the group of primarily white women gathered to build our programming, it was clear to me that the lens through which we were looking at women's advancement left out the experiences of women of color, women like me. I had experienced firsthand the exclusion and hurt that comes from not being welcomed into mostly white social networks. When I was invited, there was an unstated understanding that I was helping fulfill a quota, not being welcomed in for my ideas, opinions, and expertise. But this was my opportunity to change that. In our first planning meetings for Women's History Month, I took a bet that paid off.

With a healthy mix of corporate charm and courage, I proposed leading a bespoke event on behalf of my division that would focus on the workplace experiences of women of color. At this point in my career, I had gained confidence and earned credibility as a corporate leader. But even then I knew I needed to frame my recommendation as a limited risk proposition. How much attention could this event garner? How many women of color could I possibly bring together? Well, it was one of the most attended events that month. We hosted a panel with top female executives of color in the entertainment industry, and the event was open to all employees. It was a no holds barred, real talk about the barriers they had faced moving up in their careers. It was by women of color for women of color—we could finally hold space for each other and see each other in our journey. We held an invitation-only dinner for our female executives of color in the evening with the panelists. I still have the photo from that dinner.

To this day, the women of color in the company, including those no longer there, recall that experience as the first time many of them felt seen and valued. I'll never forget the white male manager who called me up to say, "Daisy, I don't know what you just did, but Roberta just came back from your event cheerfully talking about how wonderful it was. She has a pep in her step that I've never seen before. Please do more!" Had I not worked to help create a support system where BIPOC women not only felt welcomed but strengthened, who knows how long they would have stayed at Disney. Had I not acted on what I knew women of color needed to experience in the workplace, we would not have been able to move beyond the pervasive blind spot of women's programs only catering to white women, instead of removing barriers and clearing the advancement path for all women.

Your Road Map to Revolution

To be an inclusive, equitable, and anti-racist manager, the manager I believe you want to be, you must prioritize the support of those most disproportionately harmed by racism and white supremacy. Many talent systems and organizational cultures have built-in biases that privilege certain groups over others. These biases undermine the progress of BIPOC talent. Not all feedback and support is created equal. Design solutions that reduce obstacles for racially diverse team members, and help everyone advance in their careers.

- **Decode office politics and publicize what often goes unsaid.** Remove barriers for performance. Revamp your employee handbook and make it fun and informative! Also, be candid with employees about what, in your experience, has helped lead to advancement at your company.
- **Give employee resource groups (ERGs) the support and recognition they deserve.** While not a magic bullet, ERGs provide critical connections and career development opportunities. If invited, sit in on ERG meetings to listen to what employees really need. Offer to help take action on policies mentioned, and lend a hand when needed. Consider paying ERG leaders for their service.
- **Widen your reach.** Demonstrate an authentic commitment to propelling the careers of BIPOC talent forward by extending personal invitations to professional events and networks. Change it up by seeking new friends and connections not like you, with different life experiences.

- **Start mentoring.** It's that simple. But also foster mentorship programs focused on specific pain points, whether advancing BIPOC and other marginalized groups into executive leadership roles or developing talent in new departments.

- **Integrate external perspective.** Create a board of external diversity, equity and inclusion advisors. Pay them (!) and welcome them to help influence policy and culture change.

10 | Get to the Heart of Accountability

I have come to loathe the term "cancel culture," the practice of publicly shaming another person or institution for behavior deemed unacceptable. The term has been weaponized to derail conversations about accountability and consequences, which is really what we should be focusing on. Professor Loretta Ross, among others, has long been asking, "What if instead of calling people out, we call them in?" (Bennett 2020). She explains that being called out for accidentally misgendering a classmate, as it happened to her, or for admitting that they have long admired a cultural icon who is now under a different light, alienates people and makes them afraid of speaking up. Without psychological safety, we can't get to a place of understanding.

Instead she advocates for "calling in" with grace and patience, in a private message or simply taking a breath before commenting, screenshotting, or demanding "one do better" without explaining how. When we call someone in for hurtful words or actions, we acknowledge that we all make mistakes. We help someone discover that their behavior is harmful and how to change it. The courageous and hard conversations, compassion, and context she calls for are deeply needed in our society and in our workplaces.

Let me be clear, there are many people in power who have gotten used to getting away with horrible and often criminal behavior for so long that any semblance of consequences is seen as unfair, when in fact it's fundamental justice. Politicians and law enforcement officials who fail to live up to their oaths, executives who are serial sexual harassers, and business leaders who discriminate and abuse those under them, those people need to be called out. And there should be clear consequences for these abusers.

There are many cases, however, that are not that extreme and clear-cut. Sometimes, an executive makes a mistake, and the company issues a blanket apology or non-apology, and perhaps the important self-reflection will never occur. Where is the accountability beyond some public show of mea culpa? What would it take for the person who caused harm to understand their actions on a deeper level so they can do the work to make improvements?

We're all accountable for what happens on our watch. There is no neutral. Accountability matters, but instead of cancelling first, try calling in:

Lead with curiosity instead of anger. Ask yourself: "Am I calling out a person or systemic behavior?" "What am I hoping to achieve?"

Focus on the specific behavior, how it affected you or others. Don't let minor infractions escalate. Sometimes we don't know what we don't know.

Approach the conversation or message with respect and kindness while explaining the impact of their actions or language. If in person, which is preferable, ask, "What was your intention when you said . . . ?" "How might the other person view this situation?" "What effect would you like to have?"

If you're the person who has caused harm, think about what may make you feel defensive. Are you centering on your own feelings? Should you be doing more listening than providing feedback? Think about the difference between impact and intent. Remind yourself that words carry weight.

Accountability is sometimes used interchangeably with responsibility, which means being dependable. Being accountable is rooted in dependability. It is about examining how accountable we are to ourselves. We should be clear about what we value and how we act. We must make clear agreements about what's expected and about what happens as a result of the actions that we take. It is about committing to behave in a specific and intentional way to bring about full inclusion and equity. Everyone comes to this work with different levels of comfort, knowledge, and ability to translate good intentions into action. Everyone needs a way to start where they are individually and then build their knowledge, resources, and courage from there. I know you have it in you.

Most of us are naturally adept at deflecting responsibility, especially when things feel awkward or controversial. When that happens, the typical reaction is to revert back to our seven-year-old selves by quickly explaining ourselves out of whatever jam we're in. Too often, the first thought is, "It's not my fault," rather than accepting responsibility for our role. It's far easier to blame poor performance on others, like the team member who didn't share the information with you on time, instead of acknowledging your role in having made the ask at the last minute. Academics such as Robin DiAngelo (2018) have introduced us to multiple forms of white defensiveness including white denial, white diversion, and white fragility, and how these can derail conversations about systemic discrimination, racism, power, and privilege.

To be fair, we all fall into these traps no matter our demographic background. You do it. I do it, too. We want to avoid trouble, shame, and blame. In every situation, there are factors outside our control and factors within our control. The trick is choosing responsibility. No matter what. That's what great leaders do. You have a freedom of choice here, and I'm simply helping you find your path to exercise your agency. The decision to not use your power and privilege to enable equity and inclusion in your workplace is also a decision. But no one gets a pass. Revolutions are ripe with threatening distractions, that's just the nature of things, but you can choose how you respond.

You need to commit to the work and bring others along with you, and hold them and yourself accountable in this work. That's the only way we will make progress. When we launched our second annual DEI report at VICE Media Group, my first in my eight-month tenure in the company, I intentionally listed only one focus area for the following year: holding managers and leaders accountable to do the work. I wanted it to be clear that we needed to infuse accountability at the organizational and individual level. Nancy Dubuc, our CEO, also made it clear that DEI was a priority and a leadership challenge for our entire industry. That is accountability. And it starts with you.

Policies and best practices don't create change alone; they need people like you to own those policies, uphold them, measure their effectiveness, and hold people who defy them accountable. It means acting in the spirit of your espoused values on a daily basis. It means being a change agent. It means being willing to question your behaviors, norms, and the workplace environment to embrace the needs of diverse talent, ideas, customers, viewers, and markets. It means holding yourself responsible for actions you take as an individual (personal), with others as a team (organizational), and dismantling wider business norms that protect unearned advantages for white team members (systemic).

Now, I'm guessing you may be feeling the weight of the world on your shoulders right now. I get it. Nearly every Fortune 500 company has a chief diversity officer, chief people officer, or another title bestowed on a person (usually a woman of color like myself) who has been charged with making change and getting this work right, and who has probably failed. It's not for lack of effort, skill, or competency. We fail because we cannot do this alone. We fail because we are set up to fail from the beginning with fledgling budgets, inconsistent and shifting priorities, and lack of senior and middle management support. We fail because we are meant to somehow fix things without making white senior staff uncomfortable and without making changes to the workplace's norms and practices. And without taking too much time from the business functions of the employee body—as if DEI work is somehow extra credit and work that isn't foundational to building the best teams that can do their best work.

We fail because a single person does not win an inclusion revolution— we need everyone to do the work with us. Here's how to build your accountability muscles.

Engage the Uncommitted

One of the biggest challenges I have experienced repeatedly is the lack of a shared understanding of DEI in the workplace. This work looks and feels different at different stages. For some, it's a "nice to have," for some it's a defensive activity, and for some it's a necessity for workplace survival.

Too often, I meet managers who are worried about hiring but not about including people once they're in the door. Managers want to give BIPOC team members an opportunity to learn and grow but then discount them the second they make a mistake or do not produce fast enough results. Too often, employees assume that the solutions will come from our CEOs and senior leaders. Too often, we ignore those who can deliver meaningful and sustainable change, those in the middle. Middle managers might figure this work is on the CEO or diversity and inclusion manager to fix—or they may sometimes be uncommitted and unwilling to sacrifice the comfort, stability, and security they've gained. Some middle managers have been working in their companies and industries for years. They've seen this diversity work light up and dim down over the years. They figure the company will move on to other things. That is shortsighted.

Aubrey Blanche (2020) shared a statement that many DEI professionals have heard over the years—the average white male manager often thinks, "I'm a white man, and I feel like I can't do anything right. I'm on the wrong side of diversity." But there's no point in choosing a side here. We need everyone on board and white men to be part of the solution. We move in a world where we assume the competence of white men as a norm and where any semblance of race is perceived as less than the norm. White men are not nearly as engaged in DEI work as they should be. White men have told me they feel excluded from, targeted by, or negatively affected by DEI efforts, such as employee resource groups and inclusive hiring practices. These perceptions are harmful on countless levels.

Continuing to believe in a broken, racist workplace system that humiliates, discourages, and endangers talented people makes fools of us all. We succumb to participating in workplace theater instead of challenging the racism and misogyny that break spirits. Instead of forcing different people into existing systems, try building new partnerships and new systems. Listen to those who share, "This is what it feels like," "This is what is needed," and "This is what shared success looks like." Establish a real relationship and trusted partnership by sharing what you know (there's value in your lived experience also), your power, and your privilege. Shared power and privilege will lead to the elusive outcomes we've sought after for decades.

Start by creating a clear vision that helps others understand what's at stake and how to embody this vision in every people and business decision they make. How do you do that? Much the same way you approach launching any business initiative. You design and execute an internal campaign that introduces and explains what you intend to do and then reinforce new behavioral and operational expectations in your processes. Here's a formula to try:

Gather diverse perspectives to shape goals and priorities. Understand what your team cares most about, what motivates them, what engages and energizes them, what is missing for some. Cocreate a plan with them:

We will focus on _____ priorities, including _____, _____, and _____.

We will execute by _____ and _____.

We will measure with ____ and _____.

We will communicate through _____ and _____.

We will reward through _____ and _____ and will hold those who do not meet our expectation to _____ and _____.

These are the owners (read: accountability) _____, _____, _____. (You can consider a RACI model, or a responsibility assignment matrix, a commonly used project management tool that describes how various roles are expected to complete tasks or deliverables. RACI stands for responsible, accountable, consulted, and informed.)

Consider perspectives of champions, advocates, skeptics, and dissenters alike. Don't overinvest in those who resist the vision as they will suck you of your time and energy. Instead, identify the most influential employees—those who shape the attitudes of those around them—and get them on board; they can be your most powerful agents of change. Ask yourself:

What are the reasons why some actively engage and support this vision?

What are the reasons why others would not buy into the vision and action plans? Build your discernment skills. When some say,

"This is too much change" they generally mean, "I don't want to change" or "I'm afraid of what this change means for me."

What reasons and examples are most likely to surface?

What are their biggest fears or perceived losses?

How can you prepare and respond to the key takeaways?

When resistance appears, and it will, consider it a useful red flag—a signal of where you can perhaps apply more reflection or visioning. Creating an atmosphere of "us" versus "them" is not the goal. It's the farthest expression of this work! Instead, this is an opportunity to put into practice the lessons I've shared thus far about building bridges and connections.

Engaging everyone in the process is the key to creating a shared incentive. You can do this as an offsite, or take a note from the travel company Expedia, who hosted an Inclusion and Diversity Analytics Hackathon in 2020 (Life at Expedia Group Blog 2021). A Hackathon is an event popular at tech companies where programmers and participants get together and "hack together" a new idea, often in a crazy short amount of time like 24 hours. It's a moment for pure outside-the-box innovation, and a winner is crowned for the best idea or product.

Expedia's goal for this Hackathon was to create new products to improve their inclusion and diversity analytics. While developing products in a fun, charged up environment can be rewarding, the company's commitment to bringing the winning ideas to life left participants feeling inspired and motivated to participate. This wasn't just for fun—there were tangible, accountable results. Expedia's senior-level executives acted as judges (i.e. getting company buy-in), and the company held itself accountable for turning the award winners into real-life products.

Goals Are at the Heart of Accountability

Researchers tried to answer the question: "Can raising awareness actually reduce bias?" by studying data of racial bias among referees in NBA games in a 2014 economics study at Brookings. They found that "personal fouls are more likely to be called against basketball players when they are officiated by an opposite-race refereeing crew than when officiated by an own-race refereeing crew" (Pope et al. 2016). Once this study was widely shared and covered by major outlets, they tracked the effect of the media coverage on future behavior. What did they uncover? The bias completely disappeared, suggesting that raising awareness and publicly holding people accountable can effect change.

Like a good marketing strategy, you may need to craft a single, powerful message or tagline that you repeat consistently to remind your teams at all levels what you're trying to achieve, why, and what role they can each play in that change. Everyone will benefit from this work—define it for them, and help managers communicate it as well.

Helping others visualize these benefits and see what's possible for women of color is something that Jamia Wilson (2020), vice president and executive director at Penguin Random House and former executive director and publisher at the Feminist Press, has been doing throughout her career. She credits her board role at the Groundswell Fund, which supports grassroots organizing, for witnessing how change can be made at the executive level. At Groundswell, the board continually centered decisions on what was best for their employees. Yes, they also cared about funding and the bottom line, but this people-first approach helped Jamia understand that succeeding at both is possible.

That power can come in the form of shared goals and public commitments. Expedia (Expedia Group 2020) gives every employee at least one personal inclusion goal, P&G (Seramount 2017) continually sets and resets specific targets for their leaders, and APCO Worldwide (n.d.) rolled out an inclusivity contract for their employees that defined targets for leadership. Several media companies have committed to expanding representation of BIPOC talent, including launching inclusion riders and other diversity protocols to bolster representation in front of and behind the camera. A step beyond requiring "best efforts," Disney's inclusion standards (Dunn 2021) require that a representation standard, e.g. 50% or more of regular or recurring actors, come from underrepresented groups. That level of customization and clarity for DEI efforts, while early in practice, has the potential to motivate and sustain individual and collective accountability across this industry.

Company-wide diversity goals are typically highly publicized, such as Hilton committing that 50% (Sperance 2020) of new hire candidates will be from diverse backgrounds and Adidas investing $120 million (Creswell and Draper 2020) toward ending racial injustice.

In 2003, a law in Norway mandated that both women and men be represented at a minimum level of 40% of board of publicly listed limited liability companies (UN 2003). This law both accomplished its representational goal and narrowed the gender pay gap among board directors. Since then, others have followed suit, including California, which signed a law in 2018 requiring publicly held companies with executive offices in the state to have at least one female director on their boards by 2019 (California Secretary of State n.d.). When the bill was signed, 180 of the 650 public companies in California had zero women on their boards. Despite the law being struck down in 2022 as part of the ongoing backlash on DEI efforts, progress was made: now, over half of California's public companies have three or more women on their boards (Haridasani Gupta 2022). We can't create accountability if what we're asking people to be accountable for is not achievable or realistic. These goals provided clear expectations for what was expected, and they were achievable.

These actions matter. They turn the tide of transparency and accountability. Nasdaq now requires listed companies to disclose their diversity figures and have at least one woman and one minority represented on their board (Godoy 2023; Sorkin et al. 2020). When Apple announced, "Beginning in 2021, an environmental, social, and governance modifier based on Apple Values and other key community initiatives will be incorporated into our annual cash incentive program," the business community took note. Apple's publicly shared values (Apple Career Site n.d.) include product-led environmental practices such as using recycled materials and workforce diversity and inclusion. The board's compensation committee will apply the modifier when determining bonus payouts. That means that executive performance payouts will earn up to a 10% bonus upside or downside depending on their ability to meet their goals.

Progress and adoption of financial incentives have been slow. According to Mercer estimates, only 15% to 20% of S&P 500 companies include DEI metrics in their executive incentive plans (Passin n.d.). While many organizations are focused on building a more diverse pipeline (rightfully so), there is a critical need to hold everyone in the organization, specifically those at the top, accountable for their performance. I'm counting on Apple's and Nasdaq's moves and support from larger institutions and investors to accelerate progress and drive greater scrutiny on performance and outcomes.

Ask your manager for concrete, intersectional goals and targets against DEI initiatives and efforts. Goals involve accountability because people invest more effort when they expect that they will have to explain their actions and outcomes. Ensure that everyone can weigh in and feel that they can lend a hand to drive progress. How? Making sure everyone knows what you're trying to achieve, why, and when. People like scorecards for a reason—they provide immediate feedback about what's working and what isn't.

In crafting individual goals, tap into one's passion or talents. For someone who loves to write, add a goal of writing a certain number of internal or social media posts about the impact of diverse perspectives in your workforce. Or for those who like to organize events, you could establish a goal around internal events with a target for the communities you wish to reach and engage. Or for all, a goal could be making sure all team members have an opportunity to ask questions and share opinions, which you can track in every meeting agenda. Be clear on what achieving these goals looks like. For example, Lawrence Berkeley National Laboratory, a US Department of Energy National Laboratory managed by the University of California, shared these suggestions (Lawrence Berkeley National Laboratory. n.d.):

Goal: Participate in training that would specifically enhance my cultural competency. Goal met by: Attended LGBTQIA+ awareness training during Pride Month to increase my awareness.

Goal: Participate in professional activities that would increase my experience in interacting with people from cultural backgrounds other than my own.

Goal met by: Joined African-American ERG to support and promote their annual activities and initiatives.

Goal: Make sure that web pages, documents, forms, etc. are ADA compliant and accessible to all users.

Goal met by: Partnered with IT Department to review Division website and electronic documents to ensure ADA compliance.

Develop these together, even asking individuals for suggestions, to make this a collaborative process.

Be Accountable to Yourself

For me, success means recognizing that the buck stops with me. It means humbly acknowledging my stumbles and blind spots, as I've shared throughout this book. And it means ensuring I'm taking the same concrete actions I ask others to take on the road to dismantling inequity in the workplace. It's never easy. It can sometimes feel debilitating, like a weight on your shoulders that just won't give. But that's when I need to remind myself that the weight I carry is many times lighter because of my privileges, some of which I've earned through sweat and tears, and some, such as identifying as a heterosexual, cis-gendered woman, which I've done nothing to earn but benefitted from my entire life.

A study released by the Hispanic Association on Corporate Responsibility (HACR), called "Empow(h)er: Understanding Workplace Barriers for Latinas," aimed to shed light on what Latinas should do to advance in their careers (2020). I have been a longtime supporter of HACR and its president Cid Wilson, but I had to roll my eyes . . . not because I don't believe we need to take over ownership of our careers—that's never been in question for me. As the daughter of immigrants, everything has always been my responsibility: getting into college, securing scholarships and work-study gigs to pay for college, waitressing at every break because I couldn't afford non-paying internships, securing jobs after graduating to pay off school loans, navigating workplaces for which I had little to any cultural knowledge and even less navigational know-how. All of that.

Yet, here I am, again, being told that as a Latina *I* have to be fixed and not the system and culture that I'm working so hard to survive. The first step is flipping this imbalance. I believe you know this and are ready to go on this journey. But when in doubt ask yourself, who and what needs to change?

"What am I internalizing about the things I've heard before that I haven't been willing to accept about my company, or my role as a leader?" says Keesha Jean Baptiste, of Hearst Magazines. "What is it that I have discounted and not heard in the right way? Those questions are hard to ask of one's self and certainly for any leader that's not comfortable with being vulnerable, but we're cycling through the same problem because there is a lack of leadership accountability and acknowledgment that the problem is sometimes you" (Jean-Baptiste 2020).

When I asked Jamia Wilson to identify what's different for women of color in corporate culture from the nonprofit world, she quickly responded, "The constant hypervigilance and expectation that as a woman of color I need to fix everything immediately." What would be helpful would be for white leaders, especially those with unearned privilege and power, to understand the distinct barriers and burdens that BIPOC employees face in the work. "You have to be on the chessboard figuring out the short-term moves to protect your queen and those long-term moves that will happen at the end of the game," she says. And as BIPOC leaders, it's important to identify our values and triggers. Leadership is examining the power we hold and how it can be shared.

Be Accountable to Your Consumers, Users, and Audience, Too

Part of the reason companies with diverse teams earn larger profits comes down to a bubble analogy. When your product designers, salespeople, content creators, and marketers all look and act the same, you make decisions based on shared perspectives and blind spots. You miss opportunities by overlooking and outright neglecting a vast market! Let's start with the more commonly shared and researched assertion that diversity of thought, experience, and background drives organizational and cultural value. Examples abound; take the much-publicized issues for people of color in Google's facial recognition software or the fact that female-size crash dummies weren't used by the National Highway Traffic Safety Administration until 2003, even though studies showed that "women, having smaller bones and lower bone density, are at greater risk than men of suffering injury or death in crashes." In all these instances, the lack of diversity on the product and engineering side created major, even deathly, challenges for a huge proportion of their customers. These are dangerous blind spots.

Research has long proven that racially and gender-diverse teams enhance problem solving, creativity, and innovation. They create and design services, products, and content for everyone and bring an inclusive lens through all aspects of design, research, reach, and engagement.

Tapping into your employees' diverse perspectives and experiences can be the difference between tapping into previously unreached consumers and markets in a meaningful way or becoming obsolete. Candice Morgan, the head of Inclusion and Diversity at Pinterest, spoke to a young Pinner who shared that she felt the brand didn't present content that was relevant to her. When she searched for hairstyles or spring makeup looks, the results were filled with white women with wavy blond hair dressed ready for Coachella. Page two, page three—all the same. To get the beauty and fashion advice she sought, she told Candice she had to customize her search with words such as Black or natural hair or makeup for dark skin tones. Why would she keep using Pinterest if they made it so hard to find images that represented her? (Laurean Yates 2019).

This struck a chord with Candice, who was implementing the same search hacks. In turn, she pitched the company on an Engineering, Product, and Design project to develop more inclusive searches, and specifically for beauty and hair. Thanks to her ingenuity and perseverance, you can now personalize your skin-tone results when you search for a beauty-related idea on Pinterest. That's neat, right? This partnership between tech and diversity helped create a better sense of belonging for Pinterest's multicultural community.

Similarly, product inclusion initiatives such as Banana Republic's True Hues collection, a line of nude undergarments and accessories in eight shades, from pale to a dark espresso brown, designed to celebrate a range of skin tones delivered great results for the company. Customers and employees warmly welcomed what they had wished for years, a product that truly complemented their skin tones, not a falsely constructed definition of "nude." Social media metrics went through the roof, and sales in the first month alone increased in double digits. This work doesn't happen in silos; it requires being willing to listen to the voices of your employees and giving them agency to test and iterate on solutions that can have a timely and lasting impact.

Focus on the work behind the scenes, too. Start with your sphere of control, from your scope down. For example, supplier diversity programs—which vendors you use for supplies and services—are an external way to commit to DEI practices. Women and minority-owned businesses often can't compete with pricing and discounts from larger corporations. You can help level the playing field by changing who your company does business with.

Capital One, for example, has a robust supplier diversity program, which increases access and opportunity for minority-, woman-, veteran, disability-, service-disabled veteran-, and LGBTQIA+-owned businesses. This includes a supplier diversity mentoring program to close equity gaps for small business owners. They also have sourcing mandates for their associates to search for new suppliers (Capital One Corporate Information Site. n.d.).

Even smaller companies can audit their vendors to create change. I know a junior employee who was responsible for ordering the office supplies for her publishing company. When she looked deeper into the company who manufactured the bubble wrap they used to package their books, she discovered that the company made large donations to an allegedly racist politician. So what did she do? She shared this information with her bosses and presented a new vendor aligned with their values. They fired the bad egg, and hired the good. This seemingly small act hugely influenced her company and the new vendor whose business was boosted with this new client.

Measure Effectiveness, Always

This is not a one and done process. Like a garden, you must continue to water it, nurture it, pull out the weeds, and prune what's not growing. Celebrate the wins and acknowledge the missed opportunities or missteps. It's intimidating to get in front of a room of people and tell them where you've failed. I know, I've done it. Even though we know we are fallible humans, failing hurts. We can only move forward one foot in front of the other.

You have to critically examine your workforce data across intersectional lines, take the organization's temperature, watch out for signals and trends before they become lagging indicators, and analyze performance. Engagement surveys, listening series, and focus groups may not solve everything instantly, but they can help you gather valuable data. Revisit Chapter 7 for survey samples, but the overall goal should be to proactively look for trends, positive and negative, as to what's working and what's not. Specifically:

- Where are the most prominent sore spots?
- What are they?
- Are we measuring the right things?

Surveys are also an indication of information that your team is lacking. If you're receiving feedback that employees outside of the United States do not feel connected to the DEI strategy you have outlined, make a point to talk to them about it. Where can you shift your messaging and resourcing to allow for bespoke solutions across the globe?

Use the data to guide you and track your progress versus your plan. Data can keep you in check—use it to define areas of opportunity that can be targeted for goals and subgoals. For example, when you look at the promotion rates for women and BIPOC, external hiring rates, involuntary exit rates, what can that tell you where you have holes to mend? What are the contributing factors across the employee life cycle? Think broadly, too: share and break down company-wide goals at the division, unit, department, or team level that allow everyone to participate, and reduce bias in processes.

Then, turn the mirror on yourself. You can draw on action statements to imagine the reality you want to create as I've adapted from Bernardo Ferdman's work with Planned Parenthood (Freeman 2020). They also serve as a great way to measure your progress and check in on your accountability. Hint: these work whether you are white or BIPOC.

If you're a non-manager, try:

- I critically question and reject negative stereotypes of my colleagues.
- I amplify what my coworkers say during meetings and give them credit for their ideas.
- I bring new perspectives and ideas that are of value to my team, and I create space for others to do so as well.
- I do not let microaggressions limit my career or that of anyone else. Instead, I raise instances of indirect, subtle, or intentional discrimination with the channels (manager, HR, confidential hotline, etc.) available to me.

If you're a people manager:

- I proactively cultivate diverse networks within my organization and social circles, considering new voices, perspectives, and ideas.
- I am accountable for my actions and decisions, even when I am enforcing policy handed from above.

- I willingly seek to reduce bias about experience, knowledge, and credibility when hiring, developing, or promoting talent on my team.

If you're an executive leader:

- I use my leadership, power, and privilege to uplift others.
- I speak authentically, vulnerably, and with empathy; a veneer of perfection has no place in my leadership style.
- I seek out people on the organization's margins, find and create ways to include them in conversations and ideation, celebrate their wins, big or small, and bring their names up in meetings where they might not have been otherwise mentioned.
- I refuse to frame our journey to become a more diverse, equitable, and inclusive organization as a battle between "whiteness" and blackness," "us vs. them."
- I make open and public commitments to developing a diverse leadership bench.
- I am specific on the dimensions of diversity that I seek—race, gender identity or expression, sexual orientation, nationality, ability, etc., and why.

Idea to Steal: Try a "To-Be" List Instead of a "To-Do" List

Michael Fisher, CEO of the Cincinnati Children's Hospital Medical Center, has made it a point to create a "to-be" list. As Fisher explains: "I never purposefully gave thought to whether there's a way to be really *intentional* about how I want to show up every day. So I've added a 'to be' list to my repertoire. Today, for example, I want to be generous and genuine. I hope I'm that way every day. But today, I want to make sure it stays top of mind. On a different day this week—and look, you can see it here in my calendar—I knew that part of my job was to be collaborative and catalytic. So I pick out two qualities, two kinds of 'to be,' every morning as part of my normal routine." By holding himself accountable to how he's showing up, he engenders more trust with his team. Now imagine if his "to be" list included "Every day this week, I will amplify the voice or contribution of an underrepresented member of our team or organization, and I will pay attention to the intersectional identities of these employees" or "Today, I will reflect on my privilege and share an example with my team of a privilege that I have taken for granted and which has afforded me unearned access or power." Or "This week, I will share an invisible inequity in our workforce each day so that we can call attention to the problem and devise solutions as a team " (McKinsey Quarterly, 2022). Take a moment with me to imagine that. You can do that, right?

Accelerate What's Right, Demand Your Leaders Lead

The tone is set at the top and trickles down. Inclusive leaders have done the personal work of understanding what they want to achieve and why. They've examined their fears, assumptions, and privileges. An inclusive leader articulates a clear case for organizational change, sets concrete goals with key benchmarks, and models welcoming and respectful behavior. An inclusive leader requires structured, well-resourced, clearly articulated DEI strategies/action plans, as with any other business priority. An inclusive leader leads.

Make civility the norm. When it's not, it's a sign that the organization's culture is not characterized by respectful communication. Sometimes that can be as easy as encouraging your managers and leaders to practice respectful enquiry—the act of leaders asking employees questions about what they most need or observe in the workplace and being willing to actively listen and learn. Beyond being respectful and courteous—a practice we wish all of our managers would practice, no?—it involves relinquishing commanding control, a pervasive tool of white supremacy, and demonstrating trust in others.

Incivility can be a bug—it's contagious—but it doesn't have to be a feature, as my tech friends would say. Look internally to see if behavioral norms or operational practices need to change. For example, if your employee satisfaction surveys or exit interviews indicate that workers don't feel respected or heard by management, that needs to be corrected, now.

And if inclusion, respect, and civility have not been the norm, let employees know that things will change. Don't continue to tolerate workplace communication or behaviors that are not respectful and empathetic, and handle it as you would any kind of culture change, by modeling appropriate behavioral norms and owning issues from the past. Seek buy-in for how things will be moving forward, and focus on building accountability.

To spread accountability:

- In meetings, talk about DEI to ensure your teams know you have a personal commitment and investment in this work.
- When designing the measures most important to monitor for your strategy or performance management practices, encourage your team to integrate measurable DEI goals.
- Spend time reflecting on and taking in feedback about your leadership behaviors.
- Survey your organization to ensure that you're preserving and/or advancing efforts that employees care about.
- Take action when you witness discriminatory, exclusive, harassing, or unfair behavior.

In 2020, *Bon Appétit* magazine was one of many companies that saw its leadership fall. After a status quo social media post about how the brand stands with its Black employees, those employees, in turn, spoke up. Assistant food editor Sohla El-Waylly shared on Instagram that while she appeared in *Bon Appétit's* popular videos "as a display of diversity," unlike her white video costars, she didn't get paid. More stories came to light about a toxic test kitchen culture and a racist photo emerged of long-time editor Adam Rapaport to seal the deal. The magazine's publisher, Condé Nast, promptly fired Rapaport and his boss, Matt Drukor, likely due to the public outcry (Abad-Santos 2020).

Employee expectations in workplaces have changed as a result of these significant moments. Women are less willing to suffer sexually inappropriate behavior quietly, LGBTQIA+ employees actively demand to be treated and seen fairly, and BIPOC employees expect to be valued, supported, and given access to career growth. While the outcome was deserving, the effect of being "cancelled" can lead to a culture of fear at the top. And that fear—of repercussion, of making a mistake, of speaking out, of being caught—can diminish one's intention and accountability. It's why toxic leadership has existed without penalty until now. While you may not have the power to fire your company's leadership, there are important steps all mid-level managers and leaders can take to force a conversation and help DEI be understood as a shared responsibility.

1. **Define DEI goals.** If there is not a clearly articulated vision, set of goals, or action plan in place, ask for one. If there is, talk about it with your own team and share why diversity, equity, inclusion, belonging, and psychological safety are important to you and the business. Share this regularly with your team through various channels and platforms (email, chat, shared documents) to learn, connect, and inspire action.

2. **Find out who they listen to.** I've had plenty of bosses who are resistant to change (side note: there should be no place for people like that, but they exist). In these situations, I've had to get creative. You can't teach an old dog new tricks unless he's eager to learn, right? Instead, I think about what motivates the person. Who does my manager look up to? Who influences this thinking? Who knows him well and can give me tips on managing up? You want to make this a positive experience. In this situation, I would say, "I want to make sure that this initiative will be successful. Do you have any advice on how I could get buy-in from X?" This is not about complaining or going above someone; it's discovering the best ways to communicate with them.

3. **Speak up, even if you know there could be a fallout.** The recent rise in corporate activism and employee advocacy means that people no longer see a separation between the running of a business and the social stands taken by its leadership. Companies from Starbucks committing to hire 10,000 refugees globally, Apple's CEO op-ed calling out "religious freedom laws" as discriminatory, and

PayPal's cancelling of its North Carolina expansion plans after the state enacted its "bathroom" bill, requiring "people to use bathrooms or locker rooms in schools and other public facilities that match the gender on their birth certificate rather than their gender identity," are just a few examples.

4. **Ask for and set adequate budgets.** If something is important to your business, you invest in it. Aubrey Blanche, global head of Equitable Design & Impact at Culture Amp, calls budgets "moral contracts" (Blanche 2020). Minimal budgets, cheap, and free solutions have not remedied the problem. There is no universal structure for determining a budget for your DEI strategy: each strategy must be custom-designed to fit your company's goals. DEI warrants its own resourcing, expertise, and full-time leadership. When building your budget, account for the headcount, external vendors (targeted training and development, well-being), outreach and recruitment, and employee engagement (ERGs, programming, social impact partnerships) costs. Encourage your leaders to invest in DEI initiatives commensurate with the value they create for the business.

5. **Model civil conversations.** Your teams should engage in respectful dialogue on a variety of DEI topics such as stereotypes and judgments at work, practicing allyship, making invisible inequities visible—don't shy away from controversial issues but don't force intimacy. Host AMAs or lightning talks giving employees the room to share their own experiences and solutions. Remember that many BIPOC employees have purposely emotionally detached from their organizations to safeguard their health and safety. We spend an incredible amount of energy trying to avoid offending our white peers because we know that can be, and has been, dangerous for us. If leaders don't do the hard work of following through on commitments made in these conversations, you won't hear the truths you need to hear. The more you do, the more others will notice, and I guarantee they will follow suit.

White people are unpracticed and uncomfortable talking about racism, privilege, and oppression. It's how they're socialized: "Avoid all topics related to race because you'll look bad if you admit that you notice it in other people." Color blindness is not real and it's not a wise management strategy. Coworkers are stuck not knowing what to say or how to step in to help and often fearing for their livelihoods. I have been approached in private more times than I can count to apologize for others' bad behavior or intervene on behalf of a leader who wants their peers to stop insulting or biased behavior. But when I've asked them to join me in publicly advocating for racial equality or publicly confronting discrimination, those same caring coworkers back away unwilling to risk their relationships or expend their work capital to help me.

You'd be surprised by what I hear as a chief people officer. Or maybe not. The same executives who are quick to judge, criticize, or condemn others for not including them in a meeting or update report, or feeling that their work is over-scrutinized compared to their peers, have the hardest time confronting their peers. They jump between silently policing behavior that they feel hurts them, "I wish he would just shut up, he's terrible," and not standing up for those who are suffering the harm of being overly scrutinized or dismissed. In one week alone, I once had three executives—two white women and one white man—complain about each other, and when I asked them to share their experience with their peers they responded, "I'm afraid of the consequences. If I speak up, they'll treat me worse. It's not worth it." It never dawned on them that those below them with far less positional privilege are in far worse conditions and often incur the same if not worse behaviors.

That has to change.

The specific conversations that come next are the scary part, of course. Find courage by starting with language of possibility and understanding. Throughout my career I've often seen people enter these conversations and work with trepidation and fear. Here's the thing, we're all going to mess up, and often. What's important is that we lean on each other to learn what we don't know, push forward when we want to give up, and create a system for course correction along the way. Companies such as Culture Amp and Skillcrush published their commitments to becoming anti-racist organizations along with detailed plans and nine months later shared what they were learning on the journey.

There has been some progress. Culture Amp's stretch metric to improve the representation of Black Campers, the nickname for their team members, showed improvements, as did employee belonging sentiment. While Skillcrush did not have any hiring activity to report, their founder and CEO Adda Birnir's transparency and vulnerability in admitting they had a long way to go while continuing to tie progress to well-defined actions showed promise. "Anti-racism is a muscle and it's a muscle we hadn't been exercising, so, exercising it is, unsurprisingly, uncomfortable and we're forced to face how weak our anti-racism muscle feels." Risk of inaction is larger and makes the outcome of a diverse, equitable, and inclusive culture more uncertain.

Check In: What if you are the problem?

We experience work based on the positional power and privilege we have, or don't have. If you're at the top of the org, you may completely ignore the sore spots below you because they rarely show up in your day-to-day life. But it's those in the lower rungs of the organization, who feel the stress and demands of being disrespected, ignored, and marginalized most acutely. Failing to build perspective through constant introspection and reflection about your own behaviors, management practices and beliefs can mean that you're unable to see when you are, in fact, the problem.

I hear from many BIPOC that they feel frustrated that their manager is not connecting with them, not communicating with them, not giving them clear directions and goals, or obstructing them from advancing in their career. You may think you're talking to them, you're having business meetings with them, but not giving them the higher-up sense of what's happening to help develop their careers. Ask yourself, What have I done as a manager to help them succeed? How present have I been? Am I over focused on correcting instead of coaching some on my team and not others? If you realize that you might be part of the problem, here is some advice:

1. **Practice inclusive empathy.** Don't get defensive; try to cut to the heart of what your employees or coworkers are feeling and experiencing. Build a deeper understanding of what they need work to do for them in addition to what you need them to do for you. Be willing to dig into how your own behaviors may limit their ability to trust and engage with you.

2. **Practice vulnerability that is rooted in curiosity.** Let them know what's tripped you up in your own career and how you have overcome your own lapses. Ask for their views of what could be better and what they want you to understand about their work environment or circumstances. Be willing to admit that what works for you, as a white man or woman, may not work for a woman of color. And be willing to admit that as a BIPOC leader, the strategies that worked for you may not work for another BIPOC employee. And try to devise solutions, together. Remember, your vulnerability doesn't diminish your capacity to lead—it enhances it.

3. **Raise your team members' accountability by cocreating new community norms.** "As a team, these behaviors are acceptable, and these are not." This signals to everyone what your team accepts and promotes and what you don't. Those conversations are difficult to have, it may result in short-term pain, but you need to name it and shine light on it to solve it.

Your Road Map to Revolution

We're all accountable for what happens on our watch. We've all heard the saying: what gets measured gets managed; what gets managed gets done. Accountability can mean a lot of things to a lot of people. To me it's about equity, justice, and commitment. Making a commitment to yourself, your team, your colleagues, your company, and the world to work toward making change. There has never been a moment like now, where people are willing to put the work in to create more inclusive work cultures, to learn from past mistakes, and to do better. The future is bright, there is evidence of change across our workforce, and there is so much we can continue to do to enhance workplace culture. By enabling others to exceed their potential, we collectively rise.

- **Don't fall into the cancel culture trap.** Instead seek to empathize, educate, and revolutionize. Lead with curiosity instead of anger. Ask yourself: "Am I calling out a person or systemic behavior?" "What am I hoping to achieve?" Approach the conversation or message with respect and kindness while explaining the impact of their actions or language. If in person, which is preferable, ask, "What was your intention when you said . . . ?" "How might the other person view this situation?" "How does that land with you?"
- **Get everyone on board with the work.** Engage them by creating stronger connections to the mission and the why. Identify the most influential employees—those who shape the attitudes of those around them—and get them on board. They can be your most powerful agents of change.
- **Ask for short- and long-term goals.** Create individual inclusivity goals for team members with measurable outcomes. Look for new opportunities to create a more inclusive workforce, from a vendor supply program to innovative product development.
- **Show a commitment to civility.** How you act, talk, and walk in the workplace carries weight. Think about the difference between impact and intent. Remind yourself that as a leader, your words and actions matter.
- **Continue to measure your success.** DEI is not a one and done process. Track your progress. Celebrate the wins. When progress stalls, demand that your leaders lead. Ask for new goals, resources, opportunities.
- **Keep learning and growing.** As you near the end of our journey, ask yourself this:
  - ☐ Is my organization giving everyone what they need to thrive?
  - ☐ What role do I want to play in my organization to achieve my DEI ambitions?

☐ What beliefs or long-held assumptions hold me back from being the manager or colleague I want to be?

☐ What will I commit to do on an ongoing basis to understand white supremacy, anti-Blackness, and privilege?

☐ What can I personally do to influence change in anti-Black behaviors, systems, and culture in my workplace?

11 | Persist

I never anticipated an easy road on the journey to create more diverse, inclusive, and equal workplaces. Countless before me have fought to prevent discrimination in the workplace. Yet I quickly learned that succeeding in workplaces would still be more difficult for me than for white people, and the world told me so. I knew that the going would be tough at times, as with all things worth fighting for, but that I could make a difference, that I could add to the growing body of work fighting for justice, fairness, and equity in the workplace. Over the course of two decades as a professional and leader in some of the most admired global corporations, finding hope in progress has sometimes been difficult.

It's easy to throw your hands up. I can't tell you how many times I have felt defeated, enraged, and demoralized by my bosses, colleagues, lack of progress, broken promises, and diluted goals, and what I read in the news. We all want to be where we are supported and encouraged to grow; instead, many of us are tolerated yet not accepted. All while we're put on display for optics. Despite the good intentions and efforts over the past three decades, progress in addressing racism has been disappointingly slow. The year 2020, with its significant challenges, demanded an accelerated pace of change, yet racism remains deeply entrenched. This issue permeates even among individuals and organizations publicly committed to driving change, highlighting the complexity and depth of the problem. It's hard not to lean into cynicism when you've seen that movie play over and over again. When you see companies and new diversity leaders becoming prey to coded "make it happen" directives that lack understanding and nuance in an urgency to tick a box. This is the directive—as long as it isn't uncomfortable, risky, costs too much, or takes time away from white executives' "real jobs" as profit generators. When will we learn? I hope the time is now.

"Change is inevitable, growth is optional," says Zander Grashow, coauthor of *Adaptive Leadership* and founder of Good Wolf Group (Grashow 2018). It's important to remember that we are still building, iterating, and trying to see what is working to transform the workplace. This is not about burning down the house but living in construction. Change is not going to happen overnight, it's not going to happen the second you close this book, but if you take all that you've learned and continue to put one foot in front of the other, it will come. This is how we learn to see beyond our perspective—through the lens of others. This is how we expand collaboration beyond our closest circles. This is how we tap into collective genius to be more creative, innovative, and successful.

"Call in a friend." This is not a solo performance. So much is expected of leaders in these difficult and uncertain times. Even the most ethical decision maker and ally grapple with the weight of the multitude of social issues. When I struggle with finding the resolve to have courageous conversations or how to build common ground, I reach out to my community for wisdom and guidance.

I once texted my friend J. Bob Alotta, VP of Global Programs, Mozilla Foundation, with an SOS asking for advice. We had just released our DEI report and in our internal announcement, when referring to gains in gender representation, we said "men and women-identifying." Our LGBTQIA+ community group leaders quickly called us in about our un-inclusive misstep. "Why not also say male-identifying?" "The language is problematic because some employees may identify as female, others may identify as women." "As a nonbinary employee, I feel unseen." They were right. While we presented data charts with a nonbinary category, we did not refer to them in the employee note. When data collection and reporting practices are at odds with a person's demographic identity, the feeling that one can control one's identity and that it is seen and experienced as valid and authentic is lost. I wasn't sure how to respond without causing more harm.

After listening to me, Bob said, "I wonder about actually not trying to 'fix' this but live in the beautiful tension of it." Her advice bolstered me to create a space for dialogue, learning, and humility. I responded proactively by sharing the feedback with our communications team and drafting a note to the LGBTQIA+ community group. I acknowledged my responsibility in drafting the note, articulated the sticky points about our data collection efforts, and committed to remaining aware of and responsive to the evolving nature of people's identities. Through my immediate response and action, I regained their trust; we learned to do better in the future.

I have been tempted throughout my career to mute who I am, protect my tenuous place in the corporate pecking order, and be seen as a team player. To hold back my curiosity and ambition because it made others uncomfortable. To make myself smaller so that I could be perceived as less threatening to those who controlled my career path, whether my managers or their proteges. To scale down my empathy and passion because they were considered deterrents to making sound decisions. To not speak candidly about the assumptions, presumptions, everyday slights, and systemic inequities I faced.

Revealing my Dominican and Puerto Rican heritage has made me an insider and an outsider in corporate and social spaces. Sometimes low expectations have been laid for me before I could even reveal my credentials or know-how. Other times doors opened because I invoked a comfortable enough image with my *"India"* (read: aboriginal, non-Black) features. I let go of parts of myself in moments and stages of my career, but I found my footing and confidence along the way with the help of many friends and wise leaders. Not without incurring a few scars along the way.

The truth is that holding back who I am would have made me less of a viable candidate for the promotions I earned. It would have made me less trustworthy to leaders, peers, and those who reported to me. Most importantly, it would have made me less effective in breaking down the barriers that continually hold women and BIPOC back from professional opportunity and advancement, and make workplaces unwelcoming, unequal, and unsafe. I've persisted, iterated, and career-switched to make my mission possible, and so can you.

Despite abundant research and evidence highlighting the inadequacy of the status quo for everyone involved, its influence over us remains remarkably strong. I often yearn for a straightforward solution in which well-intentioned leaders and individual contributors join forces, embracing new perspectives, mindsets, and progressive principles, practices, and policies. However, we find ourselves contending with deeply entrenched systemic barriers that obstruct the advancement of historically marginalized individuals into leadership positions. Moreover, we must confront the enduring biases ingrained within us due to these flawed systems. Consequently, it is crucial that we actively participate and persist in our efforts to contribute toward the advancement of more equitable and inclusive workplaces.

I often hear from mentees "I heard in a panel—or was told by someone I met—that to be successful, I need to sound and look more 'white.'" Every time I hear a version of this statement, my heart sinks and my usual smile disappears. It's much easier to be who you are if everyone around you looks like you. It's much easier to celebrate someone's comments when they sound like your own. It's much harder to be the only, the first, the token. The path for professional success should not mean contorting to someone else's image of who they think you should be, who makes them comfortable and fits into their standard of what you should be. We can stop protecting whiteness. We must if we're going to build workplaces that work for everyone.

I'm no longer willing to contort myself into a caricature of white professional standards. No one should. But I still find myself sometimes providing too much comfort for those who hold social and institutional power. Despite knowing that old power structures and rules get overturned. Will we listen?

My call, my ask, my message to you is this: Instead of filling the void with short-lived promises and dropping your commitments and investments the minute pressure hits, leaders and organizations must acknowledge the impact of white supremacy on organizational culture and address the root causes of racial inequity. Managers need to look in the mirror, and then they need to listen to feedback from BIPOC and other marginalized employees without adopting a defensive stance. Companies must be willing to change their structures and practices so that all talent can gain access and opportunity to grow their careers, especially those who have been underrepresented and restricted from achieving to their fullest potential. This requires white executives to be honest about their failures and for BIPOC employees to feel safe enough to ask for what they need: institutional support. White people need to admit that they have benefited from systems that hoard institutional privilege, systemic support, and social capital. The same work-place norms that seem invisible to white people are what block BIPOC employees from success. Workplace culture is the "real job" because without skilled teams who are invested in their work and retained because their contributions are valued, companies will continue to lose profit-making talent again and again.

Many companies have made efforts to make necessary systemic changes in their DEI practices, such as diversity hiring practices, multicultural marketing, and inclusive product design. I have mentioned several throughout this book. However, it is important to acknowledge that these efforts have not always resulted in sustainable and long-term change, and many are under attack.

Companies such as Sodexo, Disney, Google, and Honda have inconsistently invested resources in DEI initiatives, and the work is far from finished. While some progress has been made, there is still a long way to go in achieving true equity and inclusion in the workplace. It requires a commitment to ongoing action and a willingness to hold companies accountable for their promises and organizational values.

Rossana Durruthy, as LinkedIn's vice president of Global Diversity, Inclusion, and Belonging, has exemplified the important of holding companies accountable for their diversity commitments (Davis 2023). She has been instrumental in driving change within LinkedIn, more than doubling the representation for Black employees (by 127%) and nearly that for Latinos (by 74%). Initiatives like the Values Match feature further demonstrate their commitment, allowing job seekers to align their values from work-life balance to DEI, career growth, social impact, and environmental sustainability with the organizations they choose to work for. Long-lasting change will require continuous investment in creating workplaces where everyone feels valued, respected, and included.

Despite films such as *Black Panther, A Wrinkle in Time, Encanto,* and *Flamin' Hot* serving as proof that megahits are possible when Black and Latinx creative leaders are empowered to hire Black and Latinx creative teams and crews and to rethink everything from lighting to hair and makeup to storytelling with a Black and Latinx lens that will appeal to broad audiences, the film industry still faces challenges in green-lighting and supporting such projects. Despite the success of these outliers, there needs to be more representation and inclusion in Hollywood studios. Many stories and ideas from marginalized communities continue to face barriers in getting the necessary support and resources to be brought to the big screen.

Why do so many organizations fail to create an equitable and inclusive environment for all employees? The answer is twofold—we underestimate the challenge of making belonging, equity, and inclusion stick as a lasting and integral part of organizational culture and have failed to explain what's available on the other side to everyone involved—the benefits and importance of creating an equitable and inclusive environment. This includes employees, managers, executives, and other key decision makers.

Making Belonging, Equity, and Inclusion Stick

To achieve real inclusion we cannot overlook the extra effort our brains have to make to include others and the level of discomfort associated with going against some of our most basic instincts. This discomfort holds true for the underrepresented employees and those in the majority. As I've shared before, underrepresented groups face the brunt of feelings of exclusion, which, according to research by Naomi Eisenberger at UCLA, "may be just as emotionally distressing as experiences of physical pain " (Eisenberger 2012). Yes, the world is at an inflection point, and change is no longer an option. But we have to take the time to understand from a deep place people's motivations and willingness to change. This is where the grappling begins.

Second, we cannot fix decades of structural inequity by tinkering at the margins. There's often a lack of incentives for involving everyone in driving change together. But here's what we must also admit to ourselves—the big, white elephant in the room—if institutions and organizations are serious about correcting wrongs and addressing structural failures, then the people in positions of power must be willing to get out of their own way and out of the way of those who can replace them. It's one thing to say that emerging leaders must be given the mentorship, sponsorship, resources, and timeline necessary to succeed. It's another to willingly give up your seat for them to do so.

Natural resistance to DEI efforts stems from people's fear of losing what they have. That is, power, unearned inclusion, status, and economic security. Achieving greater parity—meaning a small minority does not hold all the power, status, and financial security—requires those in power to recognize that, yes, you will have to give up something. How much will you give up to achieve DEI as a white manager? How much are you willing to risk to achieve DEI as a BIPOC manager?

What's Available on the Other Side

We're witness to a pivotal moment in history where existing systems are crumbling under the weight of their own doing. The problems we face in workplaces—discrimination and inequality—have been deeply ingrained in organizational structures. However, amid this time of disruption and demand for transformation coupled with extreme backlashes, there is an opportunity to create a new narrative, amplify marginalized voices and stories, and push for lasting change. White supremacy is a thing, but it's not the only dimension of change. Employees often ask me to address matters not delineated in our DEI strategies that intersect and shape their lives, including neurodiversity, religious observations, and other identity-based matters. I aim not to engage in battles over which issues to prioritize but to find the spaces of common ground, human connection, and shared resources that can move us forward. Otherwise, we stay stuck in the what-if. Many of us often dwell in that paralyzing place where our fears reside, where we numb ourselves into inaction because, at the risk of not knowing where to start, we don't—just start!

DEI is a long journey. You must be in it for the long haul—transforming systems takes time, resources, and patience. The greatest point of resistance is often the greatest learning opportunity. I believe we can, in our own spaces, be active agitators and revolutionaries. And there's a win for you, me, us.

I want BIPOC people to share in wealth creation, and live in a world where more women, POC, and underrepresented groups are richly represented in key parts of our economy and civil society. I'm not the only one. The future of work is now and our workplaces must consist of an integrated focus on diversity, inclusive cultures, equitable benefits, and fair policies. Organizations who do not advance DEI risk their bottom line, brand, and chance for success. The question is not whether we will achieve gender, LGBTQIA+, and racial equality someday, but whether we are courageous enough to reimagine and rebuild the organizational culture of the future today. I challenge you to dig for your courage reserves and exercise real courage now. I challenge you to persist.

Persist When You Make a Mistake (or Are Afraid To!)

Many of us want to change conditions in our workplaces so that everyone can thrive, yet sometimes we are terrified of messing up, saying the wrong thing, or not being able to do enough. It's where many of us often dwell. That paralyzing place where our fears reside, where we numb ourselves into inaction.

It was two weeks into my role as chief people officer at VICE Media Group when George Floyd was murdered and our nation underwent a social justice reckoning that has been long overdue. I was supposed to send an introductory email to our 2,400 global employees, but I couldn't ignore what was happening around me. I didn't yet know many employees personally, but I knew that many were experiencing pain and frustration. I was. Yet I had been working 14-hour days, and I had never felt more convinced that this is exactly where I was supposed to be: in the middle of the maelstrom, helping others figure out what to do. On May 29, 2020, here's what I wrote:

> While this is not the context I imagined introducing myself to all of you, this week has hit me especially hard, and I felt it was urgent to send a note of solidarity to my new colleagues across the world. In addition to being a proud Caribbean Latina, I have dedicated my career to leading large-scale organizational change and fostering diverse, equitable, and inclusive cultures in big and small companies. While this is just week three for me at VICE Media Group, I am personally and professionally committed to supporting our diverse teams across the world—and a big part of that is having the difficult conversations.
>
> Many of us across VICE Media Group are experiencing com-pounded trauma . . . . Many of you may be asking what you can do and how you can better support Black people on your teams, our communi-ties, and others personally feeling the impact of COVID-19 and multiple crises. We would like to inform you that in addition . . . as a company we are also currently developing an educational digital event series focused on unpacking diversity, inclusion, discrimination, and oppression; please look for more info on this in the coming month.

Sent. As I calmly waited, the replies came funneling in. "No one has even been so direct with us about these issues." "I feel like I'm being seen for the first time." The emails didn't stop. I wasn't looking for a pat on the back; instead, it became clear that everyone is terrified to talk about race and few leaders are willing to put themselves in the uncomfortable place of trying to find the words. Sometimes you will get it right (and you have a team of allies to review your message); sometimes you won't. The key is to show grace, get up, and try again. What matters is that you are willing to open the dialogue and learn from your mistakes.

A year later, I shared my experience navigating through the turbulence of that summer:

> We did not rush to make bold statements and ambitious commitments about equity in the workplace. I knew it would take time and effort across the entire organization to create real change that lasts. That is why we set about doing our work internally without fanfare. When everything around me was spinning, I was desperately trying to slow things down. When employees and leaders were clamoring for statements, I asked us to challenge our assumptions about how and where work got done, the behavioral norms and expectations across teams, how leaders led, how managers managed, and how we were structured. I embraced the opportunity of highlighting how systemic racism in practices, policies, and everyday decision-making advantages white majority employees and disadvantage BIPOC employees in regards to access to jobs, work assignments, promotions, compensation, and a sense of belonging. As a Dominican–Puerto Rican who has spent a lifetime navigating cultural and racial identity, this was also a moment of liberation for me.
>
> We doubled down on learning and skill building while the world seemed to be imploding all around us. While every single person has to see themselves in this work, we placed the responsibility on leaders and managers to address the varied sources of inequalities that exist for marginalized people at work. There's a lot of pressure for leaders to have all the answers. They don't. We provided them with the training, encouragement, and resources to meet this complicated moment.

If you're overwhelmed by a real fear of messing up, saying the wrong thing, or not being able to do enough, I get it. The key is to fail fast and recover quickly. When you make missteps, and you will, how you react is more important than what you did. How you recover says more about who you are. And know that you can't expect to be forgiven right away, because saying sorry doesn't eliminate accumulated pain. But when you persist with kind, authentic, genuine care, that pain will lessen over time.

There have been moments when I, too, haven't gotten the transformative work of DEI right. When I was the global head of Diversity and Inclusion at Moody's Investors Service in 2008, we piloted multicultural and women's groups to support underrepresented employees. In 2009, as we were about to launch our official ERGs, one of the founding members of the multicultural pilot, who self-identified as gay, courageously confronted me with one question: How can you speak about creating safe spaces for everyone and not launch an LGBT (the "Q+" would come later) ERG concurrently? The honest answer? Fear. Fear that I couldn't garner the same level of support and advocacy for a community that continued to face social exclusion, harassment, and homophobia within our hallways. Fear of endangering these employees' personal or professional safety by exposing them publicly to the company. Fear that it could risk the other ERG launches if we faced opposition. Fear of failure.

In the same way that I have asked my white friends and colleagues to step outside their own privileged experience to consider the inequities endured by women and BIPOC, I was being held accountable to do so for colleagues missing from the conversation. I made a misstep—I did not look inward to address my assumptions and fears and forgot that to drive lasting change, I needed to exert pressure on the status quo for all marginalized employees.

I have learned. I've confronted my own privilege as an abled-bodied, cisgender, heterosexual brown-skinned Caribbean Latina, and I've grown increasingly committed to intersectionality to build transformational, sustainable change—and to get it right. I'm proud to share that we not only launched multicultural, women, and LGBT ERGs all at once, but our CEO personally sanctioned the LGBT&A (Allies) ERG—an introduction to the term allies before it was en vogue. We held a safe space for LGBT employees.

He listened to their stories. And he gave his full endorsement for managers and individual contributors to create an inclusive and safe workplace where all employees could live their lives openly, without fear of personal or professional recrimination.

We righted a wrong by listening, visioning, acting, and persisting. I am asking you to do the same.

Persist When You Face Resistance

Resistance is real, pervasive, and insidious, and it can manifest in various ways, including reluctance to change, lack of awareness or understanding, and the perpetuation of discriminatory attitudes and behavior. It can be overt or subtle, individual or systemic. Overcoming resistance requires a collective effort and a commitment to ongoing education, dialogue, and action.

Here's what I tell DEI practitioners, managers, and advocates seeking support to face resistance: Fear is the root cause. Fear of losing power, status, or a place in the pecking order. Fear of messing up or of not doing enough. Fear of ceding control. You will always face resistance, and you must persist. You need to build muscles you've never flexed before—an expansive capacity for empathy, business, and personal influencing skills, and fortitude to persist. This resistance is why we haven't realized workplace diversity, equity, and inclusion. But through persistence and constant iteration, we will find the way.

Here are some insights into some of the most common types of resistance:

- **Work resistance:** Perception that DEI work is a distraction. "We shouldn't be taking employees away from their jobs to do diversity work." It is important to highlight how they contribute to organizational success by creating a more inclusive and productive work environment.
- **Resource resistance:** Revolves around resource allocation concerns. "Can you present a more cost-effective solution?" Addressing this resistance requires demonstrating the long-term benefits and return on investment of DEI efforts and explaining solutions that better align with the organization's goals and budget.

- **Fear-based resistance:** Perceived negative consequences of engaging in this work. "I don't want to lose my job for this." It's crucial to communicate that DEI efforts are about creating a more equitable and inclusive workplace that benefits everyone and reminders about non-retaliation policies.

- **Status quo resistance:** Stems from a resistance to change and a preference for the current state. "That's not how we have done things here." "_____ is not appropriate for our workplace or employees." Requires emphasizing the business case and benefits of a more diverse and inclusive workplace in driving innovation, creativity, and competitiveness.

- **Evasiveness resistance:** (Perhaps the most common resistance.) Ah, the common art of deflection or delaying action! "We've made progress." "It's not scalable." "We'll get to it when market conditions improve." "This doesn't feel right." Building a compelling case and providing concrete examples of successful initiatives can help overcome this resistance.

Shrinking from this work is not an option. The cover on racist workplaces has been blown and expectations shifted. Many of us have had to turn the mirror on ourselves, been forced to reckon with the legacy of racism and complicity, including our own. We have come face-to-face with the realization that racism is hardwired into our organizational structures and infrastructure, behavioral tendencies, leadership, and board dynamics.

Key to this work will be sustaining conversations and structural improvements beyond moments when discomfort arises, diversions occur, or you face backlash or competing priorities. There is no end to this work, this conversation; it's not a topic to be tucked away and brought out for periods of discontent or curious examination. For too long we've erred on making people, primarily white people, comfortable with change. Discomfort is a daily condition for BIPOC and other marginalized employees in your organization. This work is no longer about placating grievances but creating conditions for change that can be lasting and sustainable. Otherwise, you risk people reverting to comfortable norms that reinforce the inequalities we seek to change.

Persist When You Feel Fatigued

Diversity fatigue is real, said every DEI professional. I'm sure at times reading this book you may have felt overwhelmed—I intimately know that sense of hopelessness or frustration when there is so much work you don't know where to begin. Or maybe you're suffering from initiative fatigue and getting stuck in the PR moment. Not being able to meet your personal expectations can also lead you to feel dissatisfied, confused, and disconnected.

It's nearly impossible not to be burned out by the intellectual and emotional labor you put into this work. But I have also felt satisfaction and joy in witnessing progress over the last two decades and building community and solidarity with so many. I also understand folks occasionally needing to tune out to safeguard their minds and spirits. Let's celebrate the progress made, find sources of inspiration, joy, rest, and replenishment along the way, and continue to support one another in the journey toward a more equitable and inclusive future.

Change is slow but it is possible.

Don't give into feeling overwhelmed: Just like you can't get caught up in performative, false heroics, don't let the complexity of these challenges hold you under a spell. Pay attention to your mindset, examine your motivations, and deepen your understanding of racism and the intricate nature of identity-based differences. There will be gaps in your knowledge and experience—we don't know what we don't know. You must be willing to be comfortable in discomfort and open to learning and growth. Foster a growth mindset by seeking new resources and information to help you be a better ally, advocate, and accomplice in the fight for equity. Take your preconceptions aside to allow more space to listen and learn from the perspectives of others. Approach conversations from a place of curiosity while acknowledging and respecting the weightiness of the daily challenges faced by your team members. Addressing issues that affect our humanity is always the right thing to do. Whether you are a white manager or BIPOC, we can all find the will to challenge racism, transphobia, misogyny, and other forms of oppression.

Scientifically, this is hard. It raises our flight-or-threat response. And this happens on a continuum. We feel threatened psychologically. We worry about threat response in others. Even thinking about challenging the behavior and actions of others can result in a considerable threat response neurologically. I've felt it. Your heart beats a mile a minute. You consider a million scenarios in your head, and when you finally decide what to say and how, the meeting or moment is over. Did you know breathing is the only automatic function we voluntarily control? Breathing techniques can help regulate your brain functions, reduce anxiety and fear, and increase your ability to reason.

Try this exercise: (1) In a seated position, exhale all of your air. (2) Inhale for a count of four. (3) Hold your breath for a count of four. (4) Exhale for a count of four. (5) Hold your breath for a count of four. (6) Keep the pattern going and repeat this cycle three times. I have to remind myself to do this; it makes all the difference when I do. It dims the voices in my head and helps me see what is happening around me with a clearer lens. And the best part is that you can do it while nobody notices! Try it.

We take for granted that racial inequities are a tightly interwoven system scaffolded together through social, cultural, and institutional practices whose sole purpose is to keep racism in place. That's why what we experience at work cannot stand apart from the lives we live outside of work.

So yes, this work is hard, but picking up this book is one step to understanding and fighting for this inclusion revolution. I'm reminded of Amanda Gorman's poetry at the 2021 US Presidential Inauguration, where she delivered hope to a weary nation and reminded us of who we want to be, "There is always light if only we're brave enough to see it, if only we're brave enough to be it."

Persist by Fighting for "Us," All of Us

I'm often asked, particularly by young women of color, how I maintain my authenticity in the workplace. The ability to "bring your whole self" to work has been called a fallacy by some. I believe it is a complex matter influenced by social, political, and economic tensions. It requires a deep understanding of oneself, political and situational awareness, and a heavy dose of courage. And it's harder for anyone who holds any or multiple identities. While I have long driven DEI strategies to transform corporate cultures, remaining true to my character has been both a work in progress and a defining trait. I can be me—to be kind, bold, brave, and steadfast—because others have fought for me lovingly and fiercely.

I was reminded of this when we celebrated my father's 60th birthday on a family trip to the Bahamas. It was a perfect way to cheer a man deeply rooted in his Caribbean family.

During his birthday dinner, we all teased my father when he announced he wanted to say a few words about everyone at the table. As is typical with my impassioned "*papi*," we were all in tears, most of all him. When it came to me, he began with a story he has selectively shared over the years. He recalled the day he first saw me, when as a fifteen-year-old still discovering who he was, he was struck with a clear and distinct realization, he felt instant selfless love for his baby daughter. That fierce feeling was quickly followed by a deep sense of protection, which meant he would always fight for me, always. And fight for me he has.

The first time my streetwise father fought for me, he was about 18 years old. Fearing what would become of me if my teenage mother raised me in a midtown Manhattan community riddled with crime and poverty, he asked his parents to raise me in their home in the Dominican Republic. And so, on his next visit, he took me with him, never to return. While not a fully hatched plan, he expected some level of resistance. He did not find it. My mother relinquished me, perhaps uncertain about her parenting abilities, perhaps recognizing I could lead a better life elsewhere. In either case, in that moment, she sacrificed her needs for mine, and my father changed my life as he dared to dream for me what he couldn't for himself.

Years later, in my junior year of high school, my father was advised that I needed to complete my PSATs in the United States to improve my chances of entering an American university. He quickly bought a small house in New Jersey that he could ill afford where I moved with my grandparents who devotedly came along to help with the transition—and stayed. All so I could achieve what my father fought for since infancy—my happiness and success through education, access, and opportunity.

Knowing that I have people in my corner willing to fight for me, whether it be my father, grandparents and aunts, or the friends, bosses, and mentors who have heartily advocated for me over the years, has allowed me to stand fully and authentically in myself. And to champion the same for others.

I've been firmly anchored in who I am, often despite what others expected of me, because I've been fought for when I most needed it.

Light has been shined on me so that I can open doors and lighten the load for others.

Just like my father fought for me, I fight so that my daughter grows up to be self-assured, strong, unafraid to advocate for herself and others. My circumstances and my daughter's are far easier than that of my father's, and I have him to thank for that. Her voice, courage, and kindness are my way of honoring his good fight and lighting the path forward so that the journey toward dismantling inequity is a little less lonely, easier to navigate, and more joyful.

In Martin Niemöller's renowned poem "First They Came," he concluded with the powerful line, "Then they came for me—and there was no one left to speak for me." It serves as a powerful reminder that the fight for equality is not limited to one specific group. It is an ongoing collective responsibility that requires our unwavering commitment. When any group is marginalized or targeted, it is only a matter of time before we are affected directly or indirectly. We are interconnected, and our ability to engage with diverse perspectives informs our understanding of the world and enriches our organizations. Embracing multiple viewpoints benefits everyone and contributes to a more inclusive and vibrant society.

Many of us are wrestling with what to do and how to respond to our fraught times. There is a path forward for you to be a force for good. This will take patience, vulnerability, empathy, and courage, and it will require you to devote a large percentage of your time to the people aspect of your job. It matters. You must be willing to sacrifice your own comfort to help heal someone else. This work is about you—it starts and ends with you. You must be intentional about inclusion and belonging. Building stronger connections require knowing each other and understanding that our lived experiences differ vastly.

"What's the difference between a moment, a movement, and transformation? If you're just in it to capitalize on the moment, you will fail fast. If you're trying to create a cultural movement, that's what gets us to lasting change," says Keesha Jean-Baptiste (2020).

I know it can be hard to accept that with privilege comes unearned inclusion and harm, especially when it contradicts your values. I've heard white leaders say: "People of color just think that they can throw everything on us and that we can solve everything for them! I can't solve the world's societal problems!"

No, maybe you can't. But what you *can* do is stop perpetuating inequities within your sphere of influence. Sometimes we *are* the problem and other times, *the* solution. I've found a wall inherently up when we begin taking on the work of changing culture. It's a wall that says, "I don't care." It's a wall that says, "This has nothing to do with me. I'm not like that at all." Or "I don't have time for this; I can barely keep my head afloat."

That's what keeps the middle manager persistently stuck.

This isn't an attack on your character but an opportunity to unlock what holds you back from being the colleague, partner, or leader you want to be. This is a key step on the road to allyship. You have the power to change. And the responsibility is yours.

For my BIPOC peers and colleagues who have for far too long shouldered the burdens placed on you to succeed and make room for others, this book is also for you. I, like you, have a stake in this revolution. Many of you are exhausted from years of compartmentalizing home and work. Many of us also sit at the intersection of bias and privilege. We feel shame, doubt, and guilt about the privileges we hold. We've surpassed our parent's dreams, and yet the corporate air is often hard to breathe. And we also feel resentment, anger, and pain from bearing bias. We, too, have to determine our "what" and our "why" for doing this work. That means that we have to examine how much bandwidth we have and sometimes pause and disengage for our own mental health. That's okay, too.

We can solve racial inequity in the workplace through courageous reflection, vision, action, and persistence. It will mean making mistakes and picking ourselves up to try again.

I firmly believe that we can find a meaningful path to career success in workplaces that were not built for us but that are seeking to transform so that we can all thrive. We, too, have a role to play in making workplaces work for everyone, and we have a choice in what role we play. For some of us, it may mean building deeper bridges across communities of color and other marginalized communities. I believe in the possibility of extraordinary friendships between white and BIPOC colleagues that can lead to real and lasting change.

People can change. Systems can change. Processes can change. Institutions can change.

While the path forward may feel uncertain, workplace change is attainable. This is a moment in time to reimagine and redefine the future. By enabling others to exceed their potential, we collectively rise. I see a difference now; I see a different collective future.

To persevere in this complex and emotionally heavy work, you need to be clear on what you're trying to achieve, be willing to make tough calls, and embrace real moments of courage, as I've shown throughout this book. This is what we are up against.

Nevertheless, I persist.

And I want you to persist, too.

Don't give up on your fellow humans—persist through it all because on the other side is a more equitable future for our children . . . it starts and ends with you.

I hope reading this book has shaken you up a bit, prompted moments of introspection and revelation, and made you feel more competent and committed in your resolve to foster equity and justice in your workplace. You will have not one but a series of clarifying moments on your journey to create an equitable, inclusive, and engaged workplace, and these may include a deeper understanding of the personal practices or habits that may be (unconsciously) thwarting your efforts and the grace needed to stay the course and build the world we all want to live and work in.

My hope rests on the belief that people and workplaces can be different and that we have the agency to make that change. My hope isn't foolish or naive. It's evidence-based. We can be better, and we already have the tools.

I engage in this work because I believe change is possible. I am trying to make work safe, equitable, and inclusive—for all people—because it is possible, worthy and important. I believe you do, too. Let's strengthen our muscles together. We have a once-in-a-generation opportunity to create organizations and industries that truly reflect the world. In doing so, we can change the world. I am counting on you to help realize this shared vision. It's up to all of us to drive this change forward. Let's get the inclusion revolution started.

Notes

Chapter 1

This chapter sets up the premise that it's vital to interrogate your intentions and ask yourself, "Why do you want to do this work?" It begins with a question TV host Marc Lamont Hill asked on an episode of *Black News Tonight* in May 2021 of his conservative activist Christopher Rufo the question: "Name something you like about being white?" I have found the reflective exercises in the book *Leadership on the Line* by Ron Heifetz and Marty Linsky to be most helpful. They coined the phrase "getting off the dance floor and going to the balcony," which I relate to diversity, equity, and inclusion efforts. Stepping intentionally from the balcony to the dance floor and back can help us create powerful goals and actions. To help define your why, I looked at research from Deloitte and Culture Amp on how belonging improves retention. Evan Carr and colleagues (2019) helped quantify this in "The Value of Belonging at Work" and Francesca Gino and Katherine Coffman (2021) in "Unconscious Bias Training that Works" both published in the *Harvard Business Review*. I shared learnings from Mimi Fox Melton and Karla Monterroso's (2021) article "Equitable Workplaces Require Getting Over Fear of Conflict." I drew on findings in "Acute Social Isolation Evokes Midbrain Craving Responses Similar to Hunger" in *Nature Neuroscience*, linking the feeling of hunger to belonging (Tomova et al. 2020). I also cite psychologist Abraham Maslow's work (1943) in this discussion about the importance of creating a culture of belonging. In Maslow's hierarchy of needs, belonging and the need to connect is right there after food, water, and self-esteem. I was further inspired by "Five Classic (and Often Over-looked) D&I Mistakes" published by Korn Ferry (Tapia and Kirtzma 2019) and Kenyi Yoshino's (2006) coined term, "covering." Research from BCG Global confirms that managers have the most effect on the performance and well-being of their teams. But bias is everywhere, and there persists an *us versus them* subcurrent in the workplace, due to decades of social programming, as Mary Casey and Shannon Murphy Robinson share in their book, *Neuroscience of Inclusion: New Skills for New Times* (2017). I also talk about the need for reparations, citing Ta-Nehisi Coates's work (2014), and using that as a guide in creating a roadmap for change. Finally, I make the case for belonging, citing studies from Catalyst on the emotional tax levied on Black employees at work (Dnika, Thorpe-Moscon, and McCluney 2016) and *The Social Psychology of Inclusion and Exclusion* (Abrams, Christian, and Gordon 2007). From these works and Dr. John Powell's, there's no question that increasing inclusion and belonging at work leads to a stronger, more productive and profitable company.

Chapter 2

To begin this chapter, it is essential to understand why the workplace looks so white and why it can't be fixed by an immediate hiring spree. I lean on Peggy McIntosh's work "White Privilege: Unpacking the Invisible Knapsack" (1989), Aysa Gray's (2019) "The Bias of 'Professionalism' Standards," and Michael Sandel (2020), professor of political philosophy at Harvard University who coined the phrase "tyranny of merit," which urges individuals to look at their "meritocratic hubris"—and stop believing in their success as their own doing. I also referenced a *USA Today* article about how state laws are changing to stop natural hair discrimination, a factor that has impacted not just entry to workplaces but also the professional advancement of Black men and women (Terry and Jones 2019), as well as Aubrey Blanche's (2019) interview in *First Round Review*, "Eight Ways to Make Your D&I Efforts Less Talk and More Work," "Why Diversity is Good for Business" published in *Forbes* (Jaleel 2019), and "Why You Should Invest in Unconventional Talent" published in the *Harvard Business Review* (Ferguson and Lee 2021). Because this work not only affects large corporations, I cite Jennifer Jordan and Sonal Lakhani's (2021) piece "No One Is Talking about

This One Key Strategy to Help More Female Founders," published in *Fast Company*. That led me to ideas from Dolly Chugh (2020, 2021) and David Hekman and colleagues (2016) on how to use your privilege to create a more equitable workforce. In showcasing and determining how to set effective hiring goals, I shared a metrics framework informed from recruitment experiences and a template published in *Outsmart* by Ian Cook (2016), the extensive work Ellen Pao (2019) has done for Project Include as well as case studies from Twitter and Nike. Hiring goals always raise the question of what's legal. To answer this, I relied on my experience working with in-house counsel as well as documentation from Jackson Lewis PC (2003) on "Court Rulings Stress National Importance of Diversity Goals But Set Limits on Methods" and "Workplace Diversity—Getting it Right with Goals, Not Quotas" in *Bloomberg Law* (Levinson Werner 2020). To support these ideas, I researched critical mass theory, using Rosabeth Moss Kanter's articulation of critical mass theory as a threshold to guide organizational transformations (Childs and Krook 2008). Finally, I cite academic researchers Iris Bohnet and Siri Chilazi's (2020) work on behavior change, the will, and the way. They say you need the motivation and the skills to get the work done. The motivation can come in part through goals incentivization. Case studies from Accenture, Johnson & Johnson, Nike (LaVito 2018; Thomas 2021), and Mercer (n.d.), as well as reports from UN Women (2020) and Women 20 and the World Economic Forum (2020) discussed the power of setting big goals tied with individual accountability. CNBC reported on the success of reaching goals when you tell someone more successful than you (Stieg 2019). And Robert Livingston (2020) shared meaningful ideas in "How to Promote Racial Equity in the Workplace" published by *Harvard Business Review*. Finally, I used public reports from the Academy of Motion Picture Arts (Ugwu 2020), as well as supporting stories from *The New York Times*, to share the progress made by The Oscars organization to improve its lack of diversity.

Chapter 3

This chapter focuses on the implicit bias laden in the recruiting process. To fully understand its effect, I was informed by studies from Marianne Bertrand and Sendhil Mullainathan (2004) that support the fact that white names are more employable than non-white ones. Joan Williams and Sky Mihaylo (2020) also cite name bias in their research published in the *Harvard Business Review*. This is further echoed by Devah Pager, Bruce Western, and Naomi Sugie (2009) in their research: "Sequencing Disadvantage: Barriers to Employment Facing Young Black and White Men with Criminal Records," and Sonia Kang and her colleagues (2016) who "whitened resumes" to test the implications on the recruiting process. Not surprisingly, when BIPOC whitewashed their résumés, they were granted more access to opportunity. Why does this persist? Recruiters only spend seconds reviewing résumés, according to an eye-tracking study from Ladders (2018) and need to make gut calls. Gut, meaning biased. Applicant tracking systems can help; Forbes reports the majority of Fortune 500 companies use them (Shields 2021). But these too can fall into bias traps. Stopping the use of résumés is a smart solution. I further referenced Aubrey Blanche's (2019) *First Round Review* and an ONGIG blog piece entitled "5 Examples of Racial Bias in Hiring" (Barbour 2020). I also referenced Jopwell's gains in the PGA as described in "A Data-Driven Approach to Hiring More Diverse Talent" by Sandy Cross and Porter Braswell (2019). Research from Dave Heller (2019) titled "Work Experience Poor Predictor of Future Job Performance" confirmed the impact of bias in the selection process. One way to combat it is stopping the Friends and Family program. Survey data from LinkedIn spotlighted the fact that the majority of jobs are filled via networking (Adler 2016), while data from Public Religion Research Institute found that 75% of white Americans have "entirely white social networks" (Cox, Navarro-Rivera, and Jones 2016). Job descriptions can help attract more diverse candidates. Christina Cauterucci (2016) covered the correlation between gendered words in job descriptions and a lack of female applicants in *Slate Magazine*.

Chapter 4

The truth is bad hires happen. A study from Career Builder (2012) revealed that a bad hire can cost a company anywhere from $25,000 to $50,000. Paradigm shared research that 98 out of 100 people in candidate pools are more diverse than the ultimate hires (phone interview on October 2020). According to Paradigm staff, this was based on research in 2016–2017 across approximately 20 companies. This chapter begins with the idea that bias is everywhere. Preeminent scholars on implicit bias Iris Bohnet, author of *What Works: Gender Equality by Design* (2018), and law professor Kenji Yoshino, author of *Covering: The Hidden Assault on Our Civil Rights* (2007), confirmed this, as do Phoebe K. Chua and Melissa Mazamian (2020) who write that current hiring practices at large tech companies lead to class bias. Their paper entitled "Are You One of Us?" suggests that when BIPOC do land an interview, they may not be evaluated fairly and are held to higher double standards. It's an uphill battle: research from Giles and Rakic (2014) proves that we are extremely sensitive to those with accents. Additionally, research from Justin Friesen found that whites struggle to tell real from fake smiles on black faces, which can lead to misinterpretations and misunderstandings. To offer solutions, I sought studies to confirm that broadening your candidate pool will lead to a more diverse workforce. Research from Stefanie Johnson, David Hekman, and Elsa Chan (2016), published in the *Harvard Business Review*, found that when there's only one woman in your candidate pool, her chances to be hired are nearly zero. Further research from Catalyst (2020a) on "Why Diversity and Inclusion Matter'" and Korn Ferry Insights on "Being a True White Ally Against Racism" (Tapia n.d.) emphasize the agency we all have to solve racial inequities in the workplace. In discussing how to interview for "culture add," I sought studies from Lean In's 2020 report, "The State of Black Women in Corporate America" (Lean In 2020) and the UN (UN Women 2020).

Chapter 5

I start with Catalyst's (2020b) report on psychological safety, which notes that only 56% of Black employees were vocal about important or difficult issues in the workplace, compared with 74% of white employees. To establish a sense of belonging from the start, take a close look at your onboarding process. Karie Willyerd's (2014) *Harvard Business Review* article "Social Tools Can Improve Employee Onboarding" stressed that the first six months of an employee's tenure can determine their likelihood to stay, citing a study done by the Aberdeen Group. The company Buffer provided a great case study for how to do onboarding right, with the assignment of Buddies to new team members (Miller 2020). But it takes more than one person to create a welcoming environment. Research from Lucille Nahemow and M. Powell Lawton (1975) discusses how similarities at work can lead to friendships and stronger bonds; this can be exclusionary at its core. *Harvard Business Review* articles by Frances X. Frei and Anne Morris (2020), "Begin with Trust," and by Tsedale M. Melaku et al.'s (2020) "Be a Better Ally" showcase the value of building rich and meaningful connections on the journey to reduce racial inequities at work. Case studies from Culture Amp (Dnika, Thorpe-Moscon, and McCluney 2016; Nordwall 2020) provided ideas for how to break these bonds and create new ones; as does the book, *The Proust Questionnaire*, which provides a series of ice breakers from Marcel Proust (Carter and Servat 2005). Empathy is the fuel workplaces need to succeed. Brené Brown has written much on this, citing the four attributes of empathy from nursing scholar Theresa Wiseman (Thieda 2014). Case studies from Ford (Giang 2016), BetterUp (n.d.), and Friends with Holograms (Harding 2020) show how day-in-the-life experiences can help create a more empathetic workforce and can create a culture of belonging, which can lead to a more diverse workforce. And the reason that is so important is supported by research from David Rock and Heidi Grant (2016), as well as Matthew Corritore, Amir Goldberg, and Sameer Srivastva (2020) in their analyses for *Harvard Business Review*. Finally, I dig into the power of your words on others, and share learnings from Jennifer Sandoval (2020) on coded language.

Chapter 6

The chapter begins with a study on psychological safety, a term first coined by Amy Edmondson (1999) in her work "Psychological Safety and Learning Behavior in Work Teams." More recently, author Charles Duhigg (2016) investigated the building blocks of a "perfect team," specifically at Google, and published his results in an article for *The New York Times*. That confirmed my belief that psychological safety was a defining factor in building inclusive and equitable workplaces. Adam Grant's (2021) book *Think Again* was also a great source into what psychological safety is and isn't, as was Judith Glaser's (2016) work, *Conversational Intelligence: How Great Leaders Build Trust and Get Extraordinary Results*. Aron De Smet and colleagues' (2021) work for McKinsey highlighted the critical role of leadership development in terms of psychological safety. This led me to Timothy

R. Clarke's (2020) work on *The 4 Stages of Psychological Safety: Defining the Path to Inclusion and Innovation*. Stories from the Obama White House were great proof points for my research, like when the women became unofficial allies in meetings and when Barack had to shut down toxic masculinity behaviors that were intimidating to other employees (Eilperin 2019). I also lean on Derald Wing Sue's (2010) research, Evie Muir's (2020) "Racial Gaslights and Microaggression Can't Be Ignored Any Longer" on microaggressions, and a powerful piece by Chanel Cathay (2020), "Racism Is Real in Corporate America—I Left Because I Had Enough" published in *Fast Company*. In thinking about psychological safety and the fear of mistakes, I found this tweet from author Celeste Ng: "privilege is about who is allowed to make mistakes." This led to thoughts on using privilege for good and allyship, which can be complicated. Again, I reference Robert Livingston's (2020) "How to Promote Racial Equity in the Workplace" published by *Harvard Business Review* when considering the value of psychological safety. Research from McKinsey (2021) in "Psychological Safety and the Critical Role of Leadership Development" and Lean In (n.d.) that shows most BIPOC do not believe they have allies at work, even when others consider themselves to be allies, reinforced the need to emphasize safety in the workplace. Research from Deloitte (Smith and Yoshino 2019) shows that the proliferation of covering is a key sign of a non-inclusive culture. I read about Sam Polk (2016) writing about Wall Street's "culture of brutal conformity" to misogyny and the bro culture that forced the disrespect and exclusion of women. In "Uncovering Talent: A New Model of Inclusion," published by Deloitte (2019), Dr. Christie Smith and Kenji Yoshino take a deep dive into the widespread occurrence of "covering at work and the impacts on inclusion.

Chapter 7

In discussing the use and effectiveness of anonymous surveys, I share Gartner's most recent work on their Inclusion Index, featured in Lauren Romansky and colleagues' (2021) article in the *Harvard Business Review*. I referenced Lean In's (n.d.) "Allyship at Work," for which I was a contributor, and Kathleen Davis's (2021) "This Is What White Privilege Looks Like at Your Workplace," published in *Fast Company* when considering the role of allyship breaking away white privilege models. I read case studies on tEQuitable's website (Rose Dickey 2018; tEQtuitable n.d.) to learn more use cases of their reporting software, including the one I mentioned from Twilio. Much of this chapter leans on professional experiences through years of observation, practice and learning.

Chapter 8

Research has repeatedly shown that standard talent management practices such as performance reviews and promotional decisions, remain stubbornly in favor of white men in the workplace, with women of color receiving less support and more vague performance feedback. I read studies from Smith, Rosenstein, Nikolov, et al. (2019) on "The Power of Language," Zuhairah Washington and Laura Morgan Roberts (2019) analysis for *Harvard Business School* "Women of Color Get Less Support at Work" and Herminia Ibarra's (2019) *Harvard Business Review* article "A Lack of Sponsorship Is Keeping Women from Advancing into Leadership." While writing this book, news erupted of the firing of a Google employee, prominent AI ethics researcher, Timnit Gebru. Much was written about this, and I looked at Shelly Banjo's (2020) article in *Bloomberg* who printed the internal memo/mea culpa from its CEO as well as a Medium post from the GoogleWalkout organization. Covid-related disparate workplace impacts also began to surface, including "Performance Management Post-Covid-19: Biases to Consider" by Kristina Dorniak-Wall (2020). Several sources and studies were helpful in deducing the reasons people leave companies, especially BIPOC employees, from Amy Adkins and Brandon Rigoni's (2021) work for Gallup, and Coqual's (2021) report on "Being Black in Corporate America." The EY Belonging Barometer provided key data, including the benefit of regular check-ins (Twaronite 2019). Also, the influence of managers' performance review and feedback on their employees' motivation and morale was supported in research by Marcus Buckingham and Ashley Goodall (2021) and Katica Roy (2020). Katica also shared that only 46% of women (versus 51% of men) believe promotion criteria are fair and objective. Lean In and McKinsey and Company's "Women in the Workplace" study shared data on the prevalence of bias in reviews and promotions by gender, Through analyzing more than 25,000 pieces of peer feedback, Culture Amp (n.d.) has found that individuals tend to focus more on the personality and attitudes of women. To understand more about bias and awareness, I read a study by The National Center for State Courts (Elek and Miller 2021), which highlighted implicit bias among judges. Bias has firm implications, as shown by data from Gené Teare's (2021) article for *Crunchbase* that highlighted the lack of funding to Black founders. In researching feedback and professional development, Frances Jackson and Emma Hansen's (2016) study on "Leadership Potential versus Readiness" in *Human Resources*, Steffen Maier's (2016) "Four Conscious Biases That Distort Performance Management," and The Management Center's (2021) "Four Ways to Mitigate Bias in Performance Evaluations" were hugely valuable. I also relied on Dr. Carla Jeffries's work on feedback, why your employees want to hear the negative feedback (Jarrett 2012), and Shelley J. Correll and Caroline Simard's (2016) work on how "Vague Feedback Is Holding Women Back." A case study from Eli Lilly (Galli 2017) helped provide proof points for the need to cease the annual review. The Ewing Marion Kauffman Foundation highlighted the loan burdens faced by Black entrepreneurs (Wallace Carlson 2021). I build on the unbiasing checklist Google uses during performance reviews. The chapter ends with information on pay equity. I referenced information from Ellen Pao's (2019) *Reset*, as well as data from Equal Pay Today (2021).

Chapter 9

The leaders at Pope Consulting (2020) shared firsthand their account of the company's groundbreaking research in the 1970s on what was holding Black engineers back from advancement. This led me to research from professors Jennifer Merluzzi and Adina Sterling (2017b) that found that Black employees are more likely to be promoted when they were referred by another employee by a factor of 1.2 compared to Black employees without a referral. The 2019 report *Being Black in Corporate America: An Intersectional Exploration* by Coqual (2021) and the 2019 Lean In and McKinsey & Company's (2020) "Women in the Workplace" report provided valuable data on promotion rates based on demographics. In researching employee handbooks, I recall conversations with Freada Kapor as well as assets provided by the Valve Company Website. Culture Amp (n.d.) was a great resource for research on support systems and the impact of who you choose to spend time with, including research from Wilder and Thompson. As was "So Your Workplace Is Toxic: How Can You Fix It?" by Knowledge at Wharton Staff (2019a). I read HR Dive's report on Twitter paying resource groups to understand who was putting this idea into practice (Estrada 2020). In developing insight into why and how to expand your network, I read Dolly Chugh's (2021) *Person You Mean to Be: How Good People Fight Bias*, as well as research from Shai Davidai and Thomas Gilovich (2016) who use headwinds and tailwinds as metaphor to explain our perception of the advantages and disadvantages that we face. Internal research from Deutsche Bank came from an article in *Harvard Business Review* by Herminia Ibarra et al. (2010): "Why Men Still Get More Promotions Than Women." I also referenced publicly available responses by companies like Apple and PayPal to showcase support of employees. Cindy Pace (2020) provided case studies on mentorship at MetLife as well at Catalyst to explore what was happening at Unilever.

Chapter 10

In reflecting on cancel culture and its implications, I read Jessica Bennett's (2020) article in the *New York Times*, "What If Instead of Calling People Out, We Called Them In?" which featured the work of Professor Loretta Ross. My perspective on the dangers of cancel culture aligned with that of Professor Ross, and I found her insights on alternative methods of "calling people in" to be most helpful. To hold your team accountable, I speak on the power of cross-company initiatives and goals. Do they even matter? Research from Devin Pope and colleagues (2016) confirmed that awareness leads to action. Accountability to that awareness is even more important. Case studies on Expedia (Life at Expedia Group Blog 2021), Adidas (Creswell and Draper 2020), and Hilton (Sperance 2020) are highlighted, as well as the 2014 Economics Study at Brookings (Pope 2016), which researched the effect of bias training on NBA referees. I shared goal samples as published by Lawrence Berkeley Labs (n.d.). In studying the impact of goals, I looked to California Partners Project (2022), who published data about the new laws regarding public company boards in the state, as well as a press release detailing the positive impact of Norwegian law on corporate boards (UN 2023). Additionally, public reports on Nasdaq, Mercer, and Apple shared light on those companies' commitments. I also adapted Bernardo Ferdman's

(2020) inclusive reflection statements for individual contributors and leaders into action statements. In exploring individual accountability, I cite the Hispanic Association on Corporate Responsibility (2020), "Empow(h)er: Understanding Workplace Barriers for Latinas," as well as Culture Amp's (2021) self-published plans and goals. An *ABC News* report on how women were not factored into the equation for the automotive industry's crash tests shed light on the impact of bias in product development (Farnham 2012), while case studies of Pinterest (Laurean 2019) and Banana Republic (n.d.) provided examples of designing with an inclusive lens.

Chapter 11

In this concluding chapter, I shine a light on organizations and individuals making strides in the face of overwhelming resistance, exemplified by leaders like Rossana Durruthy at LinkedIn (Davis 2021). This dedication and efforts serve as examples of what can be achieved. At the same time, I draw attention to the sobering reality of when things aren't working, sharing research by Naomi Eisenberger (2012) at UCLA, which reveals the heavy burden of exclusion and its impact on underrepresented groups. To underscore the ongoing struggle for justice and inclusion, I reference Martin Niemöller's renowned poem "First They Came For . . . . " This serves as a powerful reminder that the fight for equality is an ongoing battle that requires our unwavering commitment. Yes, progress has been made, but it's also stalled. However, I maintain my belief that change is possible. We can make a meaningful difference in the world by remaining steadfast in our pursuit of equity and inclusion.

Bibliography

"50:50 The Equality Project—50:50." BBC News, 2020. www.bbc.co.uk/5050.

Abad-Santos, Alex. 2020. "The Food World is Imploding Over Structural Racism. The Problems Are Much Bigger Than Bon Appetit." Vox, June 11, 2020.

Abrams, D., J Christian, and D. Gordon (Eds.). 2007. *The Social Psychology of Inclusion and Exclusion. Multidisciplinary Handbook of Social Exclusion Research.* John Wiley & Sons, Ltd.

Adkins, Amy, and Brandon Rigoni. 2021. "Millennial Job-Hoppers: What They Seek." Gallup, 19 Mar. 2021. www.gallup.com/workplace/236471/millennial-job-hoppers-seek.aspx.

Adler, Lou. "New Survey Reveals 85% of All Jobs Are Filled Via Networking." LinkedIn, 2016, www.linkedin.com/pulse/new-survey-reveals-85-all-jobs-filled-via-networking-lou-adler/.

Lean In. 2020. "Allyship in the Workplace: Where White Employees Fall Short." June 2020. leanin.org/research/allyship-at-work.

"A Long-Term Plan for Anti-Racism at Skillcrush." Skillcrush, Mar. 16, 2021. skillcrush.com/blog/anti-racism-long-term/.

APCO Worldwide. n.d. "APCO: Advancing Racial Equality Blog." https://apcoworldwide.com/about/mission-values/responsible-business/accelerating-whats-right/.

"Apple to Acquire Beats Music & Beats Electronics." Apple Newsroom, Mar. 12, 2021. www.apple.com/newsroom/2014/05/28Apple-to-Acquire-Beats-Music-Beats-Electronics/#:~:text=CUPERTINO%

2C%20California%E2%80%94May%2028%2C,founders%20Jimmy%20
Iovine%20and%20Dr.

Apple Career Site. n.d. "Apple Values." https://www.apple.com/careers/
us/shared-values.html#:~:text=The%20values%20we%20share%20
at,what%20we%20believe%20matters%20most.

Atlassian Sustainability Report. 2018. https://www.atlassian.com/diver-
sity/survey/2018.

Authority Magazine. 2021. "Ragy Thomas of Sprinklr: Five Things You Need
to Know to Successfully Manage a Remote Team." January 26, 2021.

Banjo, Shelly. 2020. *Bloomberg,* Dec. 2020. www.bloomberg.com/news/
articles/2020-12-09/google-ceo-apologizes-for-handling-of-
departure-of-ai-researcher.

Barbour, Heather. 2020. "5 Examples of Racial Bias in Hiring." ONGIG
Blog, July 2, 2020. https://blog.ongig.com/diversity-and-inclusion/
racial-bias-in-hiring/.

Bennett, Jessica. 2020. "What If Instead of Calling People Out, We
Called Them In?" *The New York Times,* Nov 19, 2020. www.nytimes
.com/2020/11/19/style/loretta-ross-smith-college-cancel-culture
.html.

Bertrand, Marianne, and Sendhil Mullainathan. 2004. "Are Emily and Greg
More Employable Than Lakisha And Jamal? A Field Experiment on
Labor Market Discrimination," *American Economic Review* 94 (September
4, 2004): 991–1013.

Better Up: Hickey, Kasey, "How to be an empathetic leader in a time of
uncertainty", September 2, 2019, https://www.betterup.com/blog/
how-to-be-an-empathetic-leader-in-a-time-of-uncertainty.

Best, Emily. 2020. Video interview by the author, October 2020.

Bhalla, Vikram, et al. 2016. "*How Frontline Leaders Can Deliver Break-
out Performance.*" BCG Global. www.bcg.com/publications/2016/
people-organization-how-frontline-leaders-can-deliver-breakout-
performance.

Blanche, Aubrey. 2019. "Eight Ways to Make Your D&I Efforts Less Talk and
More Work." *First Round Review.*

Blanche, Aubrey. 2020. Video interview by the author, October 2020.

Bohnet, Iris. 2018. *What Works: Gender Equality by Design.* The Belknap Press
of Harvard University Press. https://www.hup.harvard.edu/catalog
.php?isbn=9780674986565.

Bohnet, Iris, and Siri Chilazi. 2020. "Goals and Targets for Diversity, Equity, and Inclusion: The Gender Proportionality Aspiration." Harvard Kennedy School, April 2020. https://wappp.hks.harvard.edu/files/wappp/files/dei_goals_in_us_tech_executive_summary_bohnet_chilazi.pdf.

Brand, Dalana. 2019. "Inclusion & Diversity Report September 2019." Twitter.

Brook, Timothy, et al. *Death by a Thousand Cuts*. Harvard University Press, 2008.

Brown, Bréné. 2020. "*The Power of Vulnerability*." TED Talk, June 2010.

Buckingham, Marcus, and Ashley Goodall. 2021. "Why Feedback Rarely Does What It's Meant To." *Harvard Business Review*, Jan. 20, 2021. hbr.org/2019/03/the-feedback-fallacy.

Buffer staff communications. October 2020.

Butler, Reggie. Leadership Trainings at Vice and Google, 2012 and 2021.

Capece, Kendra Claire. 2018. "Angela Davis: Making 'Radical' Imaginable." Urban Democracy Lab – NYU. New Urban Politics and the Right to the City. Blog Student Organizers. https://urbandemos.nyu.edu/2018/11/19/angela-davis-making-radical-imaginable/.

Capital One Corporate Information Site. n.d. "Supplier Diversity." https://www.capitalone.com/about/corporate-information/information-about-our-supplier-diversity-program/.

Career Builder. 2012. "Nearly Seven in Ten Businesses Affected by a Bad Hire in the Past Year, According to CareerBuilder Survey." *Press Room | Career Builder*, 2012. press.careerbuilder.com/2012-12-13-Nearly-Seven-in-Ten-Businesses-Affected-by-a-Bad-Hire-in-the-Past-Year-According-to-CareerBuilder-Survey.

Cargle, Rachel. n.d. "The Great Unlearn." Instagram page. https://www.instagram.com/thegreatunlearn/.

Carmazzi, Tom. n.d. "Creating Space for Speaking Up." Benedictine University. Video. https://cvdl.ben.edu/blog/creating-space-for-speaking-up/.

Carr, Evan W, Andrew Reece, Gabriella Rosen Kellerman, and Alexi Robichaux. 2019. "The Value of Belonging at Work." *Harvard Business Review*, Dec. 16, 2019. hbr.org/2019/12/the-value-of-belonging-at-work.

Carter, William C., and Henri-Jean Servat. 2005. *The Proust Questionnaire*. New York: Assouline.

Casey, Mary, and Murphy Robinson, Shannon. 2017. *Neuroscience of Inclusion: New Skills for New Times*. Outskirts Press.

Catalyst. 2020a. "Psychological Safety—What Is It and How Do We Promote It? London, UK." March 5, 2020. https://www.catalyst.org/event/psychological-safety-what-is-it-and-how-do-we-promote-it-london-uk/.

Catalyst. 2020b. "Why Diversity and Inclusion Matter (QuickTake)." https://www.catalyst.org/research/why-diversity-and-inclusion-matter/.

Cathay, Chanel. 2020. "Racism Is Real in Corporate America—I Left Because I Had Enough." *Fast Company*. July 2020.

Cauterucci, Christina. 2016. "Use Gendered Words in Job Descriptions? Expect Way Fewer Applicants." *Slate Magazine*, Sept. 22, 2016. slate.com/human-interest/2016/09/way-fewer-people-apply-when-job-descriptions-contain-gendered-words.html.

Childs, Sarah L., and Mona Lena Krook. 2008. Critical Mass Theory and Women's Political Representation. *Political studies* 56, no. 3: 725–736.

Chua, Phoebe K, and Melissa Mazamian. 2020. "Are You One of Us? Current Hiring Practices Suggest the Potential for Class Biases in Large Tech Companies," *Proceedings of the ACM on Human-Computer Interaction* 3, no. 143 (October 2020): 1–20.

Chugh, Dolly. 2020. "Use Your Everyday Privilege to Help Others." *Harvard Business Review*, November 19, 2020. hbr.org/2018/09/use-your-everyday-privilege-to-help-others.

Chugh, Dolly. 2021. *Person You Mean to Be: How Good People Fight Bias*. Harper Business.

California Partners Project. 2022. "*Claim Your Seat: Women of Color on California's Public Company Boards*." CalPartnersProject.org. https://www.calpartnersproject.org/wocclaimyourseat.

California Secretary of State. n.d. "Women on Boards." SB826. https://www.sos.ca.gov/business-programs/women-boards.

Clarke, Timothy. 2020. *The 4 Stages of Psychological Safety: Defining the Path to Inclusion and Innovation*. Berrett-Koehler Publishers.

CNBC. 2020. "Reddit Co-Founder Ohanian Resigns from Board, Urges Company to Replace Him with a Black Candidate." June 5, 2020. https://www.cnbc.com/2020/06/05/reddits-ohanian-resigns-from-board-in-support-of-black-community.html#:~:text=Reddit%20Co%2Dfounder%20Alexis%20Ohanian,focus%20on%20curbing%20racial%20hate.

Coates, Ta-Nehisi. 2014. "The Case for Reparations." *The Atlantic.* www
.theatlantic.com/magazine/archive/2014/06/the-case-for-reparations/
361631/.

Common People United website. n.d. "Work That Matters." https://www
.commonpeopleunited.com/about/.

Coqual. 2021. "Being Black in Corporate America." Apr. 8, 2021. coqual.
org/reports/being-black-in-corporate-america-an-intersectional-
exploration/.

Cook, Ian. 2016. "How HR Can Tackle Diversity Using the Rooney
Rule" Outsmart. https://www.hr.com/en/magazines/all_articles/the-
rooney-rule-how-can-hr-tackle-diversity-using-_im34rieg.html.

Correll, Shelley, and Caroline Simard. 2016. "Research: Vague Feedback Is
Holding Women Back." *Harvard Business Review*, April 2016. https://
hbr.org/search?term=shelley%20j.%20correll.

Corritore, Matthew, Amir Goldberg, and Sameer Srivastva. 2020. "The
New Analytics of Culture." *Harvard Business Review,* January–February
2020.

Cox, Daniel, Juhem Navarro-Rivera, and Robert P Jones. 2016. "Race,
Religion, and Political Affiliation of Americans' Core Social Networks."
Public Religion Research Institute. August 2016.

Creswell, Julie, and Kevin Draper. 2020. "Adidas Pledges to Increase Diversity. Some Employees Want More." *New York Times,* June 10, 2020.

Cross, Sandy, and Porter Braswell. 2019. "A Data-Driven Approach to Hiring More Diverse Talent." *Harvard Business Review*, December 2019.

Culture Amp. n.d. a. *6 Ways to Foster Belonging in the Workplace. Taking Diversity & Inclusion to the Next Level.* E-book.

Culture Amp. n.d. b. "Ten Companies with Great Learning and Development
Programs. https://www.cultureamp.com/blog/learning-and-develop-
ment-programs-workplace#:~:text=Pixar%20University%20offers%20
required%20training,according%20to%20Harvard%20Business%20
Review/.

DaSilva, Jennifer. 2020. LinkedIn post, March 2020.

Davis, Clayton. "Oscars Announce New Inclusion Requirements for Best
Picture Eligibility." *Variety*, 9 Sept. 2020, variety.com/2020/film/news/
oscars-inclusion-standards-best-picture-diversity-1234762727/.

Davis, Kathleen. 2021. "*This Is What White Privilege Looks Like at Your Work-place.*" *Fast Company*, February 2021.

Davis, Kathleen. 2023. "How LinkedIn's head of DEI kept the company's diversity promises where other companies failed." *Fast Company*, June 2023.

Deloitte. 2020. "Inclusion Survey: Uncovering Talent." *Deloitte United States*, 29 Oct. 2020, www2.deloitte.com/us/en/pages/about-deloitte/articles/covering-in-the-workplace.html.

DeLong, David, and Sara Marcus. 2021. "Imagine a Hiring Process without Resumes." *Harvard Business Review*, January 5, 2021.

De Smet, Aaron, Kim Rubenstein, Gunnar Schrah, Mike Vierow, and Amy Edmondson. 2021. "Psychological Safety and the Critical Role of Leadership Development." *McKinsey & Company*, McKinsey & Company, 9 Apr. 2021. www.mckinsey.com/business-functions/organization/our-insights/psychological-safety-and-the-critical-role-of-leadership-development.

DiAngelo, Robin. 2018. *White Fragility: Why It's So Hard for White People to Talk about Racism*. Beacon Press, June 26, 2018.

Dillon, Bernadette, and Juliet Bourke. 2016. "The Six Signature Traits of Inclusive Leadership." Deloitte.

Dishman, Lydia. "*Women Are Drowning in Unpaid Labor at Home. Stop Making Them Do It at Work.*" *Fast Company*, Aug. 18, 2020. www.fastcompany.com/90541130/women-are-drowning-in-unpaid-labor-at-home-stop-making-them-do-it-at-work.

D'Innocenzio, Anne. "Adidas HR head resigns as company addresses diversity issues" CTV News. June 2020.

DiversityInc Staff. 2020. "Wells Fargo CEO Works to Repair Damage from His Comments about Black Talent." September 25, 2020.

Dnika, J. Travis, Jennifer Thorpe-Moscon, and Courtney McCluney. 2016. "Emotional Tax: How Black Women and Men Pay More at Work and How Leaders Can Take Action." Catalyst. https://www.catalyst.org/research/emotional-tax-how-black-women-and-men-pay-more-at-work-and-how-leaders-can-take-action/.

Dnika, J Travis, and Jennifer Thorpe-Moscon. 2018. "Day-to-day Experiences Of Emotional Tax Among Women And Men Of Color In The Workplace." Catalyst. https://www.catalyst.org/wp-content/uploads/2019/02/emotionaltax.pdf.

Donaldson, Ben. "Selecting the Next UN Secretary-General," E-International Relations, September 2020. https://www.e-ir.info/2020/09/19/opinion-selecting-the-next-un-secretary-general/.

Dorniak-Wall, Kristina. 2020. "Performance Management Post-COVID-19: Things to Consider." Culture Amp Blog, July 2, 2020. explore.cultureamp.com/c/performance-manageme-1?x=cE1SdN.

Dufu, Tiffany. 2020. Video interview by the author, October 2020.

Duhigg, Charles. 2016. "What Google Learned From Its Quest to Build the Perfect Team." *The New York Times*, Feb. 25, 2016. www.nytimes.com/2016/02/28/magazine/what-google-learned-from-its-quest-to-build-the-perfect-team.html.

Dunn, Alessia. 2021. "Disney Continues to Push Inclusivity, Plans to Depict More Accurate Representation." Disney Blog. https://insidethemagic.net/2021/11/disney-inclusivity-accurate-representation-ad1/.

Edmondson, Amy. 1999. "Psychological Safety and Learning Behavior in Work Teams." *Administrative Science Quarterly* 44, no. 2 (Jun. 1999): 350–383. http://www.jstor.org/stable/2666999.

Eilperin, Juliet. 2019. "White House Women Want to Be in the Room Where It Happens." *The Washington Post*, WP Company, Mar. 31, 2019. www.washingtonpost.com/news/powerpost/wp/2016/09/13/white-house-women-are-now-in-the-room-where-it-happens/.

Eisenberger, Naomi I. 2012. "The Neural Bases of Social Pain: Evidence for Shared Representations with Physical Pain." *Psychosomatic Medicine* 74, no. 2 (2012): 126–135. DOI:10.1097/PSY.0b013e3182464dd1.

Elias, Jennifer. 2019. "Read Sundar Pichai's Email to Google Employees about Researcher's Departure." CNBC, December 9, 2020.

Elek, Jennifer, and Andrea Miller. 2021. "*The Evolving Science on Implicit Bias: An Updated Resource for the State Court Community*." National Center for State Courts, March 2021.

"Employee Training Is Worth the Investment." *go2HR*, Dec. 14, 2020. www.go2hr.ca/training-development/employee-training-is-worth-the-investment.

Equal Pay Today. "Equal Pay Today! OVERVIEW 2021." *Equal Pay Today!* 2021. www.equalpaytoday.org/overview-2021.

Estrada, Sheryl. 2020. "Twitter to Pay Resource Group Leaders, Saying the Work Shouldn't Be a 'Volunteer Activity'." *HR Dive*, Oct. 6, 2020.

www.hrdive.com/news/twitter-to-pay-resource-group-leaders-saying-the-work-shouldnt-be-a-volu/586489/.

Expedia Group. 2020. "Expedia Group's 2020 Inclusion and Diversity Report." https://s27.q4cdn.com/708721433/files/doc_downloads/2021/07/Inclusion-Diversity-Report.pdf.

Farnham, Alan. 2012. "Female Crash Dummies Injured More: What Car Should Women Buy?" ABC News. abcnews.go.com/Business/female-crash-dummies-injured/story?id=16004267.

Feintzeig, Rachel. "The Boss Doesn't Want Your Résumé." *The Wall Street Journal*, Dow Jones & Company, Jan. 5, 2016. www.wsj.com/articles/the-boss-doesnt-want-your-resume-1452025908.

Ferguson, D., and F. Lee. 2021. "Why You Should Invest in Unconventional Talent." *Harvard Business Review*, May 2021.

Fischer, Kristen. 2017. "These Companies Are Hiring-and They Don't Want Your Resume." *Working Mother*. www.workingmother.com/these-companies-are-hiring-and-they-dont-want-your-resume.

Fox Melton, Mimi, and Karla Monterroso. 2021. "Equitable Workplaces Require Getting Over Fear of Conflict." *Fast Company*, March 2021.

Fraser-Hill, Rebecca. 2019. "Belonging at Work Is Essential—Here Are 4 Ways to Foster It." *Forbes*, September 16, 2019.

Freeman, Bernardo. 2020. "Bernardo Freeman–led Diversity and Inclusion Training for Planned Parenthood Federation of American Board." January 2020.

Frei, Frances X, and Anne Morris. 2020. "Begin with Trust." *Harvard Business Review*, June 2020.

Friesen, Justin, et al. "Perceiving Happiness in an Intergroup Context: The Role of Race and Attention to the Eyes in Differentiating Between True and False Smiles," *Journal of Personality and Social Psychology*, published online Jan. 7, 2019.

Fritz, Annette R., "The Implications of Developing and Implementing a Staff Study in Minnesota Courts." Institute for Court Management Fellows.

Galli, Lorenzo. 2017. "Next Generation Performance Management: Interview with Alan Colquitt, Director of Ely Lilly." Science for Work, November 20, 2017.

Garr, Stacia Get al, "High-Impact Diversity and Inclusion: Maturity Model and Top Findings," Bersin by Deloitte, Deloitte Consulting, May 2017.

Gerdeman, Dina. 2017. "Minorities Who 'Whiten' Job Resumes Get More Interviews." *Harvard Business Review* Working Knowledge, May 2017.

Giang, Vivian. 2016. "How Ford Uses an 'Empathy Belly' to Improve Its Employees' Soft Skills." LinkedIn Blog, August 10, 2016.

Giles, H., and T Rakic. 2014. "Language Attitudes: Social Determinants and Consequences of Language Variation." In T. Holtgraves (Ed.), *The Oxford handbook of language and social psychology* (pp. 11–26). Oxford: Oxford University Press.

Gino, Francesca, and Katherine Coffman. 2021. "Unconscious Bias Training That Works." *Harvard Business Review*. September-October 2021.

Glaser, Judith. 2016. *Conversational Intelligence: How Great Leaders Build Trust and Get Extraordinary Results*. Routledge.

Godoy, Jody. 2023. "US Court Upholds Nasdaq Board Diversity Rule." Reuters, October 18, 2023.

Goler, Lori et al. 2018. "*Why People Really Quit Their Jobs.*" *Harvard Business Review*, January 2018.

Grant, Adam. 2021. *Think Again: The Power of Knowing What You Don't Know*. Penguin Publishing Group.

Grashow, Zander. 2018. *Statement shared in a coaching session on June 2018*.

Gray, Aysa. 2019. "The Bias of 'Professionalism' Standards." *Stanford Social Innovation Review*, June 2019.

Guynn, Jessica. 2015. "Michael Moritz Taking Heat for Comments about Hiring Women." *USA Today*, December 3, 2015.

Harding, Courtney. 2020. Video interview by the author, October 2020.

Haridasani Gupta, Allisha. 2022. "Another California Board Diversity Law Was Struck Down, But It Already Had a Big Impact." *New York Times*, May 19, 2022.

Hastwell, Claire. 2019. "How Best Companies Ensure People Can Bring Their Whole Selves to Work." Great Places to Work Blog, September 13, 2019.

Hauser, Fran. 2019. *The Myth of the Nice Girl: Achieving the Career You Want without Becoming the Person You Hate*. Harper Business, April 16, 2019.

Heifetz, Ronald A., and Martin Linsky. 2017. *Leadership on the Line: Staying Alive through the Dangers of Change*. Harvard Business Review Press.

Hekman, David R., Stefanie K Johnson, Maw-Der Foo, and Wei Yang. 2016. "Does Diversity-Valuing Behavior Result in Diminished Performance Ratings for Non-White and Female Leaders?" *Academy of Management Journal* 60, no. 2, March 3, 2016. journals.aom.org/doi/abs/10.5465/amj.2014.0538.

Heller, Dave. 2019. "Work Experience Poor Predictor of Future Job Performance." Phys.org, May 14, 2019. phys.org/news/2019-05-poor-predictor-future-job.html.

Hill, Marc Lamont. 2021. "Marc Lamont Hill in Discussion with Christopher Rufo." *Black News Tonight Podcast.* May 2021.

Hooks, bell. 1986. "Sisterhood: Political Solidarity between Women." *Feminist Review*, no. 23, 1986, pp. 125–138. *JSTOR*, www.jstor.org/stable/1394725. Accessed 11 Apr. 2021.

Harts, Minda. 2019. *The Memo: What Women of Color Need to Know to Secure a Seat at the Table*. Seal Press, August 2019.

Harts, Minda, Sarah Lacy, and Eve Rodsky. 2020. "Women Are Drowning in Unpaid Labor. Stop Making Them Do It at Work." *Fast Company*, August 19, 2020.

Hilgers, Laura. 2021. "One Simple Way Companies Can Invest in Their Diversity and Inclusion Efforts." LinkedIn Talent Blog, July 7, 2021.

Life at Expedia Group Blog. 2021. "How We Drive Inclusion and Diversity in Expedia Group." Jan 26, 2021. blog.lifeatexpediagroup.com/experiences/how-we-drive-inclusion-and-diversity-in-expedia-group/.

Hispanic Association on Corporate Responsibility, The. 2020. "Empow(h)er: Understanding Workplace Barriers for Latinas." https://www.blog.hacr.org/hri_blog/hacr-latina-empowher-initiative.

Hunt, Vivian et al. 2018. "Delivering Through Diversity." McKinsey & Company, January 2018. https://www.mckinsey.com/~/media/mckinsey/business%20functions/organization/our%20insights/delivering%20through%20diversity/delivering-through-diversity_full-report.ashx#:~:text=Companies%20in%20the%20top%2Dquartile%20for%20gender%20diversity%20on%20their,likely%20to%20outperform%20on%20profitability.

Ibarra, Herminia. 2019. "A Lack of Sponsorship Is Keeping Women from Advancing into Leadership." *Harvard Business Review*, August 19, 2019. https://hbr.org/2019/08/a-lack-of-sponsorship-is-keeping-women-from-advancing-into-leadership.

Ibarra, Herminia et al. 2010. "Why Men Still Get More Promotions Than Women." *Harvard Business Review*, September 2010. https://hbr.org/2010/09/why-men-still-get-more-promotions-than-women.

Ideal. n.d. "Workplace Diversity through Recruitment: A Step-by-Step Guide." https://ideal.com/workplace-diversity/.

Jackson, Frances, and Emma Hansen. 2016. "Leadership Potential versus Readiness." *Human Resources*, summer 2016. http://www.sheffield.co.nz/Portals/0/Human%20Resources%20Summer%20Issue%202016;%20Pages24-25;%20Leadership%20Potential.pdf.

Jackson Lewis PC. 2003. "Court Rulings Stress National Importance of Diversity Goals But Set Limits on Methods." June 24, 2003. https://casetext.com/analysis/court-rulings-stress-national-importance-of-diversity-goals-but-set-limits-on-methods.

Jaleel, Abdul. 2019. "Why Diversity is Good for Business." *Forbes*, June 3, 2019.

Jarrett, Christian. 2012. "Who Are You Protecting When You Praise a Dud Performance?" *Research Digest*, May 2, 2012. https://www.bps.org.uk/research-digest/who-are-you-protecting-when-you-praise-dud-performance/.

Jean-Baptiste, Keesha. 2020. Video interview by the author, October 2020.

Joel, Allie. 2018. "Real Talk: Fostering Diversity and Inclusion through Real Conversations." Asana Blog, November 9, 2018.

Johnson, Stefanie K., David R Hekman, and Elsa T Chan. 2016. "If There's Only One Woman in Your Candidate Pool, There's Statistically No Chance She'll Be Hired." *Harvard Business Review*, April 26, 2016. hbr.org/2016/04/if-theres-only-one-woman-in-your-candidate-pool-theres-statistically-no-chance-shell-be-hired.

Jones, Liz. 2020. Phone interview by the author, October 2020.

Jordan, Jennifer, and Sonal Lakhani. 2021. "No One Is Talking about This One Key Strategy to Help More Female Founders." *Fast Company*. March 2021.

Kang, Sonia K, Katy Decelles, András Tilcsik, and Sora Jun. 2016. "Whitened Resumes: Race and Self-Presentation in the Labor Market." *Administrative Science Quarterly* 61, no. 3. DOI: 10.1177/0001839216639577. https://www.researchgate.net/publication/

298795100_Whitened_Resumes_Race_and_Self-Presentation_in_ the_Labor_Market.

Kapor Capital Careers Site. n.d. Job Posting. https://apply.workable.com/ kaporcenter/j/1996CF88BD/.

Klein, Freada Kapor. 2020. Video interview by the author, October 15, 2020.

Knowledge at Wharton Staff. 2019a. "So Your Workplace Is Toxic: How You Can Fix It?" May 2019.

Knowledge at Wharton Staff. 2019b. "Uncovering Bias: A New Way to Study Hiring Can Help." July 18, 2019.

Labor Force Projections to 2024: The Labor Force Is Growing, but Slowly. *Monthly Labor Review.* U.S. Bureau of Labor Statistics, 1 Dec. 2015, www .bls.gov/opub/mlr/2015/article/labor-force-projections-to-2024.htm.

Ladders. 2018. "Eye-Tracking Study." https://www.theladders.com/static/ images/basicSite/pdfs/TheLadders-EyeTracking-StudyC2.pdf.

Laurean Yates, Jacqueline. 2019. "Pinterest Launches Inclusive Search Tool Beauty Enthusiasts Will Love." ABC News, January 25, 2019.

LaVito, Angelica. "Nike's Colin Kaepernick Ads Created $163.5 Million in Buzz since It Began-and It's Not All Bad." CNBC, 6 Sept. 2018, www.cnbc.com/2018/09/06/nikes-colin-kaepernick-ad-created- 163point5-million-in-media-exposure.html.

Lawrence Berkeley National Laboratory. n.d. Human Resources, Diver- sity and Inclusion Office, "Diversity and Inclusion: Sample Goals and Activities for Performance Reviews."

Lean In. 2020. "The State of Black Women in Corporate America, 2020." https://leanin.org/research/state-of-black-women-in-corporate- america.

Lean In. n.d. "Allyship at Work." https://allyship.leanin.org/#book/page1.

Lean In and McKinsey & Company. 2020. "Women in the Workplace 2020: A Crisis Is Looming in Corporate America." womenintheworkplace.com/.

Lempert, Richar. "The Supreme Court is Poised to Reverse Affirma- tive Action: Here's What You Need to Know." Brookings, June 5, 2023, www.brookings.edu/blog/fixgov/2023/06/05/the-supreme- court-is-poised-to-reverse-affirmative-action-heres-what-you- need-to-know/.

Lepore, Meredith. 2020. "You Have 7.4 Seconds to Make an Impression: How Recruiters See Your Resume." Ladders website, January 30, 2020.

https://www.theladders.com/career-advice/you-only-get-6-seconds-of-fame-make-it-count.

Levinson Werner, Julie. 2020. "Workplace Diversity—Getting It Right with Goals, Not Quotas." *Bloomberg Law*, November 2020.

Livingston, Robert. 2020. "How to Promote Racial Equity in the Workplace. A Five Step Plan." *Harvard Business Review* 98, Sept-Oct 2020, pp. 64–72.

Management Center, The. 2021. "Four Ways to Mitigate Bias in Performance Evaluations." July 28, 2021.

Maier, Steffen. 2016. *"Four Unconscious Biases That Distort Performance Reviews"*. September 2016.

Mann, Annamarie. 2021. "Why We Need Best Friends at Work." Gallup, 19 Mar. 2021, www.gallup.com/workplace/236213/why-need-best-friends-work.aspx.

Marken, Stephanie. 2019. "How a Best Friend at Work Changes Engagement in Higher Education." Gallup, July 26, 2019.

Martinez, Lucinda. 2020. Video interview by the author, October 2020.

Maslow, A. H. (1943). A theory of human motivation. *Psychological Review*, 50(4), 370–396. https://doi.org/10.1037/h0054346.

McIntosh, Peggy. 1989. "White Privilege: Unpacking the Invisible Knapsack" *Peace and Freedom Magazine*, July/August, 1989.

McKinsey Institute For Black Economic Mobility. 2023. "Corporate Commitment to Racial Justice: An Update." February 21, 2023.

McKinsey Quarterly. 2022. "The CEO Moment: Leadership for a New Era." July 2020.

McKinsey. 2021. "Psychological Safety and the Critical Role of Leadership Development." February 2021.

Melaku, Tsedale, Angie Breeman, David G. Smith, and W. Brad Johnson. 2020. "Be a Better Ally." *Harvard Business Review*, Nov–Dec 2020.

Mercer. n.d. "Using Compensation to Drive Action on Diversity, Equity and Inclusion." www.mercer.us/our-thinking/career/using-compensation-to-drive-action-on-diversity-equity-and-inclusion.html.

Merluzzi, Jennifer, and Adina Sterling. 2017a. "Lasting Effects? Referrals and Career Mobility of Demographic Groups in Organizations." *ILR Review*, vol. 70, no. 1, Jan. 2017, pp. 105–131, DOI:10.1177/0019793916669507. https://journals.sagepub.com/doi/full/10.1177/0019793916669507.

Merluzzi, Jennifer, and Adina Sterling. 2017b. "Research: Black Employees Are More Likely to Be Promoted When They Were Referred by Another Employee." *Harvard Business Review*, Apr. 11 2017. hbr .org/2017/02/research-black-employees-are-more-likely-to-be-promoted-when-they-were-referred-by-another-employee?

Meyer, Robinson. "90% Of Wikipedia's Editors Are Male–Here's What They're Doing About It." *The Atlantic*, Oct. 26, 2013, www.theatlantic .com/technology/archive/2013/10/90-of-wikipedias-editors-are-male-heres-what-theyre-doing-about-it/280882/.

Mckesson, DeRay. "'I Learned Hope the Hard Way': on the Early Days of Black Lives Matter." *The Guardian*, Apr. 12, 2019. www.theguardian .com/world/2019/apr/12/black-lives-matter-deray-mckesson-ferguson-protests.

Mckesson, DeRay. 2018. *On the Other Side of Freedom*. Penguin Books.

Miller, Nicole. 2020. "The Evolution of Onboarding at Buffer: How We Welcome New Teammates." Buffer Resources, June 30, 2020. buffer .com/resources/onboarding/.

Muir, Evie. 2020. "Racial Gaslighting and Microaggressions Can't Be Ignored Any Longer." Refinery29, August 2020.

Myers, Verna. 2014. "How to Overcome Our Biases? Walk Boldly toward Them." TED Talk, November 2014.

Nahemow, Lucille, and M Powell Lawton, M. 1975. "Similarity and Propinquity in Friendship Formation." *Journal of Personality and Social Psychology* 32, no. 2: 205–213. DOI: 10.1037/0022-3514.32.2.205. https:// www.researchgate.net/publication/232594605_Similarity_and_propinquity_in_friendship_formation.

Nellis, Stephen. 2021. "Apple Will Modify Executive Bonuses Based on Environmental Values in 2021." Reuters, Jan. 5, 2021. www.reuters .com/article/us-apple-compensation/apple-will-modify-executive-bonuses-based-on-environmental-values-in-2021-idUSKBN29A2MK.

Ng, Celeste. 2020. Tweet.

Nordwall, Stacey. 2020. "Connect with Coworkers, Make a Date with Donut." Culture Amp Blog, Aug 16, 2020. www.cultureamp.com/ blog/connect-with-coworkers-make-a-date-with-donut/.

Obama, Barak. 2020. *A Promised Land*. Crown.

O'Kelley, Brian. 2020. Video interview by the author.

Pace, Cindy. 2020. Video interview by the author, October 2020.

Pager, Devah, Bruce Western, and Naomi Sugie, 2009. "Sequencing Disadvantage: Barriers to Employment Facing Young Black and White Men with Criminal Records." *The Annals of the American Academy of Political and Social Science* 623, no. 1 (2009): 195–213. https://www.ncbi.nlm.nih.gov/pmc/articles/PMC3583356/pdf/nihms-439026.pdf.

Pao, Ellen. 2017. *Reset: My Fight for Inclusion and Lasting Change.* Random House.

Pao, Ellen. 2019. "Roadmap to Diversity and Inclusion." Medium, May 2019. medium.com/projectinclude/https-medium-com-projectinclude-targets-as-roadmap-to-diversity-and-inclusion-347e8e0b791b.

Passin, Greg. n.d. "*Using Compensation to Drive Action on Diversity, Equity, and Inclusion.*" Mercer. https://www.mercer.com/assets/us/en_us/shared-assets/local/attachments/pdf-2022-using-compensation-to-drive-action-on-diversity-equity-and-inclusion.pdf.

Phippen, Weston J, and National Journal. 2015. "With New Hires 'Daily Show' Tackles Its Diversity Problem." *The Atlantic*, September 29, 2015.

Pichai, Sundar. 2022. "Our Plan to Invest $9.5 Billion in the US in 2022." Google Blog, April 13, 2022. https://blog.google/inside-google/company-announcements/investing-america-2022/.

Polk, Sam. 2016. "How Wall Street Bro Talk Keeps Women Down." *The New York Times*, July 7, 2016.

Pope Consulting. 2020. Interview by the author, October 2020.

Pope, Devin, et al. 2016. "Awareness Reduces Racial Bias." Brookings Institute. https://www.brookings.edu/wp-content/uploads/2016/06/awareness_reduces_racial_bias_wolfers.pdf.

Powell, John A. 2017. "John A. Powell on How Bridging Creates Conditions to Solve Problems." Video transcript. Othering & Belonging Institute. November 2, 2017. https://belonging.berkeley.edu/john-powell-how-bridging-creates-conditions-solve-problems.

Purdue University HR. n.d. "Staff Promotion Guidelines." Human Resources, Purdue University. www.purdue.edu/hr/mngcareer/compguidelines/stproinc.php.

Roanhorse, Vanessa. 2020. Video interview by the author, October 2020.

Robb, David. 2020. "Anita Hill Op-Ed: Hollywood Has Made Strides To Eliminate Sexual Harassment & Bias, But Can Still Do Better." *Deadline*, Dec. 15, 2020, deadline.com/2020/12/anita-hill-op-ed-hollywood-sexual-harassment-bias-elimination-progress-report-1234656496/.

Rock, David, and Heidi Grant. 2016. "Why Diverse Teams Are Smarter." *Harvard Business Review*, Nov. 2016. hbr.org/2016/11/why-diverse-teams-are-smarter.

Romansky, Lauren, and Garrod Mia, et al. 2021. "How to Measure Inclusion in the Workplace." *Harvard Business Review*, May 2021.

Rose Dickey, Megan. 2015. "Pinterest Is Working with a Startup Called Paradigm to Foster Diversity." *Tech Crunch*, July 30, 2015.

Roy, Katica. 2020. Video interview by the author, October 2020.

Runningwater, Bird. 2020. Video interview by the author, October 2020.

Sandel, Michael. 2020. *The Tyranny of Merit: What's Become of the Common Good?* Farrar, Straus and Giroux.

Sandoval, Jennifer. 2020. Video interview by the author, October 2020.

Saujani, Reshma. 2020. Video interview by the author, October 2020.

Seramount. 2017. "Seramount Case Study: P&G's Global Diversity Goals Set and Communicate Priorities." October 10, 2017. https://seramount.com/articles/case-study-pgs-global-diversity-goals-set-and-communicate-priorities/.

Shai, Davidai and Thomas Gilovich. 2016. "The Headwinds/Tailwinds Asymmetry: An Availability Bias in Assessments of Barriers and Blessings." *J Pers Soc Psychol* 111, no. 6 (Dec. 2016): 835–851. DOI: 10.1037/pspa0000066. PMID: 27869473. https://pubmed.ncbi.nlm.nih.gov/27869473/.

Shankland, Steven. 2020. "Twitter Engineers Replacing Racially Loaded Tech Terms Like 'master,' 'slave.'" CNET, July 2, 2020.

Shields, Jon. 2021. "Report: 98% of Fortune 500 Companies Use ATS." Jobscan, 26 Feb. 2021. www.jobscan.co/blog/fortune-500-use-applicant-tracking-systems/.

Singleton, Glenn. n.d. "Courageous Conversation." Compass. https://courageousconversation.com/about/.

Slack Blog. 2019. "*Diversity at Slack*." May 2019. https://slack.com/blog/news/diversity-at-slack-2019/.

Smith, D.G., Rosenstein, J.E., Nikolov, M.C. et al. 2019. "The Power of Language: Gender, Status, and Agency in Performance Evaluations." *Sex Roles* 80, 159–171. https://doi.org/10.1007/s11199-018-0923-7.

Smith, Christine, and Kenji Yoshino. 2019. "Uncovering Talent: A New Model of Inclusion." Deloitte.

"Standing with Dr. Timnit Gebru—#ISupportTimnit #BelieveBlackWomen." Medium, Dec. 2020. googlewalkout.medium.com/standing-with-dr-timnit-gebru-isupporttimnit-believeblackwomen-6dadc300d382.

Stieg, Cory. 2019. "How to Stay Committed to Your Goals: Tell Someone More Successful than You, Says New Study." CNBC, September 5, 2019. www.cnbc.com/2019/09/05/why-sharing-goals-with-someone-helps-you-achieve-them.html#:~:text=Researchers%20say%20that%20sharing%20your,say%2C%20a%20peer%20or%20friend.

Sue, Derald Wing. 2010. *Microaggressions in Everyday Life: Race, Gender, and Sexual Orientation.* Wiley.

Suzuki Shunryū, and Trudy Dixon. *Zen Mind, Beginner's Mind.* Shambhala, 2020.

Sorkin, Andrew Ross, et al. 2020. "Nasdaq Pushes for Diversity in the Boardroom." *The New York Times,* 1 Dec. 2020. www.nytimes.com/2020/12/01/business/dealbook/nasdaq-diversity-boards.html#:~:text=Nasdaq%20will%20require%20boards%20to,within%20a%20year%20of%20S.E.C.

Sperance, Cameron. 2020. "Hilton's Diversity Strategy Underscores Recruiting Efforts in a Time of Deep Job Cuts." Skift.com.

Tapia, Andres. n.d. "Being a True White Ally Against Racism." Korn Ferry Insights. https://www.kornferry.com/insights/this-week-in-leadership/become-a-white-ally-against-racism.

Tapia, A., and F. Kirtzma. 2019. "Five Classic (and Often Overlooked) D&I Mistakes." Korn Ferry.

Teare, Gené. 2021. "Highlighting Notable Funding To Black Founders In 2020." *Crunchbase*, February 2021.

Terry, E, and C. Jones. 2019. "Banning Ethnic Hair Styles 'Upholds' This Notion of White Supremacy. States Pass Laws to Stop Natural Hair Discrimination." *USA Today*, October 2019.

Textio. n.d. Textio Corporate website. https://textio.com/.

Thieda, Kate. 2014. "Brené Brown on Empathy vs. Sympathy." *Psychology Today*, Sussex Publishers, Aug. 12, 2014. www.psychologytoday.com/

us/blog/partnering-in-mental-health/201408/bren-brown-empathy-vs-sympathy-0.

Thomas, Lauren. 2021. "Nike Sets Fresh Diversity Targets for 2025, and Ties Executive Compensation to Hitting Them." CNBC, 13 Mar. 2021. www.cnbc.com/2021/03/11/nike-sets-diversity-goals-for-2025-ties-executive-comp-back-to-them.html.

T-Mobile Career Site. n.d. "Culture and Benefits / Diversity." https://careers.t-mobile.com/culture-and-benefits/diversity-2/.

Tomova, L., K.L. Wang, T. Thompson, G.A. Matthews, A. Takahashi, K.M. Tye, and R. Saxe. 2020. "Acute Social Isolation Evokes Midbrain Craving Responses Similar to Hunger." *Nat Neuroscience* 23, no. 12: 1597–1605.

Torres, Sherrice. 2020. Video interview by the author, October 2020.

"Transform Performance Management." Gallup, Mar. 22, 2021. www.gallup.com/workplace/215927/maximize-performance-management.aspx?g_source=PERFORMANCE_MANAGEMENT&g_medium=topic&g_campaign=tiles.

Trudel, Natalie. 2017. "Yes, You Can Eliminate the Annual Review, Improve Engagement and Still Get Workforce Metrics." *TLNT*, Jan. 4, 2017. www.tlnt.com/yes-you-can-eliminate-the-annual-review-improve-engagement-and-still-get-workforce-metrics/.

Twaronite, Karyn. 2019. "EY Belonging Barometer Workplace Study." Ernst and Young, May 11, 2019. www.ey.com/en_us/diversity-inclusiveness/ey-belonging-barometer-workplace-study.

Ugwu, Reggie. 2020. "The Hashtag That Changed the Oscars: An Oral History." *The New York Times*, February 6, 2020.

UN. 2003. "Norway Called 'Haven for Gender Equality,' as Women's Anti-discrimination Committee Examines Reports On Compliance With Convention" https://www.un.org/press/en/2003/wom1377.doc.htm.

UN Women. 2020. "*Women as Drivers of Economic Recovery and Resilience during COVID-19 and Beyond.*" July 2020. https://www.unwomen.org/en/news/stories/2020/7/statement-joint-w20-women-during-covid-19-and-beyond.

"Understanding Implicit Bias." Kirwan Institute for the Study of Race and Ethnicity. kirwaninstitute.osu.edu/research/understanding-implicit-bias/.

"Unilever: Changing the Game, Unlocking the Future (Case Study)." Catalyst, Mar. 2020, www.catalyst.org/research/unilever-case-study/.

"Update on Culture Amp's Anti-Racism Plan and Goals." Culture Amp Blog, 23 Mar. 2021, www.cultureamp.com/blog/update-on-culture-amps-anti-racism-plan-and-goals/.

Valve Company Website, Employee Handbook: https://assets.sbnation .com/assets/1074301/Valve_Handbook_LowRes.pdf.

Wakabayashi, Daisuke. 2017. "Google Fires Engineer Who Wrote Memo Questioning Women in Tech." *New York Times*, August 7, 2017.

Walt Disney Corporate Site. n.d. "About the Walt Disney Company." https://thewaltdisneycompany.com/.

Washington, Zuhairah and Laura Morgan Roberts. 2019. "Women of Color Get Less Support at Work. Here's How Managers Can Change That." *Harvard Business Review*. March 2019.

Weisul, Kimberly. 2017. "Half of This College's STEM Graduates Are Women. Here's What It Did Differently." *Inc.*, May. 31, 2017.

Wilder, David A, John E Thompson. 1980. "Intergroup Contact with Independent Manipulations on In-Group and Out-Group Interaction." *Journal of Personality and Social Psychology* 38, no. 4 (April 1980): 589–603.

Williams, Joan C., and Sky Mihaylo. 2020. "How the Best Bosses Interrupt Bias on Their Teams." *Harvard Business Review*, June 15 2020. hbr.org/2019/11/how-the-best-bosses-interrupt-bias-on-their-teams?ab=hero-main-text.

Williamson, Alicin Reddy. 2020. Video interview by the author, October 2020.

Willyerd, Karie. 2014. "Social Tools Can Improve Employee Onboarding." *Harvard Business Review*, 7 Aug. 2014. hbr.org/2012/12/social-tools-can-improve-e.

Wilson, Cid. 2020. Video interview by the author, October 2020.

Wilson, Jamia. 2020. Video interview by the author, October 2020.

Wojcicki, Susan. 2016. Team communications at YouTube.

World Economic Forum. 2020. "Unleashing the power of Europe's women entrepreneurs: Six ideas to drive big change." January 2020. http://www3.weforum.org/docs/WEF_Unleashing_the_power_of_ Europes_women_entrepreneurs.pdf.

Yoshino, Kenji. 2006. *Covering: The Hidden Assault on Our Civil Rights.* Random House.

Yoshino, Kenji. 2020. Video interview by the author. October 2020.

Zenger, Jack, and Joseph Folkman. 2018. "Your Employees Want the Negative Feedback You Hate to Give." *Harvard Business Review,* Aug. 3, 2018.

Zimmer, Ben. 2017. "The Roots of the 'What about Ploy.'" *Wall Street Journal,* June 9, 2017.

About the Author

Photo by: Jeffrey Mossier

Daisy Auger-Domínguez is an accomplished executive and dynamic leader who has designed and executed organizational transformations on the leading edge of culture at Google, Disney, and Viacom, and VICE Media Group. Daisy is on a mission to make modern workplaces work for everyone. She lives in Brooklyn, New York, with her husband and daughter.

Index

A

Aberdeen Group, 87

Academy Awards, 38

Academy of Management, 28

Academy of Motion Picture Arts and
Sciences, 38

Accenture, 37, 46

Accomplices, 7, 124, 257

Accountability. *See also* Transparency;
Vulnerability
building, 236
fear and, 237
goal setting and, 36, 225–228, 280
importance of, 220
language and, 104
leadership, 133, 141, 221–222, 229
of non-managers, 233
to others, 230–232
in performance reviews, 188
personal, 229–230
promoting, xv, 67–69
reducing bias via, 77
of team members, 241

"Acute Social Isolation Evokes Midbrain
Craving Responses Similar to
Hunger" (MIT), 16

ADA compliance, 228

Adaptive Leadership (Grashow), 246

Adidas, 226

"Advancement versus Growth"
(Valve handbook), 201

Advisors, external, 213–216

Advisory boards, 214

AI, *see* Artificial intelligence

Airbnb, 115

Alargén, Alberto, 64

Allyship, 122–124
advocation and, 120, 198
in civil conversations, 238
cross-relational, 119
emphasizing, 129

Alotta, J. Bob, 246

AMA (ask me anything), 198, 238

Amazon, 54, 68

Amplification pacts, 118

Anonymity, 93, 114, 119, 127, 141, 146,
148, 149–151

Anti-Blackness, xvii, 8, 9, 17, 105, 243

Anti-racism, xvi, 14, 28, 36, 102, 240

APCO Worldwide, 226

Apple, 12, 191, 227, 237

Apple Values, 227

Applications, *see* Job applications

AppNexus, 25, 31

AppNexus Women's Network, 25, 31

Artificial intelligence (AI), 44, 63,
168, 189

Asana, 115

Ask me anything (AMA), 198, 238

Assumption trap, 78

Atkin, Ross, 33

A2020 plan, 38

297